Aquarius Rising

Aquarius Rising

The Rock Festival Years

ROBERT SANTELLI

A Delta Book

Published by
Dell Publishing Co., Inc.
1 Dag Hammarskjold Plaza
New York, New York 10017

Delta® TM 755118, Dell Publishing Co., Inc.

Printed in the United States of America

First printing—August 1980

Designed by Leo McRee

Library of Congress Cataloging in Publication Data

Santelli, Robert.
Aquarius rising.

(A Delta book)
Bibliography: p. 275
1. Rock music—United States—History and criticism.
2. Music festivals—United States. I. Title.
ML3534.S24   784.5'4'007973   80-13674

ISBN: 0-440-50956-4

For Cindy; her cooperation, guidance, and love
made this dream come true.

Contents

Acknowledgments

The primary purpose of this book is to depict the rise and fall of the rock festival phenomenon. There were many trends that evolved out of the upheaval and instability of the 1960s, but few were as compelling to those under thirty as the rock festival. Before it fell victim to violence, and before it was commercially exploited to the point of no return, the rock festival symbolized the temporary triumph of a counterculture and led to a new proliferation of rock music. The festival concept helped the music form take on a new shape and assume a much larger position in the popular music spectrum. Festivals also provided a volatile generation with a much-needed emotional outlet. For some it was the only true celebration of the age.

By examining those festivals that, in one way or another, affected the course of rock festival history, I have attempted to dig up those elements that gave the phenomenon life—and those that eventually caused its death. Some of my colleagues undoubtedly feel different about the importance of rock festivals and their proper place in the general scheme of things. *Aquarius Rising* is not meant to be the definitive work on rock festivals, but merely an interpretative analysis of the subject.

I interviewed numerous performers, promoters, and festival participants during the course of my research. From them I received significant bits of conflicting information and opinions concerning aspects of certain festivals. I have made a thorough effort to unravel the discrepancies as best I know how so that a clear account of the rock festival era may be presented.

This book could not have been written without the generous

assistance of Lou Adler, Kenny Barr, James Cotton, Shelly Finkel, Paul Grushkin and the Bay Area Music Archives, Wayne Hartman, Richie Havens, Robert Hilburn of the Los Angeles *Times*, Jim Koplik, Country Joe McDonald, Barry Melton, Joel Selvin of the San Francisco *Chronicle*, the late Lenny Stogel, and Johnny Winter. To all, a warm thanks.

I am deeply indebted to my friend and judicious editor, Sandra Choron; to Laura Wolff, her assistant; to Bob Oskam and Anne Harrison, who also helped edit the manuscript; to Craig and Robin Roberts for putting up with me when the Library of Congress was my second home; to John Santoro and the boys on Tapia Way; to Bruce Springsteen for his unknowing inspiration; to Robby Whalley for providing the lighter moments (Fast Eddie Freeman, too); to Tom and Syd Whalley for their warm friendship and confidence; to my parents Dorothy and Robert; and to Cindy, for things too numerous to mention.

A special thanks to August Kraft, who kept the faith when I didn't, and to Jack London for writing *Martin Eden*.

CHAPTER ONE

Celebration

We are stardust
We are golden
And we've got to get ourselves
Back to the garden.

　　—From the song "Woodstock"
　　　by Joni Mitchell

Woodstock. Sometimes just mentioning the word evokes all the power and glory of a generation nurtured on the tenacity of rock music and the fury of a turbulent decade. Woodstock. Just a short time after the legendary festival occurred, the term became a symbol for all those who defied outdated social values and celebrated the dawning of a new age with the exuberant sound of blaring guitars—the Woodstock Nation, as Abbie Hoffman labeled those who ventured to Max Yasgur's farm in search of three days of peace, love, and music.

In August of 1969 the name of the tiny New York State town was splashed across all the television screens and front pages of America. Over 400,000 people had endured three days of rainstorms and flirted with disaster on all fronts to hear rock demigods play the music that those of the youthful counterculture thrived on. It was indeed a sight to behold: the excited grins, the perpetual flashing of peace signs, the sea of faces stretched out across the grazing pastures of a dairy farmer who believed in the power of youth. Jimi Hendrix was there. So was Joan Baez, Sly Stone, The Who, Arlo Guthrie, and many others. And there was mud—everywhere. For three long days young people walked in it, danced in it, and made love in it. And for three days the rest of the world looked on, perplexed and incredulous.

Woodstock was undoubtedly the most triumphant and talked-about rock festival in the history of the music form. But it wasn't the only important one. Denver, Miami, Atlanta, and Monterey, California, all supported rock festivals of considerable size and significance. From 1967 to 1971, the heyday of outdoor rock events, over three hundred rock festivals attracted over three million people. Some of the festivals were huge three-day extravaganzas that featured the greatest performers in rock at the time. Others were more localized events but steeped, nevertheless, in the spirit of solidarity. Later on there were gigantic one-day rock festivals, such as the Watkins Glen event in the summer of 1973, which brought together more than 600,000 rock enthusiasts. They gathered at the popular New York raceway to hear just three heavyweight bands play rock music for over fourteen continuous hours.

What was it about rock fests that made them such spectacular events? Why did so many people flock to them?

One thing is certain. It was much more than the music. Anyone solely interested in going to a rock or pop festival, as they were often called, *just* to hear the music, quickly realized his or her mistake. These people would have fared better catching the acts in concert halls where good sound systems, decent visibility of the stage, and comfortable settings were more or less insured. The large outdoor rock festival could guarantee none of these. Although many promoters rented the most powerful and largest sound systems available, the music often drifted into the wide open spaces. Unless one was fortunate

---

The Woodstock Nation: 400,000 strong.

enough to secure a patch of ground close to the stage area, performers appeared as tiny insects to those who were, in some cases, nearly a quarter-mile from the stage. Then there was the unpredictability of the weather. Since most festivals occurred in the summer, the threat of sudden thunderstorms was prevalent. With the storms came the mud. And with the mud came the mess: huge fields of brown slop that included half-buried sleeping bags, caved-in ice chests, and a myriad of abandoned sneakers and sandals. If it didn't rain, the heat made things miserable.

Yet thousands still made pilgrimages to rock festivals. And deep down inside they knew that it wasn't only the music that compelled them to make the sojourn. Being with 300,000 or more people who espoused the same ideas and shared the same physical identities and the same insatiable thirst for the energized sound of rock music left a lasting impression. It was a good feeling. In a way the rock festival became the equivalent of a huge political convention or a large religious gathering. A spirit of community and a camaraderie was fostered. A celebration was proclaimed, and a message was sent to the outside world: We've got it together. And it all happened to the beat and the raw energy of rock music in its most passionate form.

Of course there were other, more mundane explanations for the enormous attendance figures at rock festivals. For the older, more mature festivalgoer, three days out in the country meant an escape from the anxieties of a culture overrun by violence, war, the draft, materialism, and racial prejudice. It also provided a Peter Pan effect: Being surrounded and accepted by so many young people gave one the feeling of eternal youth. Gray hair didn't matter so long as it was shoulder length. In an era when youthful splendor was glorified, older members of the counterculture found the rock festival to be a natural watering hole provided they conformed to the youthful rituals of the day.

For younger rock fans an excursion to a rock festival meant a few days of total freedom. Much of this valued time was spent fulfilling adolescent fantasies, achieving sexual conquest, and experimenting with drugs on a wide and often reckless scale. These kids had to deal with very few elements of authoritative pressure. They were on their own, free to do as they pleased. An "anything goes" attitude generally prevailed. Since most festival promoters did not invite police officers on the sites, the fear of police harassment was almost totally eliminated.

Although music was not the sole reason thousands congregated at rock festivals, its significance cannot be denied. For the major record companies the rock festival became a giant showcase in which to display new talent. Jimi Hendrix; Janis Joplin; The Who; Santana; Crosby, Stills, Nash and Young; Grand Funk Railroad; Three Dog Night; and countless others could attribute part of their success to regular appearances at rock festivals early in their careers. Older artists in the rock, blues, and folk veins, such as Chuck Berry, Little Richard, Big Mama Willie Mae Thornton, and Lester Flatt and Earl Scruggs enjoyed a renaissance of sorts as a result of their frequent participation at rock festivals.

For those who sat on a hilly field or on the outside track of a speedway, the rock festival offered a chance to catch many of the top acts in the business for a reasonable ticket price. Reasonable, that is, if one bothered to pay at all. Here was a chance to see and hear twenty or thirty groups perform on a three-day slate. There was even jamming among the artists, always spontaneous, informal, and highly treasured by the massive crowds.

The performers, however, especially the more established acts who did not need showcasing, had mixed feelings about playing festivals. On the positive side, the exchange of ideas and the reunion of old friends were always pleasant. So was the check that was handed over to the band after its performance. But the inevitable sound problems (thorough sound checks were rare), the long and tedious wait to take the stage (most festivals never followed a precise timetable), and the fact that most acts performed only short sets led to considerable anxiety.

Much has been written about rock festivals in the past decade. The news media regularly displayed numerous, lurid photos of the large crowds and interviewed festivalgoers, promoters, and musicians alike to determine what all the excitement was about. In a sense the mass media played an important role in the frenzied growth of festivals. Without continued and elaborate exposure it would have been quite difficult for rock festivals to take on such giant proportions. The media instigated the curiosity of the nation's youth to such a point that a trip to a rock festival was almost a peer-driven necessity. They also helped give the term "festival" new meaning. Newspapers and magazines constantly associated the word with drugs and long-haired kids in bell-bottom jeans trudging along a highway jammed with abandoned autos in order to experience the awesome power of rock.

In the late sixties some sociologists pointed out that the rock festival was a truly unique phenomenon that could only occur in the Age of Aquarius. While large music festivals, mass gatherings, and celebrations can be found throughout history in all forms from medieval fairs and early American camptown meetings to religious revivals and bluegrass and fiddlers' conventions, rock festivals were clearly different.

Since 1945 literally thousands of music festivals have occurred. Increased prosperity at home permitted more leisure time, and the widespread use of the automobile eliminated most travel woes. Jazz, bluegrass, country and western, folk, blues, and classical festivals were common and often repeated annually. The Newport Jazz Festival in Rhode Island and the Monterey Jazz Festival in California were highly successful festivals in that idiom. The Newport Folk Festival was just as popular. The Fiddlers' Convention in Union Grove, North Carolina, and the Ann Arbor Blues Festival in Michigan stimulated rich and energetic reactions to their respective musical genres. To be sure, music festivals had been common in America. But three distinct aspects of rock festivals segregate them from their predecessors and give credence to the theories of the sociologists who saw the differences.

The first difference involves the age group that attended the rock festivals. Never before had such a large proportion of a music festival audience been so young. Most that attended rock festivals in the 1967–73 era were under thirty, with a large majority falling into the eighteen- to twenty-five-year-old age bracket. The simple explanation for this is that rock music is almost exclusively a youth-oriented music form. This was especially true in the late sixties and early seventies. Today, as more and more of the Woodstock Nation pass on into their thirties, they carry their interest in rock music with them.

Another very important element in the rock festival tradition which was uniquely different from other music festivals was the widespread use of drugs. Alcohol was used at various festivals in the past, and marijuana and other stimulants were prevalent at twentieth-century jazz festivals; but drug use at rock festivals was far more extensive. Drugs were used openly, often without discrimination and with the idea that such experimentation was part of the overall rock festival experience. It was at these events that young people turned on to the unpredictable power of LSD, STP, and other hallucinogens.

The final factor that distinguished rock festivals from other types of music festivals was the sheer number of people they attracted. Four hundred thousand at Woodstock, three hundred thousand at Altamont, six hundred thousand at Watkins Glen. These figures rival the largest gatherings, both musical and nonmusical, in the recent history of Western civilization, barring military operations. It is this factor that stands above all others. With the post–World War II baby-boom babies coming of age, the youth culture was at its height. When summer came and school let out, there was a very large number of eager, restless kids ready to heed the call when the promise of a rock festival beckoned. Obviously not all of America's youth frequented rock festivals in the sixties or, for that matter, succumbed to the allure of the rock-music scene. But as the decade drew to a close, most accepted the genre, with a large percentage partaking of many aspects of the music and its culture and calling it their own. According to rock historian William Schaffer, "Rock, as folk music of the white middle-class American, did more than fill a cultural void or provide esthetic interests in otherwise constricted lives. . . . Rock dissolved the everyday rubbish of the young American and revealed his dream life. It flaked away the thin whitewash of outward conformity and docility and revealed basic fears and desires of the generation that grew up after Korea, after McCarthy and through the smiling placidity of the Eisenhower years. The message of rock was hardly a secret—it was a rejection of middle-class America."[1]

The rejection of middle-class America was fully symbolized by the hippie movement initiated in San Francisco after the fading out of the Beat movement there. True hippies were actually a small lot in relation to the press they received and the impact they had on the youth of the nation. Their numbers were small because their life-style was too outlandish for the American adolescent, who was ready to scrap many middle-class ideals but not willing to fully submit to a complete and radical overhaul. Instead, a huge chunk of American youth adopted certain aspects of the hippie culture as a rationalization of their beliefs in change and revolution. Long hair, drug use, and, of course, rock music were immediate and outward signs of their embracement of hippie ideals on at least a partial level. It was these young people who made up the bulk of the counterculture. And it was these young people who covered most of the hilly festival acreage at Woodstock, Altamont, and the others.

The media pounced on this change in American youth. At once they began to report in an often sensational style its impact on the nation's moral and ethical standards. When the concept of the rock festival was presented in the summer of 1967, the media treated the affairs as hippie circuses. It was not until the staging of Woodstock that the media began to take a more serious view of the rock-festival phenomenon.

In order to identify accurately the *immediate* sources of the rock festival concept, one must begin in San Francisco during the time when hippies and other young people were migrating to the Haight-Ashbury district of the city, circa 1965.

San Francisco was an ideal city in which to sow the seeds for a cultural revolution. It had a history, dating back to the California gold rush days, that emphasized permissiveness and the promulgation of liberal ideas. Nestled in the inner city during the fifties and early sixties were some of the most important personalities of the Beat movement. The North Beach section of town was home for poets, writers, avant garde musicians, and Beat fellow travelers. The straight society of San Francisco was a reluctant witness to an underground movement that would pave the way for the larger, more controversial hippie movement to come.

Aside from Bob Dylan, America's only true reply to the Beatles and the subsequent British invasion that followed (1964–5) was the emerging rock scene in San Francisco. Musicians there were well aware of the English influence on American music, but tenaciously held on to their own developing interpretations of rock. The result was labeled acid or psychedelic rock since songwriters often used LSD or other drugs for inspiration.

The music structure was indeed different from the standard pop or rock patterns of the day. More imagery was incorporated into the lyrics, and the tempo of the melodies ranged from unhurried and amorphous to upbeat and energetic. The songs tended to run much longer than the traditional two- or three-minute length, especially when performed live. Long, winding instrumental solos accounted for much of this. Finally, a dis-

Haight-Ashbury posters
for newcomers and tourists.
Summer of Love, 1967.

Sylvia Clarke Hamilton

tinct Eastern influence, often combined with country or blues themes, was found in many songs. The musical product was initially meant to recreate the audio experience of an acid trip, although acid rock quickly took on a much larger scope.

Before long, groups like The Great Society, the Charlatans, the Jefferson Airplane, and the Grateful Dead became widely known in the city. Later other bands such as Quicksilver Messenger Service, Moby Grape, and Big Brother and the Holding Company began to enjoy popularity. From across the bay in Berkeley came the satirical and political sounds of Country Joe and the Fish. The San Francisco *Chronicle* and Ralph Gleason in particular noticed the new musical trend in the city and initiated regular coverage in the newspaper's entertainment section. The *Chronicle* was ahead of its time; it was the first large newspaper in America to give serious recognition to rock as a legitimate and worthwhile music form.

In October 1965 Chet Helms, a budding rock entrepreneur and future manager of Big Brother and the Holding Company, and members of the Family Dog, a hippie group interested in the advancement of San Francisco psychedelic rock, produced the first "dance concert" at Longshoremen's Hall. Calling the event "A Tribute to Dr. Strange" (a comic book character), it featured music by the Jefferson Airplane and The Great Society, among others. The emotionalism of the music and the heated response of the audience drenched the hall with a heightened sense of euphoria. There was a demand for similar dance concerts, and soon the Family Dog moved its production organization into the Avalon Ballroom, where it would remain for most of the psychedelic era.

Two months later an impresario named Bill Graham staged a benefit for the San Francisco Mime Troupe. Graham was the group's manager at the time. The Mime Troupe needed to raise money to assist Rennie Davis, the company's leader, who was in the midst of a courtroom battle with the city over his arrest for performing in the city park without prior authorization. Graham followed the Family Dog format. The Mime Troupe benefit took place at the Fillmore Auditorium, an old dance hall used by the black community. Graham met with the same success as did the Family Dog; and the San Francisco rock ballroom scene was officially under way.

Ballroom fever caught on, and in the following months San Francisco and its music became established as the cradle of the American counterculture. The ballroom events and dance concerts eventually moved outdoors, and from then on it was just a matter of time before the term "festival" made its entrance into rock vocabularies.

One of the first times the term "festival" was used in association with an American rock event was in January 1966, when the now-legendary Trips Festival, again produced by Bill Graham, was held at Longshoremen's Hall. Basically the production was an attempt to simulate, via psychedelic rock music and wildly flashing lights, a mind-expanding experience without the use of LSD (although it was readily available there for those who wished to use it). Gleason covered the "festival" for the *Chronicle* and labeled it an "electric circus with rock music." The Grateful Dead, Big Brother and the Holding Company, and other San Francisco bands played ear-splitting "acid rock" while stroboscopic lights further battered the senses of those present.

With the success of the Trips Festival and the dance concerts, the gears were set for expansion of the San Francisco rock culture and the hippie movement. In the spring of 1966 various hip writers, poets, musicians (all amateurs) and the Mime

Vanguard Records

Guitarist Barry Melton (left) and other members of the Fish, San Francisco, 1967.

Troupe formed the Artists' Liberation Front to adopt a program designed to continue the wave of artistic creativity that was sweeping the city. One of the projects the group undertook was the informal production of the Free Faire, an outdoor, free-admission version of the Trips Festival. Rock bands performed, poets read their work, and, most important of all, the scene became set for the Human Be-In in January of the following year.

The Human Be-In was held in San Francisco's Golden Gate

Sylvia Clarke Hamilton

Janis Joplin in San Francisco's Golden Gate Park.

Park on Saturday, January 14, 1967. Labeled as A Gathering of the Tribes, the event drew close to twenty thousand people to the park's polo grounds to celebrate the emergence of the counterculture. For the first time America was able to observe hippies in full costume.

The four-hour celebration was lax in design. Most people just lounged in the grass and soaked up the sunshine while

Sylvia Clarke Hamilton

Jerry Garcia and the Grateful Dead performing at a free concert in San Francisco's Golden Gate Park, spring 1967.

listening to the sounds of Quicksilver Messenger Service, the Grateful Dead, the Jefferson Airplane, and even jazz great Dizzy Gillespie. During breaks in the music, Beat poet Allen Ginsburg led the crowd in the chanting of Hindu mantras to usher in a new spirit and a new era. Political radical Jerry Rubin, recently released from a Berkeley jail cell, made an appearance on the stage. A hat was passed to raise money for his legal defense. A satirical interpretation of "The Night Before Christmas," in which Santa Claus arrived on Christmas Eve bearing LSD and pounds of marijuana, was presented by a local poet. Timothy Leary got up on the stage and asked the passive crowd to "turn onto the scene, tune into what is happening, and drop out of high school, college, grad school, junior executive, senior executive and follow me the hard way."[2]

The crowd listened as the smell of incense and marijuana perfumed the air. A local communal group, the Diggers, gave away fruit and vegetable stew. Men and women dressed in medieval-style hippie garb raised colorful banners in the air to the sounds of bells, flutes, tambourines, and acoustic guitars.

One of the many Be-Ins in San Francisco's Golden Gate Park in the spring of 1967. The music and the vibes were always free.
Sylvia Clarke Hamilton

Hundreds of flowers were passed out and exchanged. Local merchants displayed beads and leather items. Small children, some naked, ran and played among the clusters of people, and balloons dotted the sky.

The effect of the Human Be-In on both the youth-propelled counterculture and the possible staging of larger rock-oriented celebrations, such as full-scale rock festivals, was profound. It was an overt triumph for the hippies and their followers and inspired similar events in New York, Los Angeles, and as far away as London. The Be-In forced the media to take more than a superficial glance at counterculture growth in San Francisco. Their reports ultimately provided the impetus needed to initiate the Summer of Love (as the media termed it) of 1967. As for rock festivals, the Human Be-In demonstrated that live rock music performed outdoors for large numbers of young people

had potential. There was something in the air on that Saturday afternoon that forced the observer to come face to face with a growing appetite for rock music in an unconfined, unrestrained setting. Music was a dynamic force ideally suited to bringing people together. History had proved that. The more people gathered to hear its sounds, the higher the emotional intensity. Especially if the music was rock.

The first authentic rock festival occurred in June of 1967, six months after the Be-In. The importance of the Fantasy Faire and Magic Mountain Music Festival (June 10 and 11, 1967) has been vastly overshadowed by the larger and more popular Monterey International Pop Festival, which occurred one week later in Monterey, California. Nicknamed the Mount Tam festival, the Magic Mountain Music Festival was staged atop Mount Tamalpais, across San Francisco's Golden Gate Bridge in neighboring Marin County. Tom Rounds and his partner, Ed Mitchell, sponsored and produced the two-day festival. Rounds at the time was the program director at KRFC, a Bay Area radio station.

Designed as a community project, the profits made on the festival were to go to the Economic Opportunity Council, which operated in the black ghetto area of Hunter's Point. The council had hoped to raise enough capital for the construction of child-care centers in their neighborhood. Rounds and Mitchell got involved with the organization and came up with the idea of a music festival using both local talent and a few national recording acts who would perform for a small fee. The two men recruited people in the community to help get the event off the ground. The San Francisco *Chronicle* permitted an old warehouse it owned to be used as an informal headquarters and work area. Graduate students from San Francisco State College erected prefabricated concession booths and received credit from the college for their efforts. The local underground newspaper, the San Francisco *Oracle,* donated advertisement space, and KRFC gave coverage of the unfolding plans. Other community groups donated time and funds.

The Fantasy Faire and Magic Mountain Music Festival was originally intended to take place on June 3 and 4, but inclement weather forced the producers to postpone it until the following weekend. The affair was actually two events in one: The Fantasy Faire was quite similar to an arts and crafts exhibit. The stalls built by the San Francisco State students housed the goods of various local artisans and merchants. Pop art, pottery, handmade musical instruments, leather goods, and jewelry were displayed and sold to a crowd estimated at fifteen thousand for the two days. The Magic Mountain Music Festival coincided with the Fantasy Faire and took place at the adjoining amphitheater. Eleven bands performed over the two days. Local acts included the Jefferson Airplane and Country Joe and the Fish. Also on the billing were such name artists as the Doors and the Byrds from Los Angeles, Dionne Warwick, and Smokey Robinson and the Miracles.

Admission to the festival was two dollars, and it attracted many of those people who had participated in the Human Be-In and frequented the dance concerts in San Francisco. The San Francisco *Oracle* even considered it a continuation of the Be-In. Since there was a lack of parking facilities on Mount Tamalpais, festivalgoers were required to park their cars in San Rafael and then board school buses, which took them up the mountain to the festival site. The process was reversed at the end of the day. In all, more than eighty-five school buses participated.

Barry Melton, at the time the lead guitarist for Country Joe and the Fish, recalls his trip up the mountain. "The band had just flown down from Seattle. We wanted to participate in the show at Mt. Tam so we grabbed a flight down the coast knowing full well that as soon as the show was over we'd have to fly back up again.

"When we arrived at the base of Mt. Tam a group of Hell's Angels were waiting to escort us up to the amphitheater. I had just taken about 500 milligrams of acid and was just beginning to get off when an Angel by the name of Broken Dick tells me to get on the back of his chopper. He was supposed to ride me up the mountain. Well, ol' Broken Dick looks to me like he's fallen off his bike about 300 times, and I'm thinkin' what it's going to be like when we both experience the 301st fall with me zooming on acid.

"Joe persuades me that everything is going to be all right. I get on the bike and he takes off up the mountain. We're scooting around yellow school buses and my mind begins to freak out a bit. All they were to me were yellow streaks. And the road up to the Mt. Tam amphitheater is narrow. That's one of the reasons why they didn't want so many cars going up the mountain. Broken Dick got me up there safe, but I didn't want to go back down with him."

The musical part of the two-day affair did not produce any

startling performances, as did the Monterey Pop Festival, but it did usher in the rock festival era; and as the only two rock festivals held in America in 1967—other than a handful of small, highly localized events—they are guaranteed a permanent place in rock history.

The next year witnessed a few other festivals staged in California as well as the first significant one held on the East Coast, the Miami Pop Festival.

But in 1969 the rock festival truly came of age. Highlighted by Woodstock, the rock festival assumed immense importance to the growth of the counterculture and consistently attracted huge youthful crowds. Large numbers of young people took to the highways in the summer of that year to follow the festival circuit. The same brightly colored buses and the same wildly designed communal tents were seen in Denver, Atlantic City, Woodstock, and Atlanta in 1969. The word was passed where the next festival was to occur, and the gypsy-styled caravans would be off in that direction.

It was also a great year for the music industry. Many new performers who became stars in the early seventies were showcased to literally hundreds of thousands of young people. Bands that started out in early 1969 with only local followings became superstars by the end of the year. Managers hustled to have their clients sign contracts to appear at major festivals. Promoters hastily constructed festival plans with the hope of getting rich quick. The original nonprofit concept of Mount Tam and Monterey was quickly forgotten by the festivalgoers and the musicians as well as the promoters. Money became the biggest factor for all involved. The bands and the promoters hoped to get all they could while festival fever was still hot, and many fans eschewed paying to see and hear the rock performers by resorting to gate-crashing tactics.

If there was one festival that the counterculture can look upon with abundant pride, it was Woodstock. But the glory of the event quickly tarnished some four months later at Altamont Speedway, where the innocence and idyllic triumph of the Woodstock Nation was lost forever. By 1971 local ordinances and state laws were inserted in the books that legally prevented the staging of rock festivals or demanded such stringent health, sanitary, and crowd-control strategies that many would-be promoters shelved festival plans. Festivals were still produced, but with less and less success. Rock, the organic nucleus of the youth movement, was still alive and well, but its main vehicle of presentation was sputtering as the sixties turned into the seventies.

Three years into the new decade, the decline of the traditional three-day rock festival was nearly complete. In all, more than three hundred rock festivals occurred in the period stretching back to the summer of 1967. The demand was still there for these events, but the legal hassles and the exorbitant fees charged by the top acts allowed only a few festivals to succeed. Most of these were one-day, one-shot affairs that hardly resembled the original concept on which they were based. These one-day fests usually had power-packed billings and featured high-energy music, but the communal spirit of earlier days and the sociological impact of such events were significantly diluted.

The rock festival era is over, but the memories and the over-all importance of the events live on. What follows here is a recollection of those festivals that had substantial meaning, not only for their effect on the popularity of rock music, but also for their influence on the counterculture and the maturity of an entire generation.

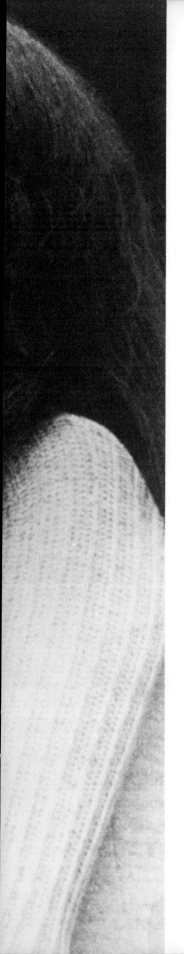

CHAPTER TWO

In the Beginning - Monterey

This is the love crowd, right?
We all love each other, don't we?
—Otis Redding
Monterey Pop Festival
June 17, 1967

The Mount Tam festival was a widely known local success, but it did not receive a substantial amount of national press and publicity. Little mention was made of the event in the entertainment trades or the music magazines. Rather, it was the Monterey International Pop Festival that was in the news in the spring and early summer of 1967. Ever since the Monterey idea had been spawned in April of that year, the hip media had nurtured and carefully surveyed its progress. Conceived on a scale much larger than that of Mount Tam, it promised to be an event of significant importance to the music world.

The notion of a large-scale pop music festival came to Alan Pariser, a sometime concert promoter and member of the pop music establishment in Los Angeles, after hearing of the San Remo festival in Italy. This foreign nonrock music festival was nonprofit in nature and was geared to the serious, creative performer who was not necessarily established in national or international circles. Pariser felt that a nonprofit music festival in the United States made up of pop and rock artists would bring together new musical ideas and concepts. It would also provide a national platform for performers not yet in the public limelight.

Pariser took his idea to Ben Shapiro, a Los Angeles booking agent. Shapiro occasionally handled big-name acts and had been in the music business since the late 1950s. Pariser hoped that Shapiro had enough contacts in the recording industry to get the festival off the ground. Shapiro grabbed at the idea but felt there was big money to be made and insisted that the nonprofit part of the idea be eliminated. Pariser reluctantly agreed, and the team began to set organizational wheels turning.

Two things that demanded immediate attention were the site and the structural format of the festival. Pariser and Shapiro believed that they should follow the general makeup of the successful jazz festivals of the day, namely the Newport Jazz Festival in Rhode Island and the Monterey Jazz Festival in California. Monterey was certainly closer to Los Angeles than Newport. It was also just a couple of hours south of San Francisco, the city that was rapidly becoming a mecca for young rock musicians and supporters of the music form. The County Fairgrounds in Monterey was the home of the Jazz Festival. It had enough arena space to accommodate seven thousand people. Shapiro and Pariser felt it was a natural choice and obtained rights to use the property on June 16, 17, and 18 of that summer.

The agreement was signed in April. The two promoters realized they had to work fast. In one of the most important moves of the early stages, Derek Taylor, the brilliant publicist who had previously worked as the Beatles' press officer, was hired to handle publicity. It was Taylor's job to "sell" the idea of a pop/rock music festival to the music world. His name and association with the Beatles carried much weight. He was, therefore, able to convince the recording industry, the press, and many established artists of the validity of the festival idea.

Shapiro and Pariser next had to concern themselves with the

various acts they wanted to have performed at Monterey. The Mamas and the Papas were one of the best-selling and biggest-name attractions on the pop/rock music scene at the time. Shapiro and Pariser approached John Phillips, the band's spokesman, and asked him if the Mamas and the Papas would like to headline the festival. The band would be paid $5,000 for its services, a sum much smaller than the group was accustomed to receiving. Paul Simon happened to be at Phillips's house the night Shapiro and Pariser made their offer. Simon, of course, was half of the duo Simon and Garfunkel, who were also big names in the business. Shapiro and Pariser offered Simon and Garfunkel a slot on the billing as well.

Phillips and Simon listened to the details of the festival idea. After a little thought they told the promoters they would have nothing to do with the festival if it was a commercial venture. However, if Pariser's original idea of nonprofit music festival resurfaced, then they would be extremely interested. The money offered to Phillips and Simon was not enough to persuade them to sign a contract. The Mamas and the Papas could easily earn twice as much on any given night, and Shapiro and Pariser were in no position to offer any more than $5,000. Phillips and Simon thought the festival could be used to further trends in popular music. It could bring together pop, soul, rock, folk, and jazz musicians from all parts of the world to jam and perform, with the proceeds going to a charitable cause.

Ben Shapiro's idea of a commercial pop music festival at Monterey was stopped in its tracks. The word would soon leak out that Phillips and Simon had refused to be associated with the event, and the impresario knew he would then find it difficult to sign other big-name acts. Shapiro, however, had already sunk $50,000 of his own money into festival plans, and he began to devise a way to recover it. Shapiro got back to Phillips and told him he was interested in selling out his interest in the venture. Phillips immediately contacted his manager and producer, Lou Adler, who, like Phillips and Paul Simon, was eager to see Monterey as a nonprofit festival. Together they set out to gather up $50,000 to buy out Shapiro.

In a matter of days John Phillips, Lou Adler, Simon and Garfunkel, producer Terry Melcher, and pop singer Johnny Rivers had each contributed $10,000 in the form of a loan to the festival. The deal was concluded when this money was paid to Shapiro. The loans were to be paid back from the gate receipts and any other money that might be generated from the festival.

Shapiro was still to be associated with the festival, as were Derek Taylor and Allan Pariser. However, after a few weeks Shapiro departed. In the May 10 issue of *Variety*, it was reported that Shapiro's ideas "were not compatible with the original festival concept." The departure eliminated his $30,000 fee for producing the event.

Allan Pariser and Derek Taylor decided to stay on. It was Pariser's original intention that the festival be nonprofit in the first place; so, he and Peter Pilafian, a good friend of the Mamas and the Papas, would coproduce the festival, while Taylor would retain his position as chief publicist. Phillips and Adler were named codirectors of the festival by the appointed board of directors, which included Terry Melcher, Andrew Oldham (the Rolling Stones manager), Johnny Rivers, Smokey Robinson, booking agent/manager Abe Somer, Paul Simon, and, of course, Pariser. Adler and Phillips cleverly enlisted Paul McCartney, Mick Jagger, and Donovan as additional codirectors in order to give further credibility to the festival idea.

When Ben Shapiro had gone to the Monterey City Council in the spring with plans for a pop festival, he told the group the event would be similar in style to the Monterey Jazz Festival. The jazz festival had become an annual affair in Monterey. It brought in needed revenue and injected the town with cultural pride. Those who attended the event were usually well-behaved and responsible-looking. There were occasional arrests for public drunkenness, disorderly conduct, and even for possession of drugs; but these problems were kept to a minimum and the town tolerated them when they occurred.

After Phillips and Adler assumed control and Taylor began to pump out publicity releases, the attitude of the Monterey townspeople began to sour. There were reports that instead of just 7,000 ticket holders showing up for the festival, there would be close to 100,000 young, pot-smoking hippies coming into Monterey. Reports also indicated that the profits from the pop festival would go to an "underground hippie cult" known as the Diggers. Actually the Diggers were a spirited bunch from the Bay Area that fed the hungry, broke kids who wandered up to the Haight-Ashbury section of San Francisco in search of the hippie life-style.

Phillips and Adler worked quickly to counteract the rising tide of opposition and ultimately saved the festival. On May 15 they appeared before the city council and promised that the proceeds from the festival would not go to the Diggers but in-

Lou Adler backstage at Monterey.

stead to various charity groups. They also insisted that the type of music to be played throughout the weekend was not the type to lure any undesirables to Monterey. Phillips impressed the council with his sincerity and intelligence. He and Adler presented enough evidence to suppress the opposition to the festival and insure that Monterey would indeed benefit from it. Mayor Minnie Coyle issued a statement that supported the festival's "charitable and educational intentions," and the council promptly backed her stance on the matter.

There is some question as to whether Phillips deliberately misled the Monterey City Council in regard to the number of people that would attend the event. The truth is that Phillips and the rest of the organization had no idea how to determine how many would show up.

The festival was broken down into five separate performances: Friday evening, Saturday afternoon, Saturday evening, Sunday afternoon, and Sunday evening. One had the opportunity to buy a ticket for one particular performance or purchase an all-festival ticket. Advance ticket sales indicated that each of the five scheduled performances would come close to selling out. But how many additional people would come to Monterey was anyone's guess. There had never been a pop music event on such a large scale as Monterey would be; a measuring device just wasn't available.

As for the Diggers, Derek Taylor had issued a press release that hinted at money being given to the commune. But he later retracted the statement, claiming it was a mistake. The Diggers, as it turned out, told festival organizers that they would not accept the money even if it were offered to them.

Phillips, Adler, and a handful of others did most of the tedious work to get the festival off the ground. The board of directors met rarely, and never were all the members present at one time. They were, however, some of the top names in the recording business, and as long as Phillips, Adler, and company didn't mind doing most of the work, the majority of the board was content merely to act as figureheads in the operation.

Lou Adler was used to working long and hard hours. He had gotten started in the music business by producing Jan and Dean and Johnny Rivers in the late '50s and early '60s. From there he set up his own production and recording company, Dunhill Records. Adler signed Barry McGuire, who had a smash hit with P. F. Sloan's "Eve of Destruction," and the Mamas and the Papas, whose singles "California Dreamin' " and "Monday, Monday" ignited a following that was still running hot at the time of Monterey.

Adler then sold the Dunhill rights to ABC Records and founded Ode Records. He promptly released a song written by John Phillips and sung by Scott McKenzie called "San Francisco," which sold well over five million copies. The tune was partly responsible for persuading thousands of kids from all over the country to journey to San Francisco in quest of the new youth culture that was sprouting in the Haight-Ashbury section of town.

Contracting artists unfamiliar with the outdoor music concept was often frustrating, but organizing ultimately secured most of the acts sought. The term "international" was added to Monterey Pop, and the event was officially called the First Annual Monterey International Pop Festival. It was international only in the broadest sense of the term, however. The Who, Jimi Hendrix (at the time based in Britain), Eric Burdon and the Animals (at the time based in San Francisco), and an obscure folksinger invited by Paul Simon named Beverly, hailed from England. The Buffalo Springfield and the Paupers were from Canada. Ravi Shankar was from India. Hugh Masekela was born in South Africa but began his career in the United States. The remaining acts were American.

The lineup included the largest and most talented group of artists in rock at that time, but three of the most influential acts would not be present. The Rolling Stones could not attend, even though Mick Jagger was a member of the board of directors. Charges had been brought against him and Keith Richards for illegal possession of hashish. (Brian Jones did attend and was a guest emcee.) The Beatles and Bob Dylan declined unofficial invitations. Paul McCartney was also a member of the board, but the Beatles were so overwhelmingly popular in 1967 that an appearance at Monterey by the band would have destroyed the festival's hope for control and order. The same held true for an appearance by Bob Dylan.

Donovan had been invited but could not get a working visa, also because of a drug bust. Chuck Berry refused to play if he wasn't going to get paid. Cream, the Young Rascals, and the Lovin' Spoonful already had concert commitments. The Beach Boys had originally intended to play but bowed out when Carl Wilson was called to appear in court in order to justify his refusal to be inducted into the armed forces.

Of all the pop music idioms, the soul or Motown sound was the least represented. Otis Redding and his backups, the Mar-Keys, and Booker T. and the MGs were the lone representatives of black music. Ironically enough, their sets were among the most dynamic of the festival. By 1967 the ubiquitous racial problem had worked its way into the pop music consciousness. Monterey was judged by certain blacks to be a honky festival set up for the sole purpose of promoting honky artists. Many black soul artists did not want to alienate fans, most of whom were also black, and, therefore, did not accept offers to appear at Monterey. Smokey Robinson was on the board of directors, but neither he nor his band, the Miracles, showed up. The Impressions and Dionne Warwick both agreed to perform, but later backed out.

Of the American acts on the bill, at least fourteen were from California (not including the Paul Butterfield Blues Band and the newly formed Electric Flag, two groups that were originally from Chicago but identified themselves with the Bay Area). Within the California contingent there was a great deal of

friction. According to Lou Adler, "There was a general philosophical separation between the San Francisco groups and all the groups and management from Los Angeles. The San Francisco musicians demanded a relaxed and loose affair with very little managerial control. They sort of resented the fact that most of the organizers came from Los Angeles. They threatened all through the weekend to put on their own festival across the street on flatbed trucks. It seemed as though the Grateful Dead were particularly opposed to anything we had planned."

Most of this stemmed from the feeling among Bay Area musicians that the Los Angeles music scene was tainted with commercialism and was a product of the recording industry's needs, which, they felt, had little to do with quality and artistic merit. A commonly cited example was the Monkees: Two of its members, Mickey Dolenz and Davy Jones, were actors, not musicians. Yet the L.A. music machine collaborated with Hollywood to make the Monkees not only teen screen celebrities, but international recording artists as well. This occurred despite the disclosure that the music on the Monkees' debut album wasn't played by them, but rather by studio musicians.

The San Francisco people had ample reasons to think as they did, but they failed to recognize that Los Angeles also had its share of innovators. The Byrds, for instance, one of the bands representing the L.A. area at Monterey, had almost single-handedly ushered in the folk-rock idiom with their renditions of Bob Dylan's "Mr. Tambourine Man" and Pete Seeger's "Turn, Turn, Turn." The Doors, who did not play at Monterey Pop but did appear at Mount Tam, were also an important band, having played a major role in the early surfacing of underground rock with "Light My Fire." The same could be said for Arthur Lee and Love and Frank Zappa and the Mothers of Invention.

Prior to Monterey, San Francisco musicians were, for the most part, isolated from the mainstream pop consciousness. Record companies did not find the city's rock music scene commercial enough to justify comprehensive attention. They were more interested in what was happening in New York, Los Angeles, London, and Liverpool. Thus, bands in the Bay Area matured without much outside interference. This finally led to the creation of a sound and music philosophy that was

Although the Rolling Stones did not perform at Monterey, guitarist Brian Jones offered his services as an emcee.
Courtesy of Lou Adler

as imaginative in design as it was distinctive in direction. The bands and personalities that fostered this new expression of American rock were put on display at Monterey. When the festival was over, performers like Country Joe McDonald, Jerry Garcia, Grace Slick, Steve Miller, and Janis Joplin had impressively carved a position in the rock world for San Francisco psychedelia.

In addition to the music, the festival staff decided to create an atmosphere that was socially and culturally representative of the people and musicians who took part in the festival. Dozens of booths brightly decorated in flashy colors and weird designs dotted the festival area. There were magnificent displays of pop art. Stands sold all the necessary paraphernalia and clothes needed to conform with the hip love crowd. Necklaces and bracelets made from multicolored beads and leather pieces, small bells bound to strings of leather and worn around the neck or ankle, hand-crafted Indian moccasins, and many different types of headbands were offered for sale. Other booths sold posters and copies of the underground papers. Flowers were everywhere.

There were a significant number of festivalgoers who drove up from southern California, though most of the attendants were from the Bay Area. Pete Johnson of the Los Angeles *Times* kept things alive in the southland by writing in the Sunday, June 4, edition that the festival had the power to elevate rock consciousness and free it from concerns of capital gain: "Its success can mean a triumph of art over money for a profit-spawned medium, the capping of a trend toward respectability which the field has been approaching for seven years."[1] Ralph Gleason commented on the festival's progress in his columns in the San Francisco *Chronicle*. Publicity was well distributed as the weekend drew near.

Work crews and volunteers arrived a week before the festival was to begin. They prepared the stage for the three-day affair and assembled the large sound system that would carry the music throughout the arena. Both Adler and Phillips had insisted on having an excellent system, one that would produce the various highs and lows of rock in the highest fidelity possible. Outdoor rock concerts presented special problems, and the technological advances that made Woodstock such an audio success were not yet available in 1967. But as it turned out, the system produced superb sound, and many performers commented that it was the cleanest they had ever plugged into.

By Friday evening close to thirty thousand people had jammed into Monterey. All roads leading into the city were swollen with cars and vans. Traffic would stand still, sometimes for more than thirty minutes, yet there was hardly a trace of the vexatious attitude that usually accompanies a crowd of people who want to go someplace and can't. In fact, people were getting out of their cars and exchanging flowers and greetings and excitedly predicting the thrills of the upcoming concerts. The police officers on traffic duty were perplexed by what they saw. Football and baseball crowds did not handle themselves like this; they behaved in the rude, aggressive manner that was expected of them. This was a totally different type of crowd. What they were witnessing was the development of a feeling that was to persist throughout the weekend, a belief in brotherhood and love. It was a genuine sensation, and all who were at Monterey that weekend felt it seep into the music and into every single human transaction that occurred.

Less than eight thousand of the thirty thousand had tickets to the Friday evening concert, and both Adler and Phillips recognized a potential problem. A decision was made to install loudspeakers outside the festival grounds so that those who did not possess tickets for the show would at least be able to hear the music outside the gates. It was hoped that this would reduce the possibility of gate-crashing or confrontations with police for lack of anything else to do. Staff members recalled reading about the Newport jazz and folk festival riots in Rhode Island some years back and wanted no part of a violent scene at Monterey. The First Annual Monterey International Pop Festival was on trial and could not afford any sort of incident that might destroy the chance of a second festival taking place the following year.

Many people who were smart enough to secure reservations in advance filled every hotel room in the city. Monterey was used to crowds taking over their streets, to seeing lines form in front of local restaurants, and to having all available parking spaces disappear for three or four days. The jazz festival had made them experienced veterans in this sort of thing. But again, the Monterey Pop crowd was different, and certainly much larger. Smiling people wearing Salvation Army castoffs were not a usual sight in downtown Monterey. Locals stared, sizing up these aliens, not knowing whether to shield their children's eyes from the women's loose and bouncing breasts

Monterey Pop was one of the few rock festivals that had reserved seating.

or scat home to prepare a defense of their property. As the weekend wore on, however, the locals not directly involved with the festival joined their neighbors in working the concession stands and the policemen patrolling the streets by turning incredulous countenances into warm grins.

By Friday all shows were sold out except Sunday afternoon's concert featuring Ravi Shankar. Right up until showtime Friday evening, Adler and the rest of the Monterey staff were busy eliminating unforeseen problems that kept popping up at the most inappropriate times. No one had previously figured out how to transport the performers who were arriving at Monterey Airport through the traffic and to their hotels so that they could rest and prepare for their performances. Where was the overflow of kids who were streaming into Monterey going to sleep? Who was going to feed them? What about the cops? Would they finally become irritated and hostile and start breaking heads for such violations as loitering and jaywalking? And what about the drug situation?

This last problem was potential dynamite. The performers could take the back roads into Monterey and hopefully make it on time. Monterey Peninsula College had agreed to turn its football field into a huge campsite for those with nowhere else to stay. The Diggers, despite disagreeing with the admission procedures and prices, showed up and eagerly tackled the task of feeding hungry kids. Police Chief Frank Marinello's men in blue were thus far keeping unusually cool and turning their heads when minor infractions of the law occurred. But drugs—what would they do when they saw their neighbor's seventeen-year-old daughter standing in line somewhere getting ready to toke on a freshly lit joint?

Luckily for everyone, they ignored it. Turned their heads. Pot was being smoked in the arena area, performers were turning on backstage, and the hip scene-makers rolled thick joints in the camping area. Arresting the offenders would have undoubtedly produced a mild tremor in Monterey. The docile and polite crowd easily could have turned into a nasty despicable bunch had the police begun hauling away all the drug offenders both in and out of the festival area. This justified reaction by the police at Monterey set a precedent in the handling of drug situations at future rock festivals. The average kid who smoked a few joints or dropped a tab of acid and could cope with its effects was, generally speaking, permitted to do so. As rock fests became more and more drug-oriented, however, the situation changed and many dealers were arrested. However, it was usually done in a subtle way so as not to disturb the sleeping—or grooving—giant.

LSD was in abundance at Monterey. Tabs of "Monterey Purple" were literally given away free to anyone wishing to experiment a little. Frequent users of acid brought their own supplies. But, as Lou Adler recalled, "We were quite prepared for any drug problems, though hardly anyone knew about this. We had knowledgeable people from the Haight who assisted in the setting up of hospital units. We also had qualified people watching over the crowd at all times, picking up anyone who seemed to be involved in a bad trip and taking him to the hospital tent where he was treated by a doctor experienced with that sort of thing."

The Monterey staff was fully aware that the media would scoop up any drug-related problems and turn them into lurid accounts of wild hippies running around out of their heads. Fortunately the press was so overwhelmed with the amicable mood of the crowd and the wealth of good vibrations that most drug inferences were buried in the middle of the report.

Derek Taylor insured widespread coverage of the festival by not declining a single request for press credentials. Both the straight and the underground press were well represented. Disc jockeys who had plugged the festival in their radio programs were also invited. Key executives of the major record companies that dealt with rock, folk, jazz, or blues attended. One of those present, Clive Davis, who at the time was working for Columbia, liked what he saw and felt at Monterey. He became especially interested in a rubber-mouthed, gangling singer from Big Brother and the Holding Company named Janis Joplin. Davis remarked in his autobiography, *Clive! Inside the Record Business*, that he and the other executives from the music world were taken by the warmth of the audience and the charisma of the musicians. He even gave a party at his hotel room to better acquaint himself with the musicians and members of the festival staff.

Prior to the festival there had existed a gap between record-company brass and rock artists. There seemed to be a mutual skepticism, and it was generally accepted that executives did not mingle with their company's artists on an informal or social level. Business was business and rock music was, well, sort of an art form. But everyone knew that rock musicians were a strange breed. Or so the myth went. Monterey changed this in many cases. At Columbia Clive Davis often took personal interest in many of the rock stars' careers as well as their personal lives. Davis was especially close to Janis Joplin.

There was a larger and much more significant result of Monterey than the formation of ties between rock artists and the record industry. Executives were given the opportunity to see their own acts perform live on a grand scale and could carefully survey audience reaction and approval. They were also able to see, firsthand, new and unsigned groups. The future of rock was on display right before their eyes and ears. Dollar signs multiplied with each wailing guitar solo and bass run. It quickly became apparent that these were the bands and this was the music that would replace the often sweet and plastic sound of rock as they had known it. They did not forget what they heard.

By Friday evening the weather had settled in for the weekend. It was damp and a bit cool, with rain a slight possibility for Saturday and Sunday. A light mist blanketed the grounds, and the tents at Monterey Peninsula College dripped with dew.

So did the flowers that someone had painstakingly attached to the goalpost at the west end of the field. The Mexican-styled serapes and the army jackets came out of the backpacks as the sun drooped over the Pacific horizon.

As ticket holders for the Friday evening show queued up, many of the hundred thousand freshly cut orchids flown in from Hawaii were handed out free at the entrance of the arena. The banner that hung from the stage spelled out the message of the weekend: "Music, Love and Flowers."

The music began around 9:30 P.M. Each act was to perform for approximately thirty to forty-five minutes. Dressed in the mod nightclub garb commonly seen in Los Angeles and New York, the Association took the stage amid welcoming applause and immediately broke into their hit "Along Comes Mary," followed by "Cherish." It was a crowd the Association were not used to singing in front of. Middle-of-the-road audiences were more their style, not flowered young people dressed in shaggy garments. Nevertheless, they plowed through their nightclub act, and the audience responded with mild enthusiasm.

The Paupers, a relatively unknown rock outfit from Canada with a knack for loud, arousing tunes, followed, along with another nightclub pop act, Lou Rawls. At first it seemed as though Rawls would be vastly out of place on the Monterey stage, even more so than the Association. Singing with H. B. Barnum's nine-piece band, Rawls mustered up all his musical energy and managed to pull off a surprisingly well-received set. Singing such tunes as "Tobacco Road" and "Dead End Street" with vigor and exhilaration, Rawls wound up playing the longest set of the evening and got a warm, sympathetic hand from the audience. Some critics later claimed that his music was too top-heavy with L.A. slickness. That probably was true, but Rawls succeeded at Monterey anyway.

Next up was Beverly, a folksinger with a soft voice and a mellow guitar style. Her only claim to fame was Paul Simon's invitation to play at Monterey. The original intention of the festival organizers had been to bring to Monterey the famous as well as the not-so-famous; the hit-makers as well as those still struggling in their creative mold. Though Beverly's appearance, like that of the Paupers, was justified, she left Monterey as unknown as she was before the festival.

Johnny Rivers, a true pop star, was next. Produced and managed by Lou Adler, Rivers was the epitome of the Los Angeles pop artist. Rivers's method for success was simple. First, sign on with a clever and audacious producer like Adler. Second, search the past for old songs with that certain energy that never failed to move people ("Memphis," "Maybellene," "Seventh Son"). Third, remold the tune and spice it up by adding the talented musicianship of L.A. session men. Fourth, add his own raspy voice to the song. The result? Usually a dash to the top of the charts and plenty of money for both Rivers and Adler. This formula approach worked most of the time. But, though Rivers was big on the charts, he never received praise from critical elements of the business. In any case his set at Monterey was adequate, primarily because of the brilliance of studio men Hal Blaine on drums and Jim Webb on piano, who, with a few others, backed up Rivers.

Eric Burdon and the Animals followed Rivers. The original band, simply called the Animals, were one of England's more aggressive and prosperous R&B bands in the early and mid-sixties. Their first big hit in June of 1964 was "House of the Rising Sun," followed by "Don't Let Me Be Misunderstood," "We've Gotta Get Out of This Place," and "It's My Life." The band that played at Monterey, however, included only Eric Burdon from the original Animals. In late 1966 the Animals had broken up, and Burdon came to the United States, ultimately landing in San Francisco. It was here that he reformed the Animals.

Burdon and his new band drew the biggest round of applause Friday night, peaking their set with an inspired version of "Paint It Black." John Wheeler traded his guitar for an electric violin and delivered one of the best received solos of the festival.

It was getting quite late when Simon and Garfunkel took the stage to round out the evening's program. Accompanied by only Paul Simon's acoustic guitar, the duo moved the audience with delightful versions of "Homeward Bound," "Sounds of Silence," "Punky's Dilemma," and the popular "59th Street Bridge Song."

Of all those who performed on Friday evening, it was Simon and Garfunkel who would benefit most from their appearance at Monterey. The secret of Simon and Garfunkel's success was the intensely rich lyrics and haunting melodies of Simon, usually interpreted by Art Garfunkel's immaculate voice. There was a distinctive charm in all their songs; a poetic clarity that was almost universally appealing.

Eric Burdon also used his Monterey success to bolster his

new, but short-lived, psychedelic image. Two songs, "Monterey" and "San Francisco Nights," were big hits for him and the Animals; but they didn't prevent the band from breaking up again, this time in late 1968. Burdon later drifted down to Los Angeles and formed the R&B funk band War.

The show concluded a bit past 1:30 A.M. It had been undoubtedly pop-oriented, and it lacked the excitement of the later shows. It did, however, demonstrate that the crowd could be responsive. Friday night represented a small victory for the L.A. Whiskey-A-Go-Go sound; but the San Francisco strain of blues-rock and psychedelia would have its say the following afternoon. And what an afternoon it turned out to be.

Things began happening early Saturday morning; at least for those who managed to tumble out of their sleeping bags and successfully rub away any evidence of Friday night's show from their reddened eyes. The smell of breakfast drifted above the football-field campsite, and everywhere people were busily preparing for the next concert, only hours away. Many were still on the road heading toward Monterey, anxiously glancing at their watches and wondering if they were going to make the show. Those listening to the radio heard a barrage of announcements advising people without tickets not to venture near Monterey. But such announcements, made to a hip San Francisco radio audience in June 1967, could hardly be expected to persuade many to stay home. Monterey was happening, man! As late as 5 P.M. Sunday evening, there were still a few people poking thumbs out into the onrushing traffic with signs reading MONTEREY propped up against soiled backpacks.

If the townspeople of Monterey thought they were swamped by flowered hippies on Friday, they couldn't believe their eyes on Saturday. A conservative estimate late Saturday afternoon by *Time* magazine measured the crowd at least 50,000. Other estimates ran as high as 100,000. But actual numbers didn't matter anymore. The fact that so many people were gathered in one place with no more serious problems than traffic was what really counted. Things were so good that Police Chief Marinello sent half his enlarged police force home. There simply wasn't anything for them to do except stand around and take the flowers offered to them by young hippies.

The crowd was as colorful and spirited on Saturday as it had been on Friday. Smiles and peace signs, flowers, and the foreign smells of incense and pot were all part of the scene. Good vibes powdered the air.

The central theme of Saturday's show was the blues. The blues, and not one black artist in the bunch except for the burly drummer in the Electric Flag, Buddy Miles! Phil Spector had publicly griped that the board of directors had failed to lure any of the rock originators such as Little Richard and Bo Diddley to Monterey. But no one, interestingly enough, had suggested that such blues greats as Muddy Waters or Mississippi Fred McDowell be present. This became increasingly apparent as one of the major faults of the festival. Where were those artists who had started it all? Why weren't they onstage performing with the younger musicians who were experimenting and creating new styles from the original form? Perhaps the Motown people were right after all: Hippies or no hippies, most of the audience was white and interested in hearing white acts. Besides, the record industry was bent on hearing new talent, not weather-beaten blacks with raw, scratchy voices and banged-up guitars.

It was an L.A. blues band that opened the afternoon concert. Canned Heat was the best Los Angeles had to offer in terms of blues-rock. Led by Bob "Bear" Hite (all 320 pounds of him), the band cranked into "Rollin' and Tumblin,'" "Big Road Blues," and a mean version of "Catfish Blues"—as if to pay tribute to the black blues artists not present. Hite was having difficulty singing in tune, as evidenced by the way he kept cupping one ear, but he still managed to put on a convincing performance. Guitarist Al Wilson wasn't having any problems at all. His stirring lead work and solid command of the blues idiom was quickly recognized by the audience. He and fellow guitarist Henry Vestine gave Canned Heat a respected one-two punch.

Canned Heat, barely a year old, included Frank Cook on drums, Larry Taylor on bass, and Hite, Vestine, and Wilson. They would release their debut album two months after Monterey and strike it big with a single from it, "On the Road Again." Canned Heat became a successful touring band, and they appeared at many festivals in the 1967–69 period, including Woodstock. They continued to prosper with such songs as "Goin' Up to the Country" and "Let's Work Together," both of which attained high positions on the charts. It all fell apart, however, with the drug-related death of Al Wilson in September 1970. One of the eight stars at Monterey who have since passed away, Wilson was the genius behind Canned Heat. When he died, Canned Heat faded into the pages of rock history.

Courtesy of Pennebaker, Inc.

Janis at Monterey.

It was still early in the day, but it was the next act that garnered the most praise of the afternoon—and deservedly so. Big Brother and the Holding Company had been the house band at Chet Helms's Avalon Ballroom since 1966. They had become quite popular in San Francisco ever since a raucous, brash, Texan folkie named Janis Joplin assumed the role of lead singer. Her voice wasn't mellow or light, but sharp and gritty. It stung its listeners rather than comforting them. She reminded people of Bessie Smith, one of her great influences.

Working herself up in a whirl of sexual crescendos, the gutsy singer gave everything she had to the music each time she walked onto a stage. She would grab at the microphone, half-buzzed from her perpetual swigging from a bottle of Southern Comfort, and proceed to churn out a blitzkrieg of blues-rock power. Big Brother members Sam Andrews and Jim Gurley on guitars filled the background with unrefined & frequently unstructured leads, while Dave Getz on drums and Peter Albin on bass nailed down the rhythm section for the band.

The sun had burned off the dampness of the previous night by the time Janis Joplin and Big Brother took the stage at Monterey. They were the first of the true San Francisco bands to perform (Eric Burdon and the Animals were not considered a true Bay Area band). Joplin wore a gold-knit pants suit with an inviting neckline and nervously fiddled with her tambourine as the band tuned up. And then one, two, three—the music began, and Joplin wailed into it with biting intensity and insane fervor. Prancing up and down the stage, she ripped through the rock-blues repertoire of Big Brother. Each note became a scorching sexual attack on the senses. The audience soaked up the power of her performance and begged for more. Janis gave them everything she had. Sweat dripped from her forehead and her brownish hair became a tangled mess. She groaned and growled and became as exhilarated as those standing on their chairs in the audience. Clive Davis was overwhelmed. During her performance he decided he *had* to sign her to Columbia. Davis wrote in his autobiography, "I knew immediately I had to go after her. I didn't tote up any executive balance sheet. I didn't care who managed her, or if she was under control to another label. I just wanted her!"

It all came together during Joplin's rendition of Big Mama Willie Mae Thornton's "Ball and Chain." Her powerful voice, with all its unfinished edges, prompted San Francisco *Examiner* jazz critic, Phil Elwood, to call her "the best white woman blues singer I have ever heard." Joplin's name appeared in *Time* and *Newsweek*. Most critics from the underground press wrote rave reviews.

Before any artist or group took the stage at Monterey, they were required to sign a legal release giving the festival exclusive rights to any filming for a future documentary or television special. Big Brother and the Holding Company, along with the Grateful Dead, had refused to sign. Both groups were concerned with the lack of control they would have in the editing room. What if the sound was poor? Who was getting the money that would inevitably be made from the film or TV special? Danny Rifkin, the Dead's manager, adamantly refused to sign the release statement. Big Brother thought it over and decided to stick with the Grateful Dead. However, after the fantastic response of the audience to Big Brother's set, the film crew and the festival staff urged them to sign the release. If they did they would be permitted to do another set, and this time it would be captured on film.

Rifkin was furious that Big Brother gave in. He had been one of the more vociferous opponents of the way the festival was being run in the first place, and he had no kind words for Lou Adler or John Phillips. While the other San Francisco bands were filling the stage at the fairgrounds, the Grateful Dead, the Jefferson Airplane, and others gave a "free festival" on the football field of Monterey Peninsula College.

The price of admission at Monterey ($3.00–$6.50) was not cheap. Members of the San Francisco contingent had opted for a free festival from the beginning. They were used to performing free, giving regular concerts in Golden Gate Park, and putting on benefits for free clinics and the underground press. They knew a large sum would be made from the festival, and they didn't trust the L.A. organizers with the profits. Part of this dissension was the fault of the board of directors. When they announced that the proceeds would go to charity, they did not explicitly name the recipients of this generosity. Had they done this, opponents of the festival might have been calmed. Unfortunately, the distribution of the proceeds was not actually determined until after the festival was over.

The San Francisco musicians, particularly the Grateful Dead, failed to realize that a free festival of the size and scope of Monterey was virtually impossible. The festival had certain expenses that needed to be met. Money had to come from somewhere to pay for the rental of the sound system, the use of the fairgrounds, the fee for police security, and myriad other bills. The money brought in at the gate would cover these expenses. The Grateful Dead had also forgotten that Adler, Rivers, Simon, Melcher, and Phillips had chipped in $10,000 apiece to get the festival going in the early stages. Gate receipts were to be used to pay them back.

Janis Joplin and Big Brother were a hard act to follow, but Country Joe and the Fish were either too stoned to care or had enough confidence in their music to take the stage in grand fashion. No one could match the intensity of Joplin's perform- ance that afternoon. But the Fish really didn't concern them- selves with intensity. Political satire and protest music, Berkeley style, were more their bag. So were songs that lauded the effects of mind-expanding drugs and the propagation of the psyche- delic culture that was growing in the Bay Area.

Never a band versed in the subtleties of musical sophistica- tion, Country Joe and the Fish instead made the lyrical sagacity of its leader the strong point of its repertoire. McDonald had been influenced by the restlessness of the times and Berkeley's role in the political activism of the early and middle sixties. The Free Speech Movement in 1964 and the numerous demonstra- tions against the war in Vietnam made their way into the lyrical scheme of McDonald's music. By 1966 the band was playing regularly at Berkeley's political rallies and at the Fill- more Auditorium. Vanguard Records saw them as a possible West Coast version of New York's Fugs and signed them to a contract. Along with the Jefferson Airplane, Country Joe and the Fish were one of the first psychedelic bands from the Bay Area to play outside California.

At Monterey, Country Joe McDonald painted his face in exotic designs and appeared onstage wearing the wildest hippie garb he could find. An American flag hung near his midsection. Playing such local favorites as "Fixin' To Die Rag," which later became an anthem for the New Left, and "Please Don't Drop That Bomb on Me," the band revealed its satirical bent. Some- times it sounded as if each member of the group were playing the same song in his own favorite key. The audience, though, never seemed to mind.

Country Joe and the Fish were another of the Bay Area bands that played the festival circuit in the years that followed Monterey. According to McDonald, "The Fish and the other San Francisco bands that went over well playing rock festivals owed much of their success to the years prior to the big rock- festival days when everyone learned the ins and outs of out- door concerts at political rallies and free appearances in Golden Gate Park. We [San Francisco and Berkeley musicians] had a definite advantage over all the other performers and bands who played the festivals with us, and it showed, especially at the early festivals."

Country Joe and the Fish peaked as a band at Woodstock, with a memorable performance of the "Fish Cheer" by more than 400,000 wildly enthusiastic kids screaming the letters f-u-c-k in cheerleader fashion at the top of their lungs. As it turned out, the Fish were one of the very few bands in rock-festival history to triumph with songs of political satire. Politics and rock music generally did not mix at rock festivals.

The blues continued after the Fish set with Al Kooper doing a solo. Kooper was formerly the organist for the Blues Project but had recently split from the band to pursue a solo career. Kooper quickly found out at Monterey that the rock establishment was not yet ready to accept enthusiastically solo careers by performers without superstar status. In the year that followed Monterey, Kooper founded Blood, Sweat and Tears, one of the first bands to experiment with a jazz-rock format.

Al Kooper came and left, and it was the Paul Butterfield Blues Band that next took the stage for their interpretation of the blues. There were no surprises in their set. This was a well-known act with a solid reputation based on their superb lp *East-West*. Released in 1966, the album had immediately become one of the definitive electrified blues albums of the decade. Paul Butterfield was one of the earliest white blues performers in the 1960s blues revival and had as much right to the stage at Monterey as anyone. Still, the excitement was generated by the younger, more aggressive San Francisco bands. Although the Butterfield Blues Band got the applause they deserved, it was given primarily out of respect for the band's contributions over the past couple of years rather than for their performance there.

Quicksilver Messenger Service had been together since 1965. John Cipollina's guitar antics impressed record companies, but, unlike Big Brother, Quicksilver did not rush into the recording studio. It may have been the result of a lack of confidence inherent in the band, or it may have represented a deliberate procrastination designed to allow time to perfect the group's overall sound. In any case their debut album, *Quicksilver Messenger Service*, on Capitol Records, was not released until the spring of 1968, more than three years after the band's inception. Many of the tunes they played at Monterey were included on their first album. Their performance was also well received, and later on in the day members of the band jammed with fellow musicians at the Monterey Peninsula College football field.

Steve Miller was another ex-Texan who had found happiness

in San Francisco. Along with good friend Boz Scaggs, Miller put together a band that confined itself to a spacy acid rock sound truly reflective of the psychedelic movement. Their appearance at Monterey was a triumphant one, and they also landed a recording contract with Capitol Records for their efforts there. The months of playing at the Fillmore Auditorium had tightened their professional edge, and the Monterey set featured the improvement beautifully.

Miller became a near-legend in San Francisco rock circles. His albums, *Children of the Future* and *Sailor*, both released in 1968, are still considered classic psychedelic albums. But while other San Francisco bands were crisscrossing the country in the late sixties and early seventies, Miller slowly faded from the picture. It wasn't until 1973 that he resurrected himself with *The Joker*. The album contained the smash hit single by the same name and helped introduce Miller to the Top 40 AM radio audience. He's been a superstar ever since.

The final act of the afternoon show was introduced by David Crosby of the Byrds. The Electric Flag was founded by Mike Bloomfield, an ex-member of the Butterfield Blues Band. The Flag consisted of Harvey Brooks on bass, Buddy Miles on drums, Barry Goldberg on keyboards, Nick ("The Greek") Gravenites singing lead and playing congas, and Bloomfield on guitar. Monterey was the band's debut live performance, and they brought the now-tired crowd to its feet more than once. Led by Bloomfield's masterful guitar solos, the blues-rock theme was absolute and energetic. Along with that of Elvin Bishop of the Butterfield Blues Band and Al Wilson of Canned Heat, Bloomfield's guitar work was some of the best on Saturday afternoon.

Saturday evening's concert promised more good rock. Thus far the festival had been smashing musically. Things were running smoothly on the organizational front, also. Lou Adler was often seen dashing to the performers' tent, shouting instructions and waving hellos in the process. Mama Cass, ever-smiling and looking a little like a performer's tent herself, chatted with friends backstage while assuming a share of the organizational responsibilities. There was a threat of rain, but few people gave it much thought. In the center of town things were peaceful as police officers with flowers pinned to their uniforms gave directions to motorists and offered parking hints.

Saturday night's crowd was the largest of the weekend. At least 8,500 people jammed into the arena, while hordes of ticketless young people milled around outside the fairgrounds listening to the music that blared from the huge loudspeakers. A large portion of these people hurried over to the football field when word leaked out that Chet Helms had set up another free concert, again featuring a few of the San Francisco bands.

Back on the stage, Moby Grape, a Haight-Ashbury band that didn't get an opportunity to play during the afternoon concert, opened the evening's show. Highlighting a swirling light show, the Grape continued the San Francisco-style bombardment begun earlier in the day. Shown in conjunction with the sounds of acid rock, light shows became an important element in the growth of what was becoming known as psychedelia. During the entire evening Head Lights, the leading light specialists in San Francisco at the time, put on a mesmerizing display of free-floating liquid colorations projected on a huge white screen hung in the back of the stage area.

Hugh Masekela, the South African trumpeter, was second on the bill and responsible for the first real flop of the festival. Masekela played the longest set of the festival—nearly one hour's worth of inconclusive jazz that finally sputtered to a desultory halt. At first the jazz idiom had provided an interesting change of pace from the blues and rock of the afternoon show, but Masekela misjudged his audience. His long-winded solos made for tedious listening, and the band ended its set to catcalls and boos from the restless crowd.

The Byrds followed Masekela. They were one of the few L.A. bands that was wholly accepted by the San Francisco musicians. The Byrds had an international following based on their reputation as trend-setters within the folk-rock movement. They were personal friends of Bob Dylan, and many hoped that Dylan would show up at Monterey to jam with his buddies. Dylan did not appear, but the Byrds, fresh from their successful gig at the Mount Tam festival, performed admirably without him.

Things, however, were not all cheery with the Byrds in 1967. There had been some intragroup squabbles that were mostly instigated by personality differences and disagreement over the band's musical direction. Gene Clark, the Byrds' principal composer, quit the band in late 1966 to pursue a solo career. The departure left the Byrds with a noticeable songwriting gap that was soon filled by Jim (Roger) McGuinn and, to a lesser extent, David Crosby. But McGuinn favored material that dealt with space exploration and other ethereal themes while Crosby urged the Byrds to adopt more political songs.

Crosby was the group's most colorful and outspoken member. Equipped with a thick, blond mustache that lazily drooped over his upper lip and ultimately became his trademark, Crosby was not one to hold back his feelings or comments. Prior to the Byrds' performance at Monterey of the tune "He Was a Friend of Mine," Crosby unexpectedly launched into a diatribe of President Kennedy's assassination investigation and chided the government for suppressing the true story as well as key witnesses.

McGuinn and the other Byrds criticized Crosby for the outburst. They were also angry at him for snubbing them backstage at Monterey. A few months later, after bickering with McGuinn had intensified, Crosby left the Byrds after a cash settlement. He was not out of work long, though. He would later turn up as one third of Crosby, Stills and Nash. The band made its second appearance as a working band at Woodstock in August of 1969.

The Paul Butterfield Band filled in for the absent Beach Boys and was followed by the second flop of the evening. Laura Nyro was an unknown nineteen-year-old songwriter from The Bronx, New York, who had just released an album on Verve Records. "And When I Die" and "Wedding Bell Blues," two cuts from her first lp, later became huge hits for numerous artists, including Al Kooper's Blood, Sweat and Tears and the Fifth Dimension. But at Monterey Nyro's talent was hidden behind a frozen expression of fear when the first signs of the audience's lack of interest in her music became apparent. Dressed in a black evening gown, Nyro attempted a cross-section of gospel and blues that might have been successful if the complex musical arrangements had not baffled her backup band. The sound that came from the stage was confused and lacked even the smallest amount of direction. After being hissed at, an intimidated Laura Nyro left the stage with tears streaming down her cheeks. The music scene might not have been ready for Laura Nyro in the summer of 1967, but time was on her side; by the early 1970s she began receiving the critical raves she so thoroughly deserved.

The Jefferson Airplane took the stage next, and the anxious audience warmed up to one of San Francisco's more innovative bands. The band was in the midst of riding a crest of commercial popularity with the success of its second album, *Surrealistic Pillow* on RCA. Replacing vocalist Signe Anderson with Grace Slick, previously a singer with The Great Society, gave the band's music a more acid-rock feel. She had brought with her two of perhaps her greatest songs, "Somebody To Love" and "White Rabbit," both of which were big hits in 1967. The former openly advocated the use of hallucinogenic drugs and hinted at them being one of the main forces behind the Airplane's music. Slick quickly became the band's preeminent figure. Her notoriety took limelight away from Marty Balin, the Airplane's other lead vocalist, although his contribution to the Airplane's music was never less than important.

The audience called for an encore after the Airplane completed their set, but it was getting late. Backstage, Otis Redding nervously peeked out at the audience and wondered why he had decided to sing at Monterey. He had heard the boos generated by Masekela's and Nyro's performances. He had heard the shouts of approval and elation elicited by the Byrds and the Airplane. Where did a black soul singer fit in? Many of his black colleagues had decided against playing the festival. Redding asked himself out loud if he shouldn't have done the same. He had played in front of a few white audiences before, but never had he been able to get the same fired excitement from them as he had from black audiences. One of his most successful encounters with a white audience had come at a gig at the Fillmore Auditorium in 1966. He hoped his luck had not changed since then.

The festival organizers and the Monterey City Council had agreed on a set curfew of midnight for the evening shows. Friday night's performance went way past the curfew, and it was rapidly approaching 12 o'clock when Booker T. and the MGs and the Mar Keys took the stage for a short instrumental set. They finished with an enthusiastic round of applause. This gave Otis Redding—the Crown Prince of Soul, as he was known then—the courage to give it his best shot.

"It's been a real groovy day and a great evening," announced emcee Tommy Smothers. "Let's bring on with a great hand Mr. Otis Redding."

"Shake! Let me hear you!

"Shake! Everybody say it!"

Redding blasted into a rousing version of the song "Shake." Instantly people moved into the aisles, dancing to the music. Even those with half-closed eyes, weary from over ten hours of music, managed to shimmy and shake and let every ounce of energy left in their bodies transform into the upbeat drive of rock 'n' soul.

"Respect," a Redding original made popular by Aretha Franklin, was next. Again the results were startling. When the song was over, Redding, panting and sweating, asked the crowd, "This is the love crowd, right? We all love each other, don't we?" The response was thunderous. Here was a black man in the summer of 1967, when racial tension in America was thick and ugly, telling a screaming crowd of white kids that we all love each other. Redding pulled it off by masterfully involving the audience, making them an important element in his act. He was performing *with* them, not for them. No one, with the exception of Janis Joplin, had ignited the audience like Redding had.

"I've Been Loving You Too Long" and one of the best soul versions of "Satisfaction" ever heard live climaxed his memorable performance. Those not in the aisles dancing were up on their chairs clapping their hands. Redding single-handedly turned the Monterey fairgrounds into a soul madhouse.

Unfortunately, he would not live long enough to fully capitalize on the triumphant performance. On December 10, 1967, just five months after Monterey, Redding was killed in a plane crash in Wisconsin. At the age of twenty-six Redding was just on the verge of receiving the credit he deserved. For years he had written songs that such artists as Aretha Franklin and Arthur Conley ("Sweet Soul Music") turned into money-making hits. "Sittin' on the Dock of the Bay," posthumously released, was perhaps his biggest hit of all. Redding's most gratifying honor in 1967, aside from Monterey, was when *Melody Maker* named him the best male vocalist of that year. If one man ever deserved the honor, it was Otis Redding.

All anyone could talk about on Sunday morning was the Otis Redding set of the previous night. Many found it hard to sleep after such a commanding performance and, instead, had gone over to the football field, where music was played all through the rainy night. The Sunday afternoon concert would be something wholly different from what the crowd had seen and heard during the past two days. Instead of hearing a number of groups and artists, they would hear just one. Instead of focusing in on guitars and amps, they would see exotic stringed instruments, the most familiar being the sitar. Instead of listening to the strains of blues and rock, the audience would hear the delectable sounds of the Indian raga.

David Crosby had done some experimenting with the sitar;

Otis Redding.

Courtesy of Pennebaker, Inc.

the Beatles had used a touch of the raga style on the *Sergeant Pepper* album. When George Harrison told the rock press he was studying under the master of the sitar, Ravi Shankar, the venerable Indian musician was cast into the international spotlight. While interest in Eastern religion had always been alive in the bohemian culture of the late fifties and early sixties, the psychedelic movement took that interest one step further and incorporated it within its music.

Shankar had the entire afternoon to himself. Those who came to Monterey for the sheer exuberance of rock or the power of the blues stayed away. As a result, there were a few tickets available for the performance right up until showtime. Just prior to the commencement of the music, Shankar asked the audience to refrain from smoking or talking loudly. Concentration by both the musicians and the audience was essential if the music was to be fully appreciated. Marijuana was stashed away and incense was lit instead. Throughout the performance Shankar periodically stopped and explained to the audience the nature of the music and the techniques he used to achieve such effects. Shankar was accompanied by a musician playing tabla (a tuned pair of small hand drums) and another one playing a tamboura (an instrument resembling a lute in appearance but containing no frets).

For three hours in a lightly falling rain, Shankar played Indian music for a hip crowd. When he finished, he received the festival's longest standing ovation. Three times he returned to the stage to receive the approval of the audience. He gave flowers to members of the crowd, and he remarked how much he enjoyed playing for them.

"I want you to know how much I love you and how happy I am to be loved by you . . . Even if it is not pop music, I am happy my music has become a popular music." The audience clapped louder. Shankar's smile widened.

It would have been difficult for Shankar to accomplish what he did without the Beatles connection. Chances are the audience would not have lasted the three hours. But it was chic now to enjoy Indian music, and many listened attentively. Shankar had added a new dimension to pop consciousness. After Monterey he was in considearble demand for concerts, lectures, and other rock festivals.

At the conclusion of the afternoon concert, many people went back to their hotel rooms or campsites and packed up, ready to head back to the city as soon as the evening show ended. Others

At Monterey, Ravi Shankar added another dimension to the pop consciousness.

stayed and slept in Monterey on Sunday night. The festival's almost nonstop music had drained the energy of many. Most people had gotten only a few hours of sleep on Friday and Saturday nights, and this was simply not enough to maintain the pace.

It took an invigorating dose of hard-edged rock 'n' roll to keep the interest blazing. The Grateful Dead opened Sunday evening's show. The Dead had as large a following as the Airplane in the Bay Area, although they were not nearly as well known on a national scale. They had played twice at the football field on Saturday, and their sets there were much more successful than the forty-minute one they played Sunday evening. Forty minutes was hardly enough time for a group like the Dead to get warmed up. Their Monterey set seemed to come to an abrupt halt just as the band was getting comfortable on stage.

The Blues Project followed the Dead. Like the Butterfield Blues Band, they were members of the "old guard"—experienced bluesmen with a knack for the stage and an innate drive to carry the blues feeling to a more sacred level. Unfortunately, most people had had their fill of the blues by Sunday evening. A memorable "Flute Thing" temporarily alleviated this feeling, but people were fading fast. What they needed was an act that would overwhelm their fatigue, make them forget how tired they really were. They needed the passionate moans of Janis Joplin or the fury of Otis Redding to jar them into more than a wakeful composure. What they got was The Who, and they turned out to be much more than any hoped for.

The Who slammed into their set. Roger Daltrey sang with dynamic energy. Keith Moon pounded away at his double bass drum kit. John Entwistle jerked notes out of his bass, and Peter Townshend built up steam with authoritative, powerful chords rather than note-infested solos. He shook his guitar like an angry madman.

The Monterey crowd quickly came to life. The Who were power-packed musicians who demanded reaction. "Pictures of Lily," then "Summertime Blues," and a superb "Substitute" preceded "My Generation" and rocked the audience. It was during this song that The Who demonstrated their potent brand of rock emotionalism. Just as the song was ending, Moon began throwing his sticks up into the air and catching them in perfect stride. The power that rose out of Townshend's guitar rapidly skidded out of control. Daltrey's voice ached for a stronger release. All at once a smoke bomb exploded on stage, and Daltrey let his microphone fly out of his hand and into Moon's drum kit. Townshend turned from the audience and rammed his guitar into the wall of amps. There was a flash, and more smoke belched from the destroyed amplifiers. Moon continued to kick his drums until they lay scattered over the stage. Townshend picked up his battered guitar and violently smashed it on the stage floor. When there was nothing left to demolish, The Who walked from the stage. Just like that.

The audience was numb with bewilderment. They enthusiastically cheered and shouted, but few in the crowd grasped the meaning of it all. Never before had so many come so close to the raw power of rock and the emotional reactions it was capable of evoking. The Who had jammed their music and their force down the throats of the Monterey audience. They made their presence known, like it or not.

It took courage to take the stage after The Who's set. Anyone else would have failed miserably. Anyone except Jimi Hendrix. All Hendrix did was take the rabid, frenetic energy

The Jimi Hendrix experience.

of The Who one step further. Brian Jones of the Rolling Stones introduced the Jimi Hendrix Experience. Out of the wings came a wild-haired black dressed in flaming red pants and a brightly ruffled shirt. He spoke in jittered bursts of broken words and bent syllables. He muttered something about boring the crowd for six or seven minutes. Boring? Hendrix broke into Dylan's "Like a Rolling Stone" with a freight train full of muscle. The full sound of the Experience (Noel Redding on bass and Mitch Mitchell on drums) was staggering. They tore sounds from their instruments that were previously thought possible only with a full band playing at full volume. The three musicians were a full band, however. The trio idea, lying dormant since the days of Buddy Holly, had resurfaced on the music scene. Most bands in 1967 employed a lead and a rhythm guitarist and a keyboard player as well as a drummer and a bass player. Hendrix's guitar work made up for the lack of another guitarist. He played enough chords and lead riffs to fully stretch the sound of his instrument without losing the immediacy of its power.

Like Joplin, Hendrix worked up a sexual frenzy on the stage. He stroked his guitar one moment, kissed it the next, and rapidly humped it until it exploded in an ecstasy of piercing high notes. He worked the guitar behind his neck and rammed it through his legs. He played a solo with his teeth. Just before climaxing with "Wild Thing," Hendrix told the audience, "I'm gonna sacrifice something that I really love, man. Don't think I'm silly doing this, I don't think I'm losing my mind. This is the only way I can do it. Don't get mad, *noooo*, don't get mad. This is it, man, there's nothing more I can do. *Ooh*, look at those beautiful people out there."

Hendrix raced his fingers up the neck of the guitar, producing screeching notes. He then took the guitar and placed it between his legs, swinging it madly. All at once the guitar turned into a flaming torch. Hendrix had doused the instrument with lighter fluid and set a match to it. In just a few seconds the crude, raw power of rock had again been released with apocalyptic intensity. Was Hendrix a madman or a genius? Certainly his guitar work and mastery of the instrument were beyond doubt. No one at Monterey had come close to Hendrix's charismatic and authoritative style of rock guitar. He delivered an unparalleled explosion of wild energy delicately bordering on bedlam. Yet he never let the music fly completely uncontrolled. In that respect he was a true genius.

But the theatrics and violence were very controversial. Was there room on the rock stage for destruction and violence? The critics were divided on this point. Robert Christgau wrote in *Esquire* magazine: "Hendrix's act can be seen as a consistently vulgar parody of rock theatrics, but I don't feel I have to like it." Commenting on The Who's set, Christgau wrote, "The destructiveness of the Who is consistent theatre, deriving directly from the group's defiant, lower-class stance."[2] Many felt that the destruction of the instruments used to make music was the ultimate release of rock 'n' roll energy. Violence on the stage took the music to a higher, more passionate state. For Hendrix and The Who, the destruction onstage was a sacrificial act. The boldness of Hendrix and The Who later found its way into the style of many other bands and artists who felt the need for a visual release.

After the Hendrix spectacle the remainder of the show was anticlimactic. The Buffalo Springfield filled the stage with four guitarists, including David Crosby of the Byrds. The band's music was well executed, considering the circumstances, but

Courtesy of Warner Brothers Records

Jimi Hendrix: "I'm gonna sacrifice something that I really love, man."

the audience found it nearly impossible to give them their un-divided attention. Their minds had been tampered with, and their musical awareness had been stolen by the power of Hen-drix's performance. The Group With No Name followed the Buffalo Springfield. They were branded "The Group With No Talent" and were promptly added to the festival flop list.

It took the sweetened pop sound of John Phillips and the Mamas and the Papas to bring everyone back to earth. Mama

Cass's presence onstage was undeniable as her massive frame swayed with the music. Sharing lead vocals with Phillips, Cass's voice sounded angelic compared to the barbarian sound of The Who and Jimi Hendrix. Scott McKenzie joined John Phillips and the band for a version of the hit single "San Francisco." The final number of the festival was a joyous and triumphant "Dancin' in the Streets." A host of thank yous and good nights, and the First Annual Monterey International Pop Festival was history.

The festival might have been over, but it remained newsworthy. Critics wrote columns praising the work of Lou Adler and John Phillips. The national magazines reported on the colorful sights of an exposed counterculture. Music periodicals gave detailed accounts of the wide range of musical styles exhibited and the introduction of such new faces on the scene as Janis Joplin and Jimi Hendrix. D. A. Pennebaker, who had filmed *Don't Look Back,* a documentary of Bob Dylan's 1965 tour of England, had hours and hours of film footage of the Monterey Pop Festival, which he was busily editing for either a full-length film or a television special. And then there was the matter of deciding what to do with the profits realized from the extravaganza.

It had cost approximately $300,000 to stage the festival, but, with the profits gained from the sale of the film rights, the festival organization wound up with almost $200,000 in charitable proceeds. Since the festival's inception, no one had come up with any practical ideas as to what group or groups should receive financial assistance. It was decided that all those who had performed at Monterey would be required to submit a statement indicating their choices. Due to the commotion and excitement backstage, this idea was never carried out. Thus it was left to Adler, Phillips, and Paul Simon, along with the rest of the board of directors, to determine what to do with the profits.

As it turned out, Jerry Wexler of Atlantic Records received a large amount of money for the Sam Cooke Memorial Scholarship. A donation was made to the Monterey Symphony Orchestra, and a token amount was handed over to the Los Angeles Free Medical Clinic. Money also went toward the purchase of

---

Mama Cass and Michelle Phillips at Monterey.
Courtesy of Lou Adler

guitars and the setting up of music lessons in Harlem and other inner-city ghettos in New York. Small donations were made to other organizations as well.

The remainder of the money was kept in an account with the Bank of America until the board decided on the last round of recipients for the proceeds. At the time Sandra Beebe, who was working as a bookkeeper for the Monterey organization, figured out a clever way to embezzle more than $51,000 of the account. All checks were supposed to have both Phillips's and Adler's signatures on them. Phillips had signed a number of checks in advance, and Beebe forged Adler's signature. She wrote out a check to a bogus organization in New Mexico, which was cashed by her husband. Before anyone realized what had occurred, Beebe had vanished and so had the money.

The story was picked up by *Rolling Stone*, the new rock periodical out of San Francisco, as a cover story. Immediately there were cries of inept and improper regard for the money. It was determined that the Bank of America was liable for the theft. Rather than face a lawsuit and court battle, the bank paid back to the organization most of the embezzled money. A warrant was issued for Beebe's arrest, but there is no information available on whether she was ever apprehended.

Pennebaker's film was made into a full-length documentary and opened to rave reviews. It was the first documentary of rock music to achieve commercial success on an international scale. The film concentrated on the performers and the music, and accurately captured the thrilling performances of the best acts. *Monterey Pop* paved the way for numerous other documentaries on rock and its festivals.

The Monterey Pop Festival stands out as one of the most important happenings in rock history and in the development of a large-scale, youth-dominated counterculture. For years rock had been reaching out for serious recognition as a legitimate music form, but it always wound up in the shadows of the more conventional pop music of the day. The Beatles had forced rock to the surface due to the overwhelming popularity and success, but even their ascendance could not completely topple pop music as the reigning musical genre in America in 1967. What was needed was an event that would solidify the importance of rock in the 1960s. The Monterey International Pop Festival fit the order perfectly.

Monterey set off a frenzy of signings as record companies

realized the commercial value of hard rock. Not only were groups and artists such as Janis Joplin and Big Brother, Steve Miller, and the Paupers signed immediately after the festival to handsome contracts, but, more importantly, Monterey set off a widespread hunt for more talent all over the United States and England. The pop establishment was overthrown as rock forced its way to the center of the stage. Top-40 AM stations were besieged with songs by bands formerly considered too radical for their playlists. FM stations began springing up regularly and played the music that had been heard at Monterey. Moby Grape, the Electric Flag, and Country Joe and the Fish, among others, quickly became national acts. Joplin, The Who, and Jimi Hendrix began a speedy rise to superstardom.

Monterey was the first of the large rock-oriented music festivals. Perhaps more than anything else it demonstrated the huge marketability of the new rock sound. Record companies came to view the festival concept as an excellent means of exposing new talent and promoting established acts.

But the unveiling of the new rock and the new counterculture was not without a price. The roots of Monterey Pop—the free outdoor concerts, the numerous be-ins, Mount Tam—and the nonprofit, celebratory theme were soon debauched, distorted, and forgotten. The vision of large profits that arose from the excitement over the commercial viability of the new music and the festival format caused the perversion. Things would never really be the same again.

CHAPTER THREE

Growing Pains

The pop festival is revolution in microcosm.

> —Tom Rounds, festival promoter,
> Miami, 1968

The huge success of the First Annual Monterey Pop Festival instigated a substantial amount of speculation as to when and where the event would occur in 1968. John Phillips and Lou Adler were frequently hounded by the rock press to give statements concerning any future festival plans. At first the festival organizers felt that the annual event should be permanently rooted in Monterey. But Phillips later hinted to the media that, if the festival was to retain its international stature, the site should be changed: Phillips mentioned London, New York, or even Stockholm as possible future sites. When the word spread that the Monterey Pop Festival was considering alternative sites, a group of Australian entrepreneurs proclaimed that they would pay all expenses if the festival based itself in Melbourne.

Meanwhile other rock promoters began formulating plans for their own festivals. Sid Bernstein, a noted and well-respected concert promoter and businessman, circulated plans for a huge festival in New York's Central Park for June of 1968. Bernstein told *Billboard* in the fall of 1967 that "there's a big need for a festival here in New York. It would bring together the British scene, the West Coast scene and the East Coast scene and reconfirm New York as the music capital of the world." Bernstein hoped to attract upward of a quarter-million people to a three-day event that would be similar to Monterey. Another promoter toyed with the possibility of a Boston pop festival. And in southern California impresarios began to plan the staging of a large rock festival in southern Orange County.

European promoters were just as busy as their American counterparts in concocting grandiose plans for international or European rock festivals. Czechoslovakia hurried plans through the developmental stage and actually pulled off the First Annual Czechoslovakian Festival of Rock Music. Held in Prague in December 1967, the event marked the first time that the Czech government had allowed rock music to be heard on a large scale. For three days Czech rock bands played to twelve thousand young people in Prague's Lucerna Hall, competing for a grand prize that was awarded to the best act.

Plans were also discussed for the staging of the First European International Pop Festival, scheduled to take place in Rome in February of 1968. Promoters promised a huge array of talent, mostly British and American rock acts. All proceeds were to be handed over to needy international charitable groups, and a theme of worldwide peace and love was to be openly promulgated. Unfortunately the promoters claimed that many of the top groups would appear before they were actually signed to contracts, and thus lost much of their credibility. The festival did ultimately take place, but not on the scale that the festival promoters had originally hoped for.

After long talks concerning the relocation of the Monterey Pop Festival, Adler, Phillips, and other members of the festival organization finally decided that Monterey should once again host the 1968 festival. The organizers had only pleasant things to say about Monterey and its citizenry, and the site was close enough so that extensive planning and logistics could be handled with ease.

The city of Monterey, however, had second thoughts on the proposal. Police Chief Frank Marinello, who had previously assured those who attended the Monterey Pop Festival that they were his friends and were always welcome in Monterey, retracted his statements upon hearing of the festival's decision to return to his domain. He pointed to excessive drug abuse and acts of questionable morality, such as boys and girls sleeping together, as reasons why the festival was not welcome to return. The mayor of Monterey, allegedly angered at not having her name added to the festival's board of directors, also refused to endorse plans for a second pop festival. Local businessmen who did not prosper from the first festival and irate residents who were inconvenienced for three days voiced their opposition at town meetings.

Legally speaking, the city of Monterey could not prevent the festival from occurring without a formal county denial of request to festival organizers. The fairgrounds were owned by the county, and county officials were thus responsible for the final decision on the matter. Of course, Monterey townsfolk knew that if they complained loudly enough, officials would see it their way.

After a series of meetings with Adler and Phillips, the city council of Monterey surprisingly decided to endorse the festival if its organizers agreed to a series of demands and restrictions. According to Michael Lydon, who covered the issue for *Rolling Stone*, some of the demands presented by the city council were that the organizers of the festival were to take out an insurance policy that would protect the city from any suits evolving out of false-arrest charges; that stringent time restrictions be placed on the music; that a curfew be enforced by the local police; that religious services be held on the festival site on Sunday morning; that segregated campsites be designated for males and females; and that a sizable donation be made to Monterey's antinarcotic program.

Some of the demands were valid and could be met by the festival's organizers, but others were simply not compatible with the concept of the festival. Segregated campsites would be scoffed at by young people and arguments would inevitably be raised about the limitations on the music. But the most serious demand was the insurance policy that would give the Monterey police department a free hand to round up at will anyone who offended them without the opportunity for the victims to lodge a complaint legally. The possibility of the police abusing this unlimited power was great, and Adler and Phillips considered approval of these demands to be an egregious mistake. The duo made one last attempt to secure permission to use the festival grounds without the demands but failed to make any headway. Subsequently plans for the Second Annual Monterey International Pop Festival were permanently dropped.

The Newport (California) Pop Festival

While Richard Nixon and his supporters encountered rising opposition from Nelson Rockefeller and Ronald Reagan at the Republican National Convention in Miami, close to 100,000 young people gathered in southern California for the start of the summer's largest rock festival. While members of the California state legislature finalized a bill that increased the punishment for possession of LSD and marijuana, Newport Beach and Costa Mesa police officers were busily frisking anyone suspected of holding drugs outside the grounds of the Newport Pop Festival.

Aside from the Sky River Rock Festival and Lighter Than Air Fair, the only significant rock festival that occurred in the summer of 1968 was the Newport Pop Festival. Not to be confused with the Newport Folk and Jazz festivals of Newport, Rhode Island, the two-day rock festival was staged some fifty miles south of Los Angeles in Costa Mesa, California, on the first weekend of August. Newport Beach borders on Costa Mesa, and for some unexplained reason the festival promoters decided to use the fashionable resort community's name as the official site of the festival. It is possible that the promoters hoped to link the Newport Pop with the Newport Folk and Jazz festivals in order to attract a sizable crowd.

Earlier in the year many rock people had predicted a whole slew of festivals for the summer months, but the general mood of the country and a steady rise in young people's interest in politics diluted the festival spirit. Plans for a second Monterey Pop Festival had fallen through, and interest in other large rock festivals also waned. Instead of attending huge, rock-oriented celebrations, the youth of the nation seemed to be more concerned with antiwar demonstrations or protesting at political conventions. Both the Republicans and Democrats were to choose presidential nominees in August. The war in Vietnam had been dangerously escalated. Robert Kennedy and Martin Luther King, Jr., recently had been assassinated. Draft quotas were raised. All these events directly affected America's youth. Instead of passively protesting the problems of the country as they had throughout most of 1967, people who had been only mildly affiliated with the New Left movement or other socio-political groups in the past took to the streets in 1968.

Whether it was as a volunteer worker for Senator Eugene McCarthy's bid for the Democratic nomination or as a member of the revolutionary Yippies, young people with activist blood in them forgot about rock festivals for the summer. Actually the most important "festival" of the year was the Yippies' "Festival of Life," staged in the streets of Chicago to counteract the "Convention of Death," staged, according to the revolutionary group, by the nation's Democratic politicians. The Chicago Democratic Convention was the target, the battleground where the forces of the counterculture met Mayor Daley's men in blue in a fight over the future direction of America. There were no feelings of celebration as bloodstained protesters fell victim to the poundings of police billy clubs. The sounds of police sirens were heard far and above the strains of rock music during August of 1968.

But earlier in the month the youth of southern California found some time to forget political issues for a weekend and to gather en masse to groove on rock. The Newport Pop Festival was produced by a group of local concert promoters who had successfully presented a small weekend rock fest in Los Angeles the previous summer. Therefore, the lack of planning that accounted for numerous inconveniences suffered by the majority of festivalgoers at the Newport Pop was more a product of neglect than of inexperience.

The Orange County Fairgrounds is a huge, flat, dusty, dry, open field that is more suited for a flea market or swap meet than it is for a rock festival—especially one that was to attract 100,000 attendants. Perhaps the festival would have been more enjoyable if the promoters had spent a little extra money and rented chairs, so that the crowd wouldn't have to sit on the dusty field. The lack of seating was just one item in a series of cutbacks designed to save money for the promoters.

As more and more people converged on the festival grounds that weekend, more and more dust was unsettled. The combination of ninety-degree temperatures with the perpetual blowing of dust made for many parched throats. By noon of the first day, almost all the available water had been consumed by thirsty festivalgoers, and a serious water shortage was in effect. The Costa Mesa Health Department was correct when it claimed that the lack of water was due to poor planning by the promoters. Sanitation facilities were also in short supply, as were camping facilities. Many people arrived on Friday expecting ample campgrounds. They were wrong. Those who did not have hotel reservations or had not planned to commute back to Los Angeles after each concert were without a place to sleep. Many wandered down to the beach and established campsites there, but sooner or later they were escorted away by the police.

Fortunately Costa Mesa city officials realized the severity of the problem and designated a thirty-two-acre area of unfenced fairgrounds to be used as an emergency campsite. Portable toilets were hastily set up, and water tanks were brought in to handle the basic necessities. Those who were unable to secure a campsite merely slept at the concert site in the dust and litter that was strewn all over the field.

It seemed that an inordinate number of people had come to Newport for everything but the music. In the middle of the day, it was not uncommon to see people sleeping on rolled-out sleeping bags or just generally loitering about. Blank expressions and apathetic reactions were often visible. Drugs were used extensively and unwisely by people who were too immature to handle the unpredictable consequences. Many cases of drug overdoses were reported, numerous young runaways were picked up by the police, and almost one quarter of those arrested for drug possession were minors.

The music began on Saturday afternoon, August 4, with a lineup that included Sonny and Cher, Steppenwolf, the Chambers Brothers, Tiny Tim, the James Cotton Blues Band, Canned Heat, and a San Francisco contingent made up of Country Joe and the Fish, the Electric Flag, and the Paul Butterfield Blues Band.

The Newport Pop Festival might have been lacking in sanitation and camping facilities, but there was no deficiency in the musical output on Saturday afternoon.

Oddly enough, the act that drew the most applause was Tiny Tim. A music critic for the local newspaper, the *Daily Pilot*, sized up the vaudeville performer this way: "He looks like Joan Baez's sister. He talks like a canary with a cough and he walks as uncertainly as a high-wire artist who just dropped his umbrella."

It could have been the kisses he constantly blew at the audience, or maybe it was the way he imitated Rudy Vallee when he sang "The Good Ship Lollipop" through a megaphone. Whatever the reason, Tiny Tim undoubtedly enjoyed a moment of glory at the Newport Pop Festival. The Electric Flag sweated through a power-packed set, and the James Cotton Blues Band gave a memorable performance, but it was Tiny Tim who captured the hearts of the crowd at the Orange County Fairgrounds.

Sunday's show was highlighted by sets by the Jefferson Airplane, the Grateful Dead, and the Iron Butterfly. The latter group performed its rock epic "In-A-Gadda-Da-Vida," and received two standing ovations in the course of the song. Iron Butterfly, at the close of 1968, were finishing up a triumphant assault on mainstream rock. The two albums the band released that year were heavy favorites with rock audiences. Their second lp, *In-A-Gadda-Da-Vida*, was one of the first rock albums to achieve platinum (million-seller) status. In concert the title song frequently lasted over thirty minutes as crashing guitar solos, winding keyboard riffs, and pounding bass and drum blasts echoed the true spirit of psychedelia.

None of the other acts on Sunday matched the flamboyance and musicianship of the Dead, the Airplane, or Iron Butterfly. During the performance of Eric Burdon and the Animals, Burdon attempted to achieve the visual wizardry of performers like The Who and Jimi Hendrix, but failed miserably. Burdon had viewed with amazement the response these two acts had received at Monterey, and tried to imitate their visual styles. During "Sky Pilot" a smoke bomb was set off, much to the disturbance of the crowd, who had already found it difficult to breathe with all the heat and dust. Later on, as the band finished up its last number, Burdon lost control of the situation and poured beer all over himself, rolled off the stage and climbed back up with some women from the audience for an impromptu dance contest. He came off looking foolish and desperate.

Blue Cheer, a band that packed much aimless energy into three or four chords and a blitzkrieg of sound, fared as badly as Burdon and the Animals, while the Byrds and Illinois Speed Press were only mildly captivating. Perhaps it was the dusty and uninviting location that killed the enthusiasm at the Newport Pop Festival. The lack of such basic necessities as water, portable toilets, and sleeping facilities surely caused

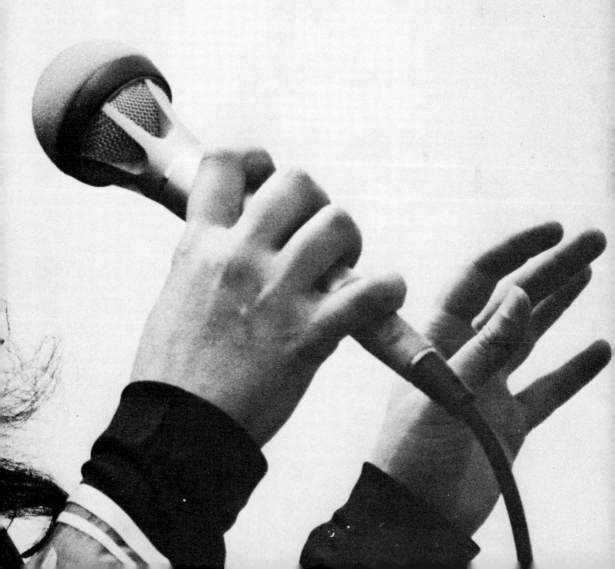

Lead singer Gracie Slick of the Jefferson Airplane. The San Francisco
band was a regular at many of the early festivals.
Courtesy of RCA

considerable discomfort for many in the large crowd. The heat undoubtedly played a key role in the not-so-impressive performances of many of the big acts. In the summer of 1968, rock festival crowds were not yet prepared to sacrifice worldly comforts to hear the music. The enduring qualities that made Woodstock such an astounding success one year later, in spite of rain, mud, and lack of food and water, were simply not part of the rock festival consciousness in 1968.

The Newport Pop Festival presented a preview of the problems large rock festival crowds would face in coming years. As more and more festivals became commercial ventures rather than nonprofit cultural gatherings, promoters attempted to curb their overhead by supplying only minimal services. Nevertheless, compared to some of the rock festival disasters in 1970 and 1971, the situation at Newport in 1968 wasn't all that bad. At least not on some levels.

The Sky River Rock Festival and Lighter Than Air Fair

Betty Nelson's Organic Raspberry Farm had the reputation of harvesting the finest crop of berries in a sixty-mile radius. Located just outside Sultan, Washington, the farm is an hour's drive from Seattle. Many of the residents of Sultan (population: 960) voiced their displeasure with Betty Nelson when they found out that she intended to lease some of her acreage to the New American Community. The liberal organization, it seemed, was interested in staging "some sort of rock 'n' roll thing" to raise money for American Indian human-rights groups.

The New American Community had appointed John Chambless, a local college professor, to head the event. After securing a lease from Nelson, Chambless met with townspeople in an attempt to quiet their fears of an invasion of long-haired hippies. Chambless promised that the festival would not be widely advertised, and a large turnout was not to be expected. He also convinced them of the worthiness of the cause. The town fathers reluctantly decided not to fight the festival's legality in court and adopted a wait-and-see attitude.

The Sky River festival drew only a fraction of the number of people who had attended the Newport Pop Festival in early

Jorma Kaukonen of the Jefferson Airplane.
Courtesy of RCA

Construction of the Woodstock stage.
New York **Daily News**

August. This was mostly due to the bad weather that settled in over Washington that weekend. Its importance, however, lies not in its size but in the fact that it was the only truly successful rock festival of the summer of 1968 in which major acts headlined. The three-day festival occurred over the Labor Day weekend and attracted an estimated fifteen thousand people.

The formal and complete name of the event was the Sky River Rock Festival and Lighter Than Air Fair. The overall format of the affair was strikingly similar to the Fantasy Faire and Magic Mountain Music Festival (the Mount Tam festival) presented just outside San Francisco in June 1967. Like Mount Tam, Sky River was a combination of music and art. The Lighter Than Air Fair was a conglomeration of local and Seattle-based hip merchants and artists. Throughout the weekend these artisans displayed their work and sold whatever they could to interested festivalgoers. Also involved in the nonmusical aspect of the event were such avant-garde theatrical groups as the San Francisco Mime Troupe.

It is interesting to note that the Sky River Rock Festival was the first significant festival actually to be called a rock festival. In the past, most events were called pop festivals—Monterey Pop and Newport Pop were two. But the rock-festival label was actually a misnomer for the Sky River festival, since the bill was, at most only half filled with pure rock bands. Of the forty acts that performed, a majority were steeped in either the blues, folk, country, or jazz idioms.

The music began early Saturday morning, August 31, and continued until midnight of September 2. Country Joe and the Fish, the Grateful Dead, It's A Beautiful Day, and an up-and-coming local Bay Area band, Santana, drove up from San Francisco to play. Other performers included Muddy Waters, the James Cotton Blues Band, Big Mama Willie Mae Thornton, Ramblin' Jack Elliott, the New Lost City Ramblers, Dino Valenti, the Youngbloods, and Mark Spoelstra. The rest of the lineup comprised lesser-known acts and local Seattle bands.

Obviously Sky River did not possess a billing that could even remotely compare to Monterey or Newport. But the informality of the setting and the comparatively small size of the event permitted the bands to perform a bit longer, mingle with the crowd with no hassles, and jam more often than at other festivals. The atmosphere was amicable and relaxed. With only fifteen thousand people on hand, everyone could hear and see the acts on the stage. It was a perfect example of what a rock festival could really achieve if the crowd was limited and proper organization and planning were in effect.

Unlike the previous festivals, where the *rock* acts controlled the tempo of the music and elicited the most response, it was Big Mama Willie Mae Thornton who dominated Sky River. Introduced onstage as the woman who made the song "Hound Dog" popular so that Elvis Presley could become rich from a similar rendition, Big Mama Thornton steamrolled into a gutsy, rough-edged volley of the blues. Big Mama could really sing. Anyone who followed the blues genre knew that. But for the younger rock fans, her name and harsh vocal style were new and exciting. Appearing twice in two days, Thornton received write-ups in *Rolling Stone* and *Downbeat* for her efforts.

Bluesman James Cotton reflected on her performance at Sky River: "I known the Big Mama for a long, long time, ya see. Anyways, she comes up to the festival with no band. So I says, 'Big Mama, what you doin' with no band? How you gonna do your thing with no band?' She said, 'James, now why don't you come up onstage with me and bring your band and we'll do some jammin' if you know what I mean.'

"Me and the band go up on the stage with the Big Mama, you see, and we begin to play the blues. I remember Willie Mae from the time she did 'Hound Dog', but this was one of the best times I ever heard her do the blues. We showed the people at Sky River that the blues ain't all sad like 'my woman gone and left, so what I'd do now' thing. The blues ain't all laid back, you see. There's happy blues and then there's sad blues. We did a lot of happy blues that day. I think we played for close to two hours doin' nothin' but the blues. A funny thing happened when we was playin'. I don't notice nothing peculiar until the crowd in front start laughin' at somethin'. So I looked over at the Big Mama and see this nude fella dancin' with her while she was singin'. This dude didn't have a stitch. I just said to myself that the blues can do *strange* things to people."

Thornton used her triumphant appearance at Sky River to begin a successful run of the rock-festival circuit. She was one of the first of the older blues performers to enjoy a rebirth of popularity, especially with the younger, more rock-oriented audiences.

The Sky River Festival and Lighter Than Air Fair drew widespread acclaim from the rock community. The festival grossed nearly $55,000, of which a substantial portion was handed over

to needy Indian groups. As was the case in Monterey in 1967, the locals were highly impressed by the organization of the event and by the good behavior of the crowd. Chambless spoke of repeating the festival the following year, and the locals warmly endorsed the proposal. The area merchants had made more money over the 1968 Labor Day weekend than at any other time of year. A few of them even hinted that they would like to see more people at the next festival.

Sky River was one of the very few rock festivals to occur two years in a row. The Sky River fest of 1969 was not held in Sultan because the rains that swept down upon the area for two of the three days during the 1968 festival transformed the raspberry farm into a sloppy mud path. Betty Nelson, who was not too happy with the condition of her acreage and had a difficult time getting it back up to par, didn't feel like risking her property a second time. Chambless also realized that the success and press coverage of the event would guarantee a much larger crowd, and he wisely sought a larger site for 1969.

The Sky River Festival marked the first successful semilarge event to occur outside California, and it was the first festival to use a truly pastoral setting. Both Monterey and Newport were located in or near sizable population centers, but the Sky River site was exclusively rural. As the return-to-nature theme became more pronounced in counterculture philosophy, other rock festival promoters chose similar settings.

The Miami Pop Festival

The successful production of the Miami Pop Festival was further proof that the rock-festival concept could indeed survive outside the boundaries of California. The three-day event (December 28–30, 1968) was the first major rock festival staged on the East Coast, and the first major one with personal profit in mind to succeed on all fronts.

Formally billed as the First Annual Miami Pop Festival, the event attracted over 100,000 festivalgoers, almost all of whom lived in the Miami–Fort Lauderdale area. In 1968 it was still uncommon for groups of young people to travel long distances to attend rock festivals. Only the Monterey Pop Festival had

Muddy Waters at the Sky River Rock Festival.
Courtesy of Cameron Organization

attracted festivalgoers from outside the immediate vicinity of the site, as a result of the wide-scale publicity the event received prior to the festival and also because of the novelty of the event. The promoters of the Miami event, however, cleverly realized that if the festival became an annual affair as they hoped, it would attract hordes of college students from the Midwest and Northeast who pilgrimaged to southern Florida during their Christmas break.

The Miami Pop Festival was actually located outside the city limits of Miami in the town of Hallandale. The festival site was Gulfstream Park, one of the largest racehorse tracks in all of Florida. Promoter Tom Rounds, one of the men responsible for the first rock festival at Mount Tam, and his associates acquired the use of the Gulfstream Race Track for a meager five thousand dollars in rental fees and a 5 percent gross of the gate. The small fee guaranteed that if the festival grossed less than had been anticipated, Rounds and his partners could still hope to clear their expenses.

Since they saw the festival as a long-range money-making investment, Tom Rounds, Mel Lawrence, Ron Jacobs, Tom Moffatt, and Mitchell Fisher went about actively securing both community and political support. Rounds managed to get an official endorsement from Florida's Governor Claude Kirk, who deemed the pop festival a cultural event of significant importance to his state. The promoters also received backing from various community groups in and around Hallandale. When Rounds notified Mayor Ernest Pinto of Hallandale of the diminishing availability of sleeping facilities in the area due to the presence of tourists and football fans for the Orange Bowl game, the mayor went out of his way to help. Pinto himself made telephone calls to all the parks and beaches in Dade and Broward counties in an attempt to get permission to use their facilities for possible emergency camping space. No one, however, offered to help.

The lack of sleeping facilities was the only major difficulty encountered at the Miami Pop Festival by either the fans or the promoters. Fortunately it was not as large a problem as was originally anticipated, since many festivalgoers commuted back to their homes after each day's show. The element that directly led to the overall success of the festival was the general layout of the grounds rented from the racetrack. The promoters smartly used every bit of acreage at their disposal to maximum advantage. The most important new concept in rock-festival production was the use of two stages. One of the stages was set up in front of the racetrack grandstand, while the other was located in a grassy area near one of the large parking lots. Several hundred yards separated the stages. In between the concert areas were a number of concession booths as well as an art show that displayed exotic pop sculptures on which people were permitted to climb. Each act performed for approximately forty-five minutes, with a fifteen-minute intermission between sets so that people who wished to do so could move back and forth between the two stages. The staggered performances kept the crowd moving throughout the day.

The continuous-music idea coupled with the two-stage concept eliminated the long delays between acts. It is unfortunate that the technique was not used more often in later festivals. Numerous incidents at some of the larger festivals might have been avoided, and the fans would have had a better chance of getting closer to the music.

The Miami Pop Festival's three-day lineup represented just about every form of contemporary popular music. Folk, blues, country and bluegrass, jazz, soul, top-forty pop, and rock all had suitable interpreters. Only the Monterey Pop Festival had been able to claim such diversity. Rounds was careful not to weigh the festival down with a lopsided dose of any one music form, although there was a higher concentration of rock acts than any other.

Representing the folk idiom were Buffy Sainte-Marie, Richie Havens, Joni Mitchell, and Ian and Sylvia. The collection was a particularly fine lot. With the possible exception of Joni Mitchell, they were all seasoned with stage and recording experience.

The blues lineup was to consist of the Paul Butterfield Blues Band, the James Cotton Blues Band, Canned Heat, and Booker T. and the MGs, who bailed out at the last minute due to an attack of the flu affecting three members of the band. Except for Cotton, all the acts had played Monterey in 1967.

The jazz representation was weak. Only Hugh Masekela and the Charles Lloyd Quartet performed. Masekela's reputation had been marred by a perfunctory showing at Monterey, but Lloyd's outfit had always been popular with rock audiences, especially those of San Francisco. Lloyd was one of the first artists to successfully mix jazz improvisation with a hard-rock beat. He was slightly ahead of his time, however, and never received much recognition.

The Iron Butterfly at the Miami Pop Festival.
Wide World Photos

The soul contingent at Miami was close to the strongest ever assembled at a major rock or pop festival. It is quite possible that up to that time Marvin Gaye, the Box Tops, Junior Walker and the All-Stars, and the Joe Tex Revue had never played to such a large white audience. Marvin Gaye was the most popular soul performer on the billing. He was still riding the charts with "I Heard It Through the Grapevine," while the Box Tops were following close behind with "The Letter." Otis Redding was dead, but his memorable performance at Monterey had opened the door for black soul artists to appear at predominantly white pop festivals.

The bluegrass representation was admittedly scanty; only Lester Flatt and Earl Scruggs were invited to play. But that they were invited at all illustrated the perceptiveness of Rounds and his partners as to the important role that bluegrass and country would play in the future growth of rock. More bluegrass and country artists found their way onto rock-festival slates as the genres became closely allied in the early seventies. The advent of country rock and the gradual success of such groups as the Flying Burrito Brothers, Poco, and late incarnations of the Byrds encouraged rock fans to explore the sound of the fiddle and banjo. Dylan helped solidify the bonding of country and rock when he and Johnny Cash teamed up on *Nashville Skyline* in 1969.

Top-forty acts were not in short supply at Miami. José Feliciano, the Turtles, the Grass Roots, and Three Dog Night all performed, with the latter group stealing the show on Saturday night. Three Dog Night had begun as a syrupy rock band in southern California that eventually upgraded its sound and delivery by maximizing the voices of three lead vocalists. At the time of the Miami Pop Festival, the band had just finished recording their debut album for ABC Records. The lp was released in January of 1969 and contained the band's first huge hit, "One." For some hard rock fans at Miami, Three Dog Night was just another California top-forty band, but their bristling stage act and compelling vocal charm smoothly worked its way into the hearts of many festivalgoers. After their Miami appearance the band took off. They belted out fourteen gold albums, along with an additional ten gold singles. In all, they sold close to fifty million records before they finally fizzled in 1976.

The rock lineup was both familiar and obscure. British rockers included Terry Reid, Procol Harum, and Fleetwood Mac.

Reid's name was known only to those who remembered when he opened for Cream during their farewell concerts, but both Procol Harum and Fleetwood Mac had been on the record charts. Procol Harum's "Whiter Shade of Pale" was released as a single from the band's debut album of the same name in the summer of 1967. It immediately settled into a top-ten position for the latter part of July and nearly all of August. In September of 1968 the band released its second album, *Shine On Brightly*. Although this album did not sell as well as the first, Procol Harum's position was established in rock circles.

Fleetwood Mac's name might have been placed in the blues category, since the music they played at the time of the Miami Pop Festival was very blues-oriented. However, the band gradually strayed from the format when guitarist Peter Green left the band in 1970, and today they are best known as a rock band.

The American rock acts consisted of Country Joe and the Fish, the McCoys, Pacific Gas and Electric, the Grateful Dead, Sweetwater, Iron Butterfly, Chuck Berry, and a host of lesser-known bands that were only local in stature. From Canada came Steppenwolf. Only a few of the rock acts were big stars at the time. Country Joe and the Fish and the Grateful Dead had established themselves at Monterey, but the McCoys ("Hang on Sloopy"), Sweetwater, and Pacific Gas and Electric were not nationally known acts with large followings. Even Chuck Berry was not yet enjoying the renaissance in 1968 that he would experience a few years later. None of the big three from Monterey was present: The Who, the Jimi Hendrix Experience, and Janis Joplin (she had just separated from Big Brother and the Holding Company and was in the process of forming the Kozmic Blues Band). Neither were the Jefferson Airplane or the Doors. Rounds instead chose to headline some of the newer rock bands that were rapidly taking their places next to the older, more established giants. John Kay and his band, Steppenwolf, had two top-selling singles in 1968, "Born To Be Wild" and "Magic Carpet Ride." The former became somewhat of an anthem for the youth in America and epitomized the furious energy and arrogant conviction of the band. Along with Iron Butterfly, Steppenwolf was one of the reasons 35,000 people showed up for Saturday's concert and 46,000 for Sunday's despite rain in the late afternoon.

But not all the attention went the way of Steppenwolf and Iron Butterfly at Miami. Pacific Gas and Electric stunned the promoters and the fans alike and became the Cinderella group at the three-day festival. The Los Angeles band performed a total of four times, with each set concluding to thunderous rounds of applause.

As one reads through the pages of rock festival history, it becomes apparent that one or two acts stand out at each festival above all the others. Frequently enough the act was not well known and not necessarily the one that performed the best. American audiences, whether in sports, politics, or the arts, like to pull for the underdog or the little guy; the David in a world of Goliaths. At Monterey it was Joplin. Newport had Tiny Tim, Sky River had Big Mama Willie Mae Thornton. Grand Funk Railroad, Santana, and Johnny Winter stole the show at other festivals. At Miami it was Pacific Gas and Electric. Unfortunately the band was never able to capitalize on their triumph. It was true that the band developed a sizable reputation on the West Coast and later released a couple of acclaimed albums, but their overall popularity never went beyond a large cult following elsewhere in the United States.

Rolling Stone capped a story by Ellen Sander on the Miami Pop Festival with the headline, THE MOST FESTIVE FESTIVAL OF 1968. Indeed it was. The compliments paid to Rounds and his group were numerous. As was previously mentioned, the lack of sleeping facilities was the only problem of any significance. It was one that needed to be remedied if the Second Annual Miami Pop Festival was to be as successful as the first. Parking at the festival site was not actually a problem, just a hassle. So was the traffic. But these two menaces occurred at any large public event, and thus were accepted as inevitable.

Tom Rounds and his associates began preparations for a second Miami festival in the spring of 1969. Rock-festival fever was hot then, and many promoters sought advice from Rounds, who had always gone with the philosophy that the most important item in the production of a rock festival was the environment and not the music. A favorable setting had to be created and continued throughout the event.

Rounds had had a favorable setting and an excellent cast of musical acts at the Miami Pop Festival in 1968. He planned an even bigger and better one for 1969. Hallandale gave him the go-ahead to begin planning, and in July the city council officially issued the festival permit. However, with all the hoopla that surrounded the Woodstock festival in August, the Hallandale governing body panicked and retracted Rounds's permit for the staging of a second Miami Pop Festival in December of 1969. The council feared that more than 500,000 kids would converge on Hallandale and disrupt—maybe even destroy— the peaceful way of life there. Rounds fought the issue, but he was never able to convince the city council to rescind its decision.

CHAPTER FOUR

1969 The Year of the Festival

*Texas never looked like this
when I lived here, man.*

—Janis Joplin
    Texas International Pop Festival
    September 1, 1969

Nineteen sixty-nine was the year it all came together—and began to fall apart. After two years of rapid maturation, the rock festival came of age. No longer was it deemed just a weekend outing for hippies and long-haired youths who grooved on the sounds of acid rock, as in 1967. No longer was it just a series of outdoor concerts that generated newsworthy performances by powerful rock acts, as in 1968. Instead, in 1969 the rock festival became a sociological and musical phenomenon that echoed the energy and vitality of an action-packed decade.

More rock festivals were staged in 1969 than in any other year. More than one million festivalgoers attended huge rock extravaganzas in every corner of America. Thousands of kids roamed the nation's highways in search of rides that would ultimately land them near a festival. Like an army on the move, the youthful counterculture marched to wherever the promise of a rock celebration existed.

The rock festival had changed considerably since Mount Tam and Monterey baptized the concept in the early summer of 1967. The most obvious change was its size. Attendance figures at large rock festivals swelled to six-digit numbers with amazing ease. The average festival in 1969 attracted anywhere from 100,000 to 150,000 festivalgoers. The Atlantic City Pop Festival attracted 130,000 people. Newport '69 at Devonshire Downs in California claimed 150,000 in attendance, and Altamont surpassed the 300,000 mark. Close to a half million showed up at Woodstock. Many "smaller" festivals attracted crowds of 30,000 to 75,000 people.

The large number of festivals occurring in 1969 had a two-fold effect on the music industry. On the positive side, successful acts were able to command exorbitant fees for their services on the stage. Many of rock's top acts at the time—Janis Joplin; the Jefferson Airplane; Jimi Hendrix; the Grateful Dead; Sly Stone; Crosby, Stills, Nash and Young—traveled the festival circuit throughout the summer months. It was reported by *Rolling Stone* that Jimi Hendrix received $100,000 for his appearance at Newport '69 at Devonshire Downs. (He had played for free at his first festival.) In all, promoter Mark Robinson spent $282,000 on entertainment for the festival.

The money, the brilliant performances, and the glamour of it all helped usher in a new term in the rock vocabulary. Record companies and managers of rock performers saw the rock festivals as a tactic designed to assault the music world with a concentration of big-name artists. As these stars received more and more recognition and money, their status reached new levels as well. The rock scene had become saturated with "stars," and for those who were yet bigger, a new title was created: "superstar." These superstars were idolized by the rock masses. When they took the stage at the large festivals, the earth shook in response to the bellowing applause they received.

Record sales also increased as a result of the large number of festivals staged in 1969. Just after the Texas International Pop Festival, Dallas record retailers reported to *Billboard* magazine a dramatic increase in the number of albums sold. Registering particularly high sales figures were albums by artists who had previously been unknown or at least not very popular in the area. The retailers pointed to Grand Funk Railroad as an example. The band had made its initial appearance in the Southwest at the Texas festival. One week after the festival a large record store reportedly sold 2,200 copies of the band's debut Capitol album and had ordered an additional 6,000 to keep up with the demand.

Record companies and outlets all across the country attributed the breaking on the scene of so many new acts in 1969 to the multitude of rock festivals in the summer of that year. Retailers referred to the financial merits of a "relatively unknown (or new) act receiving strong attention through a festival event, which in turn creates extensive market interest and sells records that the retailer had not even stocked before."[1]

On the other side of the picture, rock festivals almost spelled disaster for small club owners and local rock concert promoters. Simple economics dictated that it was indeed practical and much cheaper for the rock fan to pay, say, $15 for three days' worth of music performed by sometimes more than thirty acts, than to pay $5 to see one or two acts perform. This situation was compounded by the reluctance of some groups to sign contracts to play at small and medium-size concert halls. In 1969 the real money and prestige for rock bands was at the large festivals.

Newport '69 at Devonshire Downs

The first large rock festival of the summer season was held just outside Northridge, California, on the third weekend in June. The actual festival site was a huge, wide-open field and picnic area called Devonshire Downs. Principal promoter Mark Robinson opted to call the festival Newport '69 in an attempt to link his festival with the one that had occurred in Newport Beach and Costa Mesa the previous year.

Like the Newport Pop Festival of 1968, Newport '69 suffered from numerous and unexpected problems. When the festival was over, the promoters claimed losses of nearly $150,000, most of which resulted from personal property damage.

The fact that there was any property damage at all was a major surprise. Just about all of it resulted from the first overt acts of violence to occur at a large rock festival. Rock festivals had miraculously avoided widespread violence in the past. There had always been problems, usually drug-oriented in nature. These problems, however, were isolated incidents involving the police and a suspected drug possessor. Never before had rock festivals been subjected to large-scale gate-crashing, as Newport '69 was. The gate-crashing led to violence and the violence led to property damage. And the love and peace theme was temporarily tarnished.

But Robinson and Newport '69 ran into trouble even before the festival had begun. George Wein, the producer of the Newport, Rhode Island, folk and jazz festivals, did not take kindly to Robinson's decision to use the Newport name for his festival. Wein complained that the Newport tag was exclusively his and feared that people would associate the rock festival in California with his folk and jazz productions on the East Coast. Some unknowing members of the press had done just that when they reported on the Newport, California, festival in 1968. Two days before the festival a Los Angeles Superior Court judge permitted Robinson to use "Newport" in his festival title but restricted its use by him in the future. Robinson was also told to make clear that Newport '69 was in no way associated with Wein's Rhode Island festivals.

The music began on Friday evening, but not before gate-crashers had toppled a sizable portion of the hurricane fence that had been erected to keep them out. By 9 P.M. a segment of the fence had been thoroughly destroyed, and people passed through the gaping hole at will. There were minor scuffles with the police all evening, but few people were actually arrested and only a small amount of damage, aside from the fencing, had occurred. The situation remained the same throughout Saturday. But on Sunday, the final day of the festival, the situation went from stable to critical. The police and members of the Street Racers, a motorcycle gang that had been hired by the promoters to act as a security force, had managed by mid-afternoon to curb most of the gate-crashing. Still hundreds of youths milled around the festival entrance, demanding to be let in free of charge. First rocks were thrown and then bottles as the gate-crashers launched a final assault on the fencing. The police fought back, and when it was over some three hours later, sixty-seven gate-crashers had been arrested, fifteen police officers had been injured and taken to the hospital, and thousands of dollars was assessed in personal property damage in the neighborhood adjacent to the festival site.

Courtesy of Cinema Five

Tina Turner—and Ike—performed at Newport '69 and at the Seattle Pop Festival during the summer of 1969.

It was difficult to determine what had caused those without tickets to initiate acts of violence. At first police suspected provocation by radical leftist groups, but no evidence was found to justify this. If anything, the violent eruption was a spontaneous reaction to the commercialism of the festival format. Many in the crowd outside the festival site who battled police demanded that the music and the festival be set free from its capitalistic chains. Others, of course, looked for any excuse to avoid paying the ticket price.

The trouble many went through to crash the festival really wasn't worth it. The sound system was not powerful enough to fill the huge field with music. Many times during the three days the music was in direct competition with the loud, irritating noise of police helicopters surveying the unruly crowd outside the festival gates. Visibility wasn't much better. The distance from the stage to the audience area was too great for many in the large crowd to see the performers.

The festival lineup was predominantly rock-oriented. The top acts included Jimi Hendrix, Janis Joplin, Jethro Tull, Steppenwolf, Creedence Clearwater Revival, the Young Rascals, the Chambers Brothers, Joe Cocker, Ike and Tina Turner, Three Dog Night, Spirit, Taj Mahal, and Johnny Winter. In all, thirty-three acts performed during the three days.

Of all the acts that appeared, it was Jimi Hendrix whom the audience was most excited to see and hear. In 1969 Hendrix was again crowned rock's most gifted guitarist. But he was running into trouble coping with his new superstar stature. His most recent studio album, *Electric Ladyland*, was a huge success both financially and critically, but Hendrix seemed to want more out of his music and his band. *Electric Ladyland* was the last album Hendrix made with the Experience (Noel Redding and Mitch Mitchell), and it featured guest appearances by Al Kooper, Steve Winwood, Buddy Miles, and Jack Casady. The album had been released late in the summer of 1968, and by the beginning of the following year Hendrix had dissolved the group. Many cited the personality clashes and musical differences that existed between Redding and Hendrix as the main reason for the breakup. Most of the problems, however, centered around Hendrix's insatiable desire to jam with other musicians or to team with old army friend, bassist Billy Cox, rather than play with the Experience.

Occasionally Hendrix's personal problems got in the way of his music when he performed onstage. At Newport '69, for example, Hendrix called the crowd there "immature" when they didn't react to his music the way he had expected them to. When he played his guitar, more often than not it was a quasi-religious experience for him, especially at large rock festivals where the union of the large crowd and his music was steeped in emotional intensity. When the climactic moment was anything less than spectacular, Hendrix became disappointed not only in himself but also with the crowd for failing to achieve a musical orgasm.

Hendrix often magnified his role at rock festivals. He seemed to view himself as the high priest of the event, whose mission it was to guide the musical experience of those present. Because of this Hendrix pushed himself and his guitar playing beyond the limit, and his performances seemed much more dramatic and expressionistic than those of other artists. He gripped and then choked the neck of his guitar to squeeze out the right riffs. He seemed obsessed with fruition and power as he sought to galvanize the rock spirit. He was never without a sense of urgency. He revealed phallic come-ons; he was intensely public in front of all those people. Some of the greatest moments in rock history occurred when Jimi Hendrix played his guitar on a festival stage.

Although Hendrix's initial performance at Newport '69 was

less stimulating than past festival appearances, he returned later to join singer Tracy Nelson of Mother Earth and drummer Buddy Miles in a jam that brought the cheers and shouts of approval he was accustomed to hearing.

Newport '69 demonstrated that rock festivals were not immune to violent eruptions and gate-crashing, as was previously thought. Newspaper reports did not point out, however, that those who had purchased tickets for the festival did not partake in any of the rioting. The large crowd inside the festival grounds behaved just like former festival throngs, showing respect for others' property, and not once during the three-day festival were police called in because of disorder. Those who battled the police represented a fraction of the young people at Devonshire Downs for the weekend. Unfortunately it was this band of rowdies who received all the ink.

Denver Pop Festival

The Denver Pop Festival met with the same fate as Newport '69. The second large festival of the summer occurred one week after the Newport fiasco and was also raked with violence and gate-crashing, making it two festivals in a row at which the celebratory spirit of the rock festival turned sour. Once again the media spread the word of violence as newspaper accounts told of pitched battles between police and long-haired youths. This time, however, they were correct in depicting a battle scene.

Unlike Newport '69, there was strong evidence that at least part of the violence at the Denver Pop Festival was the result of radical political activities. In town the same week as those who came in for the rock fest were members of the American Liberation Front, a leftist organization that consisted of Students for a Democratic Society (SDS), Young Socialists, radical clergy members, and other smaller groups that proclaimed themselves against oppression and the war in Vietnam. The ALF had received a permit from City Hall to stage a series of protests and demonstrations at City Park. The group planned a week of free rock concerts, guerrilla theater performances, guest speakers, and political discussions. The activities would culminate with a July 4 march through downtown Denver.

The leaders of the ALF hoped to persuade those who were going to the festival to join their ranks. The attempt marked the first time New Left leaders actively sought an alliance with that portion of the counterculture that was more interested in rock music than in politics. For over a year New Left leaders had haggled among themselves in an attempt to formulate a policy that would effectively politicize the youthful masses at rock festivals.

When Denver city leaders realized the possibilities of a merger between the ALF and the rock festival crowd, they quickly embarked on a plan to prevent such a union. The day before the festival began, Denver's city council had allocated camping space to festivalgoers on a city-owned baseball field instead of in City Park. ALF leaders had hoped festivalgoers would be granted permission to use the facilities in the park so that they could partake in the political activities sponsored by the radical group. City leaders realized that the numeric strength of the radical group might swell beyond the controllable limit if the ALF plan was allowed to be carried out. The city, therefore, enticed festival campers to use the baseball field by promising them free transportation to and from the stadium where the festival was to take place. Many weekend ticket holders took them up on the offer.

Barry Fey had been Denver's most active and successful rock concert promoter. He was the man responsible for the presentation of major acts at Denver's Auditorium Arena as well as the outdoor Red Rocks amphitheater. It was only natural that he be responsible for the Denver Pop Festival. Fey was one of the first festival impresarios to use an athletic stadium for a large three-day rock festival. Mile High Stadium wasn't the ideal location for those interested in the total festival experience, but it was a perfect setting for the promoter. Everything was at his disposal: bathrooms, water supply, electricity, seating, fencing. All he had to do was stage the event and collect the tickets.

Fey presented a billing including a number of acts that had performed at Newport '69 the previous week. Jimi Hendrix was the most prominent; others included Creedence Clearwater Revival, the Mothers of Invention, Taj Mahal, Joe Cocker, Johnny Winter, Three Dog Night, the popular local band

---

Frank Zappa (second from the left, rear) and his Mothers of Invention. The Denver Pop Festival was one of their earliest festival performances.

Courtesy of Warner Brothers

Zephyr, Poco, Iron Butterfly, and Big Mama Willie Mae Thornton.

Thornton opened the festival on Friday evening wearing a ten-gallon hat and a Western-style shirt and singing the blues the way she had at Sky River in 1968. Following Thornton was the Flock, a seven-member Chicago band that featured Jerry Goodman (who later teamed up with guitarist John McLaughlin to form the Mahavishnu Orchestra) on electric violin. Next was Three Dog Night, which had catapulted into national prominence since their highly successful appearance at the Miami Pop Festival in December 1968. After Three Dog Night came Frank Zappa and the Mothers of Invention, and Iron Butterfly.

There were only isolated incidents of gate-crashing on Friday evening. One or two young people would occasionally attempt to scale the high chain link fence, only to be rebuffed by the police and security guards. The music was loud enough to be heard outside the concrete structure, so that most of the crowd that gathered in front of the stadium's main gate were content to sit and listen. Throughout the evening members of the ALF passed out literature and spoke to those who showed any interest in the evils of domestic oppression.

Saturday evening was an entirely different story. The second concert of the three-day festival was scheduled to begin at 6:30 P.M. Two hours before the gates opened, a large crowd of young people had gathered at the south end of the stadium, away from where those with tickets patiently stood in line. At approximately 5:30 P.M. Fey's people began collecting the tickets as the crowd was let into the stadium. All at once those at the south end of the arena charged the fence in the first large gate-crashing attempt of the evening. Police and security guards rushed to the scene and repelled the crowd, but more than a hundred kids had successfully avoided the police and entered the stadium grounds. By 7:30 another group of young people had assembled outside the main gate and were joined by those from the south end of the stadium.

The small group of police assigned to the stadium was no match for the large, restless crowd that had grown to over 350 people. When a squad of police reinforcements arrived on the scene in full riot dress and gas masks, the crowd erupted in a fury of protest. First came a barrage of rocks, then came bottles and beer cans. Those who had crashed the fence successfully at the south end of the stadium and were now inside climbed to the top of the grandstand and hurled objects down on the police below. Political slogans were heard amid the shouting, and ALM members who had been passing out leaflets before the disturbance began became part of the unruly crowd.

One police officer was knocked to the ground by a large wine bottle, and the police decided that the situation was now serious enough to use tear gas. The canisters were shot into the crowd, only to be thrown back at the police by brazen members of the throng. The southerly winds picked up the fumes and carried them into the stadium. As the crowd inside the stadium realized that their wet eyes and parched throats were due to gas fumes, many people ran for cover. The scene inside the stadium bordered on bedlam as Johnny Winter played on and Chip Monck, the festival's stage manager, tried to calm the fears running through the people close to the stage.

Outside, the battle between the police and the young people intensified until Fey reluctantly agreed to open the gates at the request of the Denver Police Chief. The kids swarmed into the stadium yelling victory chants and radiating triumph.

Gate-crashers take to the fences at Mile High Stadium during the Denver Pop Festival.

Denver Post Photo by Ed Sielsky

A young gate-crasher is apprehended outside the Denver Pop Festival.

Fey was angry that the police had not been able to control the crowd and emphasized that he would not open the gates on the following night. But a precedent had been set, and on Sunday evening a larger crowd assembled at Mile High Stadium demanding to be let in for free.

Sunday's show consisted of Joe Cocker; Aorta; Three Dog Night; Zephyr; a gospel singer, the Rev. Cleophus Robinson; and the headliner, Jimi Hendrix, whose presence was undoubtedly responsible for the size of the crowd both inside and outside the stadium. But this time the police were determined not to falter in their defense. The previous night's activities had embarrassed them. The newspapers seemed to indicate that the police had been whipped by a mob of long-haired kids. Retaliation was in the air. Police dogs were placed around the perimeter of the stadium, an extra platoon of Denver policemen donned riot gear, and a portable weapon called a pepper-fog machine, which effectively pumped clouds of tear gas and skin-burning mace in the air, was made ready.

Things were quiet until a bit after seven P.M., when a group of officers at the bottom of the hill, who feared an outbreak similar to Saturday night's, moved in the pepper-fog machine. Whether they intended to use it on the crowd unjustifiably is not known, but the crowd reacted with violence. Rocks were thrown at the police at the bottom of the hill and people shouted obscenities.

If the police were looking for an excuse to use the machine, they quickly got it. Using the pepper-fog like a machine gun mowing down a retreating enemy, the police stormed the hill. The crowd moved back and then scattered. Firecrackers and bottles were thrown in the direction of the police. As the police moved up the hill, the crowd moved around and down it and raced for the fence in the evening's first scaling attempt. The police reversed their direction and ran down the grassy embankment to ward off the gate-crashers. Those caught in the act of climbing the fence were dragged down. Those who violently resisted the police were clubbed and arrested. The Denver *Post* reported that some of its staff saw several instances in which fellow officers told others to cease unnecessary beatings. One case was reported where an officer pulled a young man down the hill by his hair until another officer intervened. A photographer trying to capture the scene on film was knocked to the ground.

Again the police requested that Fey open the gates to avoid further trouble, and again Fey unwillingly acquiesced. As a result, over three thousand gate-crashers caught the last few acts of the festival, including Jimi Hendrix. During the final number of his set, the energized crowd raced across the outfield toward the stage. Hendrix cut the song short and escaped from the stadium in a panel truck.

The violence at the Denver Pop Festival ended any future plans for rock festivals there. In the days after the festival, both the press and city officials searched for an explanation for the violence. The police, Fey, and the gate-crashers were all partially saddled with blame. However, the main reason, city officials reckoned, was the nature of the event itself. Large-scale rock festivals were uncontrollable affairs that should be either severely curtailed or permanently banned. Rock music was fine in small doses, but any unusually large concerts or festivals would not be tolerated in Denver. City officials had

A tear-gas canister explodes outside the Denver Pop Festival.
Denver Post Photo by Duane Howell

the backing of the public; thus Denver became off limits for promoters interested in future festivals there.

1969 Newport Jazz Festival

The 1969 Newport Jazz Festival was the third event of the early summer to fall victim to the violent tactics of gate-crashers. Traditionally George Wein's annual folk and jazz festivals at Newport were orderly affairs that attracted a regular festival crowd year after year. There had been isolated cases of violent incidents in the history of the two music festivals, but Wein had always managed to comfort city leaders with promises of calm, orderly events.

For years the Jazz Festival had consisted of only jazz acts. Occasionally the definition of jazz was stretched a bit, but Wein always selected these special acts with care and good judgment. In 1969, however, Wein strayed from past festival formats and invited several rock bands to perform side by side with jazz outfits.

It was the biggest mistake Wein had ever made. Later he told *Downbeat* magazine that "the festival was sheer hell—the worst four days of my life. The festival was an artistic experiment and a calculated risk. I wanted to interest Newport goers of long standing in the new music—the best rock groups—but the kids destroyed the event and the experiment was a failure."

The damage done by gate-crashers and rock fans was not high in pecuniary terms, but Wein's integrity had suffered a low blow, and Newport ultimately sent the festival looking for a new home. The atmosphere at the four-day annual festival was tense and hard-edged. Jazz enthusiasts complained of the presence of rock acts on a jazz stage. Rock fans voiced their disappointment over the lack of freedom normally enjoyed at rock festivals and rock concerts. Townspeople were disgruntled with the abnormally large crowds that swarmed into Newport (78,000 for four days; the previous high was 59,000). Some members of the music press labeled Wein a promoter more interested in the capital gains that would surely result from the presence of rock acts than in the presentation of good jazz. No one seemed content with the temporary merger of rock and jazz.

Wein had booked almost a dozen rock groups of various

prominence to play at Newport. The opening show on Thursday evening (July 3) was the only one that did not include a rock act. It was also the only show that did not sell out beforehand. The concerts took place at Festival Field, an outdoor amphitheater with enough seating to accommodate nineteen thousand people. There was such a large demand for tickets to the shows that included rock acts that Wein received permission from the city to set up an additional three thousand seats. It would be a tight fit, Wein realized, but he did not want the expected large turnout of young people to amass outside the festival site, angered and frustrated over not being allowed in. During the past two weekends newspapers had reported on the violence and gate-crashing incidents at the Denver Pop Festival and Newport '69. Wein hoped the current gate-crashing trend would not affect his festival.

Friday night's July 4 show was billed as "An Evening of Jazz Rock" and featured Jeff Beck; Blood, Sweat and Tears; Jethro Tull; Ten Years After; and two jazz artists, Steve Marcus and Roland Kirk. Wein's choice of rock bands was good. He cleverly selected those groups that borrowed substantially from the jazz idiom and included musicians who were well versed in the capacities of their instruments. Jeff Beck and Alvin Lee of Ten Years After both were highly technical rock guitarists who peppered their solos with jazzlike improvisations. Ian Anderson of Jethro Tull often sounded like a jazz flautist in a rock band. Al Kooper's Blood, Sweat and Tears was the result of the first commercially successful attempt to blend equal parts of jazz and rock. The band had a potent sound that appealed to both rock and jazz audiences.

Twenty-four thousand festivalgoers, mostly rock oriented, squeezed into every available section of the festival amphitheater. Outside the festival site, more than ten thousand people gathered with no prospects of acquiring tickets. They could do nothing except hang around and listen to whatever strains of music escaped the amphitheater. The situation was ripe for a gate-crashing extravaganza.

Wein hoped to avoid any trouble before it began. Using the festival public address system, he admonished the outside crowd of the dangers of gate-crashing and reminded them of the two disturbances that had occurred the previous month at Denver and Northridge. Wein flatly stated that if any such violence occurred in Newport, future festivals would most likely be banned. He told the crowd outside to sit in the grass, listen to the music, and have a good time. But he begged their co-operation in preventing any violent episodes from occurring.

Wein's warning was enough to at least preclude a mass attack on the fencing that separated the outside crowd from a view of the performers. There were frequent instances of fence jumping, but the evening's show was miraculously unmarked by any significant disturbance.

A Saturday matinee show consisted of a combination of jazz and rock acts. Representing rock were Frank Zappa and the Mothers of Invention and John Mayall's latest band. Again Wein's wise choice of rock acts helped bridge the gap between music forms. Mayall's outfit went over well with the predominantly jazz audience; John Almond's flute solos received numerous rounds of applause. Perhaps, thought Wein, the festival could make it through the weekend without violence setting in.

Wein's luck ran out on Saturday evening. A crowd of over twenty-one thousand once again jammed into the festival amphitheater to hear a mostly jazz lineup. Sly and the Family Stone was the only major rock act on the billing which included such jazz artists as Art Blakey, Gerry Mulligan, and Dave Brubeck. From the start things looked grim. Throughout the first portion of the concert, the large crowd that once again gathered outside the amphitheater showed signs of restlessness and frustration that were not so dramatically present on Friday. Fireworks exploded dangerously in the crowd, small fires were set, and an excessive amount of liquor was consumed by many in the crowd to celebrate the Fourth of July. When word spread that Sly and the Family Stone was the next act to take the stage, a large segment of those outside the amphitheater pushed right up to the fence.

Just before the band took the stage, a boisterous portion of the outside crowd stormed the main gate at the far end of the festival grounds, ultimately knocking it down as they raced into the amphitheater. Others in the crowd, realizing a gate-crashing assault was in progress, climbed the fence unchecked. A gate used by the performers was torn down. A few people used a discarded broken ladder as a battering ram to make holes in the ten-foot-high fence.

There was little room for the three thousand or so who forced their way into the festival. Most of them grouped by the picket fence that separated the press and the audience. The crowd pressed tighter along the fence when Sly and the Family Stone took the stage almost a half-hour late. Midway through the first number rain began to fall. As it became a steady downpour, the confusion near the press area grew worse. Quickly the picket fence succumbed to the pressure from the crowd, and the press people were swamped with zealous rock fans. Wein pleaded with the people to move back and settle down, but in vain. Pandemonium ruled, and the concert came to a precipitate end.

The following afternoon, just before the James Brown concert, Wein announced that Led Zeppelin would not appear that evening as previously scheduled. The promoter cited an illness of Robert Plant, the lead singer, as the reason for the band's cancellation. Actually, none of this was true. Wein hoped that the announcement would discourage the rock crowd from sticking around for the evening's show. Aside from Led Zeppelin, Johnny Winter was the only rock act that was scheduled to appear.

The ploy worked well, as many people left Newport prematurely. Then, in the middle of the evening show, festival officials unexpectedly announced that Led Zeppelin would play after all. The band was furious when they heard what Wein had told the afternoon audience. They considered it a cheap shot by the impresario and credited the flagrant lie as the main reason the band's set was less than spectacular.

Three days after the festival ended, the Newport City Council canceled an appearance in Newport by the supergroup Blind Faith scheduled for July 11. They also ruled out all rock acts at future festivals in the city. There was much speculation that the council would scratch the Newport Folk Festival slated for later on in the month, but after lengthy deliberation the group allowed folk-festival plans to proceed as originally scheduled.

The reaction to the 1969 Newport Jazz Festival did not end at Newport City Hall. In a heated article written by Dan Morganstern in *Downbeat*, the author urged jazz promoters to "leave rock where it belongs: in the circus or in the kindergarten." Jazz critic Leonard Feather was less critical in a piece written for *Melody Maker*, although he warned that rock and jazz were not yet ready for wholesale integration.

Atlanta Pop Festival and Seattle Pop Festival

The reports of rioting and gate-crashing at the Newport Jazz Festival over the Fourth of July weekend were offset somewhat

Some of the greatest moments in rock festival history occurred when Jimi Hendrix ran his fingers down the neck of his guitar.
Courtesy of Warner Brothers

by two peaceful pop festivals held in Georgia and Washington. The Atlanta Pop Festival attracted 140,000 rock fans from all over the Southeast for a two-day July 4 extravaganza that featured twenty-one acts. And at Gold Creek Park, located a few miles outside of Seattle, the Seattle Pop Festival was the second successful major rock fest to occur in Washington within less than a year.

The Atlanta festival was staged at the Atlanta International Speedway. Like most festival lineups in 1969, the one for the Atlanta Pop Festival was excellent. Appearances were made on the first day of the festival—Friday, July 4—by Pacific Gas and Electric; Delaney and Bonnie and Friends; Sweetwater; Ten Wheel Drive; Creedence Clearwater Revival; Canned Heat; Johnny Rivers; Johnny Winter; the Paul Butterfield Blues Band; Dave Brubeck and Gerry Mulligan; Blood, Sweat and Tears; Booker T. and the MGs; and Ian and Sylvia.

Saturday's lineup featured repeat performances by five of the acts heard on Friday plus Janis Joplin, Led Zeppelin (they flew to Newport, Rhode Island, early Sunday morning with Johnny Winter to play at the jazz festival there), Spirit, Joe Cocker, Chicago Transit Authority, Tommy James and the Shondells, and the Staple Singers.

One of the most important and intriguing results of the Atlanta Pop Festival was the warm reception the festival received from the neighboring city of Atlanta. In spite of the recent news concerning riots and gate-crashing incidents at rock festivals held in Denver and Northridge, California, the attitude in Atlanta was congenial. The day before the festival began, the Atlanta *Journal* published an editorial that dissipated the fears of many long-haired youths who had second thoughts of going to Georgia to attend a rock festival. The editorial was titled "Pop Festival" and read as follows:

> The Atlanta Pop Festival is being publicized as having something for everyone, from Tommy James and the Shondells to Dave Brubeck. In the middle, and on top as far as blues fans are concerned, is Janis Joplin, a young woman who puts so much into a song that you wonder if anything's going to be left of her when she's through. Fortunately Janis Joplin seems to endure.
>
> There have been "festivals" around here before. We're glad to note that the people who have pulled this one together have signed performers who would rather sit back-

stage than do less than top performances. Certainly Miss Joplin is such a singer, and so are Ian and Sylvia, Johnny Winter and Delaney, Bonnie and Friends.

A full music diet is good for a city. Pop music is important and expressive of our times. We hope the Pop Festival Friday and Saturday at Atlanta International Speedway will not be a one-shot thing. For many people, gatherings such as this are their only opportunities to hear live pop concerts.[2]

The Seattle Pop Festival was the second rock festival to fare well in the Washington media. It attracted some seventy thousand festivalgoers and was promoted by Boyd Grafmyre, who had previously worked with the New American Community at Sky River in 1968. Assisting in the production were numerous other people from that organization, including Sky River producer John Chambless. Grafmyre's festival was one of the first not to use any regular or off-duty police officers as a security force. Instead, he brought in more than 150 youthful volunteers from Seattle's Head Start Program and other black youth groups. They were used as ticket collectors, maintenance personnel, and security guards in exchange for free admission and a chance to escape the city's summer heat.

The festival ran so smoothly that Grafmyre grossed over $300,000, against a total festival expense of some $200,000. Unlike the Sky River festival, the Seattle Pop Festival was a commercial event; the profits were not earmarked for needy organizations. The huge success of the event pointed out that if a rock festival was properly run by experienced promoters, a profit—and a large one at that—could be realized.

Atlantic City Pop Festival

The Atlantic City Pop Festival was the second major pop festival of the summer to successfully use a racetrack as a festival site. Herb Spivak, part owner of a popular Philadelphia discothéque called the Electric Factory, along with three of his brothers and another business associate, Shelly Kaplan, leased the Atlantic City Racetrack for the first weekend of August. The event introduced rock festivals to the New York/New Jersey/Pennsylvania area, a region populated by millions of young people. The promoters judiciously picked a site within easy driving distance of the three densely populated areas. The attendance figure of some 110,000 for the three days was a slight disappointment, although it was dubious whether the facilities at the racetrack could have accommodated much more than that. The disappointment was magnified when, just two weeks later, the Woodstock festival at Bethel, New York, attracted four times as many festivalgoers.

The promoters reserved a large portion of land located directly west of the racetrack for festival campers. It was becoming increasingly popular for festivalgoers to spend the entire three days of a festival on the site itself, even though, as was the case at the Atlantic City fest, many could have commuted to and from with ease. The nonmusic aspects of festivals had assumed greater importance for many young festivalgoers these days, and this trend was augmented after the Woodstock festival. The nonmusic scene included drug experimentation, round-the-clock partying, and celebration of the warm feelings that resulted from being with so many others who thought, looked, and acted the same way you did.

The music at the Atlantic City Pop Festival began in late afternoon on Friday, August 1. The day's lineup consisted of Joni Mitchell, the Chambers Brothers, Iron Butterfly, Aum, Dr. John the Night Tripper, Mother Earth, Procol Harum, and Chicago Transit Authority. There were a number of acts at Atlantic City that regularly followed the festival path. Iron Butterfly, Chicago Transit Authority, and the Chambers Brothers were frequently seen on the festival stage in 1969. On the Saturday billing the very familiar names of Booker T. and the MGs and the Jefferson Airplane were featured. These veteran festival acts stretched back to the Monterey festival of 1967. Sunday's lineup included even more familiar names from Monterey: Canned Heat, Janis Joplin, Paul Butterfield, Hugh Masekela, and the Byrds.

An incident during Joni Mitchell's set accurately portrayed the lesser role music was beginning to play at rock festivals. Joni Mitchell had not been known by the vast majority of the rock-music world in 1969 as she would be in the early '70's. She had just released her second album, *Clouds*, in April of that year. To artists in the field, Mitchell was already highly respected as a composer and performer, but it would not be until her third release, *Ladies of the Canyon* in 1970, that she received widespread attention from the rock masses. The album included the singer's interpretation of the meaning and spirit behind rock festivals and Woodstock in particular. The song was simply titled "Woodstock," and although Crosby, Stills, Nash and Young's version received widespread airplay, Mitchell was never really accorded critical acclaim for writing the tune.

Joni Mitchell was onstage at Atlantic City for just over ten minutes and was midway through "Cactus Tree," a song from her first album, when she unexpectedly stopped playing.

"I sang that verse twice and nobody noticed," Mitchell said to the crowd. No one *did* seem to notice. Mitchell looked up from the microphone and saw numerous people in the crowd talking with one another and generally not paying attention or really caring about what transpired on the stage. Perhaps this was due to the fluttering sound system, hoped the offended singer. She finished the song. The sound system had been temporarily mended, but the attitude of the audience remained the same as Mitchell perfunctorily completed two other songs. With tears building in her eyes, she suddenly exited from the stage and refused to return. Folksinger Biff Rose, the master of ceremonies, muttered something to the audience and then moved to the piano. He sang a few of his own songs to fill in the time until the next act could take over.

This was not the first time a festival crowd had disregarded a laudable performer. And it would not be the last. Usually loud, aggressive rock bands escaped this problem by overwhelming audiences with power and sound, but for those like Mitchell, whose soft, intimate music demanded attention and concentration, a festival stage could easily become a snake pit. As music became a slightly less important ingredient in the rock festival format, performers like Joni Mitchell found it increasingly difficult to succeed at such events.

The Atlantic City Pop Festival was not without its gate-crashers and violence. In all, festival organizers estimated that more than two thousand people climbed the fence and entered the festival site free on Saturday night alone. Fortunately no battles with the police occurred, since the bulk of the festival's security staff was a group of five hundred young men armed only with peace buttons. Their crowd-control tactics were nonexistent, and they sorely lacked the respect of the crowd. Thus, festivalgoers and gate-crashers generally did as they pleased for the three days.

Unlike the Atlanta Pop Festival, the people who attended the Atlantic City event were met by locals harboring mixed emotions concerning their presence. The Atlantic City Chamber

Locals view the sights outside the
Texas International Pop Festival.
Wide World Photos

of Commerce officially endorsed the festival, but many community members did not warm to the idea of over 100,000 long-haired kids roaming the area for three days. A few local restaurants shrewdly imposed dress codes on their customers, and a number of gas stations placed "out of order" signs on bathroom doors. Those who did not find camping space available at the festival hoped city fathers would be generous enough to permit them to sleep on Atlantic City beaches, but local police strictly enforced ordinances that prevented such things. As a result, thousands of young people strolled the famous boardwalk until 6 A.M., when they were legally able to get on the beach. From then until closing some twelve hours later, clusters of colorful sleeping bags and tired young people speckled the beach.

The press, particularly the Philadelphia *Inquirer*, was unsure of how to view the festival. After running stories that praised the behavior of festivalgoers, the *Inquirer*, two days after the festival's conclusion, ran a story with a headline that read: MASS DRUG ORGY AT 3 DAY ROCK FESTIVAL. The story began: "Local officials and state police charged that last weekend's Atlantic City Rock Festival was a disgraceful orgy in drugs, and they moved Monday night (August 4) to insure that the event would not be repeated in Atlantic County."[3] Ordinances were ultimately passed that restricted rock gatherings, and no other festivals were ever held in southern New Jersey.

New Orleans Pop, Texas International Pop and the Second Annual Sky River Rock Festival

The summer of 1969 officially ended with the staging of three rock festivals held during Labor Day weekend—Texas International Pop, the Second Annual Sky River Rock Festival, and New Orleans Pop. The last of these was the smallest. Held in Prairieville, Louisiana, at the Baton Rouge International Speedway, only 30,000 rock fans showed up, a far cry from the 400,000 who had shown up at Woodstock that past month.

The festival was small and orderly, but a number of festivalgoers were arrested and booked on drug-related charges. Law-enforcement agents dressed as hippies circulated through the festival grounds. When they spotted a drug deal in progress, an arrest was quickly made. Those who were arrested—some for simple possession of marijuana—were held on $50,000 bail. Possessing or selling drugs in Louisiana in 1969 was a serious offense. At the time the state's law called for a maximum sentence of fifty years in jail for those convicted of selling marijuana.

The Texas International Pop Festival was billed by the local rock press as a homecoming for Janis Joplin and Johnny Winter, two of the state's home-grown rock stars (Winter is from Beaumont and Joplin was a native of Port Arthur). Both artists were completing highly successful runs of the summer festival circuit. Joplin's appearance was her first in Texas with her Kozmic Blues Band.

The festival featured several bright moments in addition to memorable performances by Winter and Joplin. B.B. King, James Cotton, and Freddie King, all masters in the art of blues musicianship, turned in sets that received standing ovations. Led Zeppelin marked the end of their highly acclaimed American tour. The appearance of Santana and Grand Funk Railroad at the festival was their first in the Southwest. And Sam and Dave, the festival's only soul act, received an unexpectedly heated response from the mostly white audience.

The festival was held at the Dallas International Motor Speedway in Lewisville, Texas. Located just twenty miles north of Dallas, the town was a growing suburb known for its lakes and camping facilities.

The drug scene was particularly intense at the Texas International Pop Festival. Headliner Johnny Winter remembered when he first arrived at the festival site.

"First off let me tell ya, neither me nor Janis Joplin wanted to go back to Texas, man. That place was a thing of our past. We had some good experiences there and some bad ones. I, for one, looked upon that homecoming bit as a bunch of crap that the promoters rigged up.

"The drug situation was pretty heavy as I recall. It probably wasn't worse than any of the other festivals, but this one, everything went wrong for me. It seemed like everyone was blown away on acid even before the music started. I told myself before I even arrived that I was goin' to stay clear of any drugs. When I got to the stage area, the prettiest blond-haired girl I'd seen in a long, long time came runnin' up to me and threw her arms around me. A second later she opened my mouth wide with her mouth and tongue and slid 'bout three tabs of acid down my throat."

The Second Annual Sky River Rock Festival was one of three festivals to take place over Labor Day weekend, 1969.

117

"I said, 'Girl, why did ya have to do such a thing?' She just smiled and said, 'My, are we goin' have a good time tonight.' I kept thinkin' to myself, 'Oh, God, not another one of those nights. Why'd that bitch have to do such a thing for.'

"Turned out I had a great time, but I was blown away for two fuckin' days, man. For two days I didn't even know my name. People like that girl thought she was doin' me a favor. As a matter of fact, more people were dosed at that festival than at any other I played at."

On Sunday the Lewisville mayor announced that he would no longer stand for the use of drugs or the nude bathing in the lake area. He ordered the police to begin a crackdown and arrest those who broke the law. The police smartly carried out the order in only the most blatant of cases. They did not wish to create a situation that could result in a riot; therefore, only a small number were actually arrested. Nevertheless, fear had been injected into the minds of people at the festival, and by the last day only 25,000 people remained for the concert.

The Second Annual Sky River Rock Festival and Lighter Than Air Fair, or, more simply, Sky River '69, took place on a 360-acre ranch outside Tenino, Washington. The 1968 Sky River fest had been held in Sultan, Washington, on a local raspberry farm, but due to the expected large response to the second festival and also because the rain that had accompanied the first festival had turned the site into a swamp, promoter John Chambless opted for a new location.

After being denied space at numerous preferred sites, the sponsors of Sky River, the New American Community, settled for Tenino. It fit the needs of the festival, except that the ranch was divided by a line of the Northern Pacific Railroad. The railroad people insisted that it would be too dangerous to hold a rock festival anywhere in the vicinity of the stretch of track. They pointed out the speed of the trains (60–75 mph), the frequency with which they passed through the ranch (an average of 30 times per day), and the danger of festivalgoers possibly climbing the hill on which the tracks sat in order to get a better view of the performers as reasons for holding the festival elsewhere.

The Tenino townsfolk did not want the festival, either, and sided with the railroad people. The town's governing body decided to fight the issue in court. They succeeded in acquiring a court order banning the festival for the Labor Day Weekend. But Chambless and the New American Community fought the injunction. They had spent two weeks preparing the site: a stage was erected, concession booths were built, and large tents had been rented. And they did not intend to forfeit the site without a battle.

Twenty-four hours before the festival was to begin, the State Supreme Court of Washington lifted the injunction and granted permission for the nonprofit festival to proceed as scheduled. The Northern Pacific Railroad had agreed to slow down trains to less than twenty-five miles per hour when they passed through the ranch if the promoters promised to keep people off the tracks.

The festival did take place. Close to forty thousand people showed up for the three days, but it was not enough for the festival to claim success. *Variety* reported that the festival ended up in the red, and very little money was given to the nonprofit groups who were expected to benefit from the event. Performers at the festival only received $50 per person for their efforts, but court fees and numerous other expenses caused the financial loss.

No real attempt was ever made to produce a third Sky River festival in 1970. Many counties in Washington had passed laws restricting large musical gatherings in the wake of Woodstock and Sky River '69. Although the locals in both Sultan and Tenino had only good things to say about festivalgoers after the 1968 and 1969 events, they feared a return of the young people. Like the rest of the country, residents of the state of Washington feared another Woodstock. The legendary festival had exaggerated the definition of "rock festival." After August 1969, Woodstock represented the norm rather than the exception in the eyes of those who had the power to pass local ordinances and state and county laws concerning the control of rock festivals.

CHAPTER FIVE

Woodstock: A New Nation

Will Daisy Johnson please go to the Hog Farm kitchen.
Sammy Cohen wants to marry you.

—Announcement from the
   Woodstock stage,
   August 16, 1969

John Roberts met Joel Rosenman in 1967. Roberts, a recent graduate of the University of Pennsylvania, had just taken a job as a reporter for a small news service until he figured out what he wanted to do with his life. Money was the least of his problems. His father, Alfred Roberts, was president of Lydia O'Leary Inc., a large cosmetics firm. His mother had died when he was a child, leaving him a trust fund of over four million dollars. The money was to be handed over to her son in three installments: on his twenty-fifth, thirtieth, and thirty-fifth birthdays.

Joel Rosenman had recently graduated from Yale Law School, and he too searched for something meaningful to do with his life. That was part of the reason Rosenman and Roberts hit it off so well the first time they were introduced to each other. Rosenman's father was a Long Island dentist with perhaps enough capital to get his son started in business or involved in a legal practice, but Joel leaned more toward a career in entertainment.

The two men quickly became good friends, and within a month they were roommates. They hung out together, both looking for something to get involved in that would be fun and profitable. In 1968 they decided to put an advertisement in the *New York Times* that read: "Young men with unlimited capital looking for interesting and legitimate business enterprises." In less than a week, Roberts and Rosenman, who had recently formed Challenge International Inc., received close to five hundred replies to their ad. Some were preposterous, others enterprising and adventurous, but none of them totally captured their fancy or enthusiasm.

One day a lawyer friend of Joel Rosenman introduced him and John Roberts to two "shaggy-haired individuals with a great idea that needs financial backing." The two long-haired men turned out to be Michael Lang and Artie Kornfeld. Their idea was simple and promising: the building of a rock star retreat in New York State which would include an elaborate recording studio, living quarters, and a peaceful atmosphere where rock composers could write and exchange musical ideas in comfort and style. Lang and Kornfeld suggested the site be near or in Woodstock, New York. The town, they explained, was fast becoming a countercultural hotspot, especially with rock musicians. It was located just a couple of hours north of New York City, and it was the home of Bob Dylan.

After the studio and retreat had been constructed and ready for business, Kornfeld suggested that a large concert and gala press party be staged to introduce the structure to the media and rock world. Kornfeld figured that if all went well, such Woodstock locals as Dylan, the Band, and Tim Hardin could headline the concert.

Artie Kornfeld and Michael Lang had met when Kornfeld was working with Capitol Records and Lang approached him with a tape of a band he was managing at the time. Prior to his position at Capitol, Kornfeld was a part-time producer and lyricist for a top-40 band, the Cowsills. He had also served as an A&R (artists and repertoire) man with Laurie Records. Lang had once owned a head shop in Florida before moving back to New York to take up managing rock bands. Both men were hip to the music scene, at least more so than either Roberts or Rosenman.

Lang and Kornfeld had come to Roberts and Rosenman simply because they lacked the capital to transform their idea into a profitable reality. They explained to Roberts and Rosenman that they had the connections and knew the youth and music market enough to handle thoroughly the business aspect of the idea. All Roberts and Rosenman had to do was put up the cash. The profits, of course, would be split by all four.

The cash that Lang and Kornfeld talked about was Roberts's money, not Rosenman's. Roberts would soon be receiving the first allotment of his inheritance and was eager to invest it. Because Rosenman was his friend and roommate, Roberts decided to cut him in on any investments he made. But Roberts was no fool. He didn't feel good about handing over a few hundred thousand dollars to a couple of long-haired hipsters for them to invest in a field he knew next to nothing about. Still, for some reason, he liked the idea.

Roberts came up with a modified idea. What if they expanded the concert idea into a two- or three-day rock festival? The profits could be used to finance the rock retreat and recording studio. Roberts would invest a portion of his money to get the festival idea off the ground, but it would be a smaller sum than the original idea called for. Lang and Kornfeld had nothing to lose. Neither did Joel Rosenman. The four agreed on a basic strategy, and Woodstock Ventures Incorporated was formed.

The Woodstock festival was, first and foremost, a business venture. John Roberts and Joel Rosenman had absolutely no ties with the counterculture. Mike Lang and Artie Kornfeld wore their hair long, spiced their conversation with "groovy, man" and "far out," smoked dope, and were involved in rock music, but their motive for staging the Woodstock festival was quite similar to that of Roberts and Rosenman. None of the four promoters ever even remotely envisioned the power and significance behind their event until the festival was in full swing.

Kornfeld, Lang, Roberts, and Rosenman hoped to attract fifty thousand young people to their festival, which they scheduled to take place in August of 1969. In the early part of that year, it was decided to use a substantial amount of money to begin advertising the event. Ads were placed in underground newspapers across the country, in rock music periodicals, and on progressive rock radio stations. Most of the advertising was done in the Northeast, with special emphasis on New York City. But ads were also placed in Los Angeles, San Francisco, Chicago, and other large cities, and judging from the different license plates seen at the festival, the ads worked.

The bank that sheltered the trust fund of John Roberts permitted him a huge credit line. All he had to do was guarantee the bank in writing that the withdrawal of money would be balanced by a lien against his inheritance. Because of this, Woodstock Ventures had virtually unlimited capital. With finances established, the promoters went searching for a festival site.

The village of Woodstock was out as a potential site. Nowhere within its limits could a suitable area capable of accommodating fifty thousand people be found. Instead, the promoters checked nearby Middletown, where the township of Wallkill, fifteen miles from Woodstock, was located. The most appropriate site they found there was the Mills Industrial Park. The property was owned by Howard Mills, who told the promoters they could lease the land for $10,000 provided they got approval to stage the festival from the Wallkill Zoning Board. It was agreed that Mills's land would need some work to make it conducive to a rock festival, but otherwise the fallow fields and gently sloping hills would make for a fine location. There was even a grove of apple trees that the owner would put at the festival's disposal.

Lawyers representing Woodstock Ventures explained to the Wallkill Zoning Board that the Woodstock Music and Art Fair was to be mostly an art festival that would have musical entertainment. Most of the performers would be folksingers or jazz artists, they promised. The Wallkill officials liked the idea of hosting this sort of cultural activity and granted Woodstock Ventures permission to begin preparations on the site. Within a month the promoters hired crews to pave roads, erect fences, and design the general festival site.

Things were working smoothly until the middle of July, when a rebellious group of Wallkill residents known as the Wallkill Concerned Citizens Committee demanded that the Zoning Board abrogate the permission granted to Woodstock Ventures to hold a festival at the industrial park. They cited evidence that the Woodstock Music and Art Fair was a cleverly disguised title for a large hippie rock festival. The lawyers who had originally represented Woodstock Ventures at the zoning board meeting had not been instructed by the promoters to resort to mendacity to obtain a permit. The promoters *did* intend to present an art fair and *some* folk music *was* to be played. Woodstock Ventures argued its case before the zoning board, but the irate citizens had presented a petition of some two hundred signatures that demanded an immediate repeal of the permit. Not only did the residents feel they had been deceived by Woodstock Ventures, but they also feared a general disruption in the town if more than fifty thousand hippies invaded their streets. The town, they argued, could not cope with the traffic that would undoubtedly snarl local streets and highways.

The Wallkill Zoning Board bowed to the pressures of its citizenry and obtained a court injunction that banned the festival. To make doubly sure that the festival would not occur, the local governing body passed a resolution regulating the assembly of persons in public places.

Four weeks before the festival was to take place, and after the sale of fifty thousand tickets at a price of $18 for the entire weekend or $7 per day, the event was without a site. The thought of canceling the festival was briefly discussed, but too much money had already been spent. When word leaked out that the festival's organizers were looking for a new site, offers and ideas from people all over the country inundated their headquarters in New York City. According to Roberts and Rosenman, they were offered "riverfronts, mountainsides, wilderness areas, ski jumps, and even airstrips. One guy went so far as to suggest draining a fifty acre lake on his property and selling it to us. He said it would make a real nice amphitheater."

Meanwhile Michael Lang had been roaming through Sullivan County, New York, on his motorcycle in search of a new site. He had come across a dairy farmer by the name of Max Yasgur, who owned a six-hundred-acre farm with an adjoining four hundred acres of pasture and woodland. The farm was located at White Lake in the town of Bethel. Yasgur had worked his dairy farm since 1948 and had been responsible for supplying a large segment of Sullivan County with its dairy needs.

Yasgur took an interest in young people. In 1968 he had leased a portion of his property to the Boy Scouts of America for their annual National Jamboree, and things had gone well.

He had heard about the problems the music festival faced in Wallkill, and when Lang approached him, he invited the promoters to inspect the farm and talk business.

Lang called the festival headquarters in New York and told Roberts and the others to drive to Bethel as soon as possible. The town was seventy miles north of New York City, and when Roberts and a lawyer got there, they found a warm and amicable farmer who expressed sincere interest in seeing the festival occur in Sullivan County. He was also sincerely interested in seeing a load of cash before the deal was concluded. Yasgur told the promoters he would rent his farm for the weekend of August 15 for $50,000 plus an additional $75,000 that was to be put in escrow to cover any damages to the farm or his herd. He also listed three demands that had to be met before he signed the contract: (1) Woodstock Ventures must obey the zoning ordinances of the town of Bethel; (2) the festival plans must be approved by the local board of health and police department; and (3) Woodstock Ventures must agree to limit the number of people that would attend to forty thousand.

Max Yasgur drove a hard bargain. The price was steep, but the promoters had little choice. The $50,000 that Yasgur demanded was five times as high as the amount asked for by John Mills. Time was running short. If they declined Yasgur's offer, who knew whether another site could be found? And if they had to come back to Yasgur after turning him down the first time, what would prevent him from raising the rental fee higher and adding to his list of demands? Yasgur had the promoters over a barrel; they were going to pay his fee and do things his way or they weren't going to do it at all.

The promoters knew they could never limit attendance to forty thousand people, since they had already sold fifty thousand tickets. But Yasgur did not seem to be truly concerned with that demand as long as the others were met and the money paid. Therefore, the promoters kept the ticket sales low key. Yasgur had promised to use his influence in acquiring zoning and board of health approval (he was the town's wealthiest and most popular citizen). When unhappy residents planned a boycott of Yasgur's dairy products, Yasgur calmly explained to them the value of having the festival staged in their town. He spoke of how the festival would inject life into a dying local economy and pointed to the various commercial facilities that had been doing poorly in the last few years. He promised the locals that the festival would put Bethel back on the map and hinted that a bristling tourist trade might result. The locals now thought twice about a Yasgur boycott. Maybe he was right. The town did need *something* to revitalize it. Perhaps the festival was just the thing. The town backed Yasgur's decision to rent his land to the Woodstock promoters, and the festival was set to go.

Thursday, August 14

Traffic. Slowed, but still moving. "Creeping" was probably a better word. It was only Thursday evening, the start of the music was a full twenty-four hours away, and the traffic was rapidly approaching a critical stage. The promoters had expected a crowd of approximately 200,000 people. But at the rate traffic was building, actual attendance would easily top the estimated figure. The New York State police kept careful tabs on the Thruway, the main artery that linked New York City and New Jersey with the festival. The situation looked grim. Troopers on the opposite end of the Thruway voiced similar sentiments as festivalgoers converged on Bethel from Boston and other points north. The roads were lined with beat-up heaps, VW buses and bugs, family station wagons on loan for the weekend, sports cars, pickup trucks and vans, and wildly painted converted school buses and hearses. All of them passed slowly in the night.

For those coming from New York City and New Jersey, the directions were simple: Get on the New York Thruway and head north until Exit 16. Then take the Quickway (Route 17) until one saw signs indicating the festival site. For those coming from the north, the directions were equally simple. It sounded *so* easy that those who left home early Thursday afternoon thought they would beat the inevitable traffic jam.

They thought wrong. Many of those people were still in their cars on the Thruway or Quickway when the sun came over the trees on Friday morning. But somehow they kept their festive spirits alive. From the looks of things, the festival was going to be *big*. It seemed as though every rock fan and freak east of the Mississippi River was converging on the town of Bethel. Also included was a pretty fair representation of young people from the western and southern parts of the United States. License plates from California and Colorado were so common that it seemed as if someone had picked up and moved the two states somewhere near New York without telling a soul. The whole scene made one feel important; kind of like being an eyewitness or even a participant in some big, historical event.

Part of the traffic problem resulted from a lack of police officers near the site to direct traffic. Woodstock Ventures had hired more than three hundred New York City off-duty policemen to handle security and assist the state police with traffic snarls. They were to be paid $50 per day. But at the last minute the New York City Police Commissioner forbade the men to honor their contracts with the promoters of the festival. He cited a clause in the police code that prohibited police officers from moonlighting as security guards outside the city limits. Many of the officers feared reprisals by the department or even layoffs if they worked the festival and so decided not to go. Others disregarded the commissioner's statement, but their presence was not sufficient to curb the traffic mess. There just were too many cars.

Along with the New York City police officers, the Woodstock security staff was made up of volunteers—fifty ushers from Bill Graham's Fillmore East in New York City, and one hundred members of the Hog Farm.

When it was all over, Roberts and the other promoters could not thank the Hog Farm commune enough. Without their invaluable assistance the Woodstock festival would have undoubtedly succumbed to disaster, the threat of which hung so precariously over the event for the entire weekend. The group performed all sorts of public services. They fed those who were hungry (brown rice and beans cooked in giant caldrons) and compiled a daily news sheet that, among other things, listed lost festivalgoers, messages from home, and the location of medical tents. They assisted in the distribution of free food that was flown in by Air Force helicopters when the festival site was on the verge of being called a disaster area. Most importantly, they helped take care of all those suffering from bad acid trips and drug overdoses.

The Hog Farm commune was formed in the mid-sixties on a hog farm north of Los Angeles. The group's philosophy was simple and straightforward: Help those that need help and advance the messages of the counterculture—love, brotherhood, peace, and harmony with nature. Their leader was Hugh Romney, better known as Wavy Gravy. Romney was a former poet in the Beat era as well as a former Merry Prankster who traveled the country with Ken Kesey. Romney was an outstanding organizer and crowd appeaser who, during the course of the festival, was usually found onstage calming crowd fears about an impending disaster.

It was one of Michael Lang's friends who suggested that the promoters fly the entire commune in from New Mexico to help with security, drug bummers, and food distribution. At first the idea sounded absurd. But the friend explained that the commune was well respected in the counterculture ranks and that the Woodstock crowd would relate much better to them than they would to regular police officers or other establishment authorities. At a cost of over $17,000, Woodstock Ventures flew the entire commune to New York City in a chartered Boeing 727. As they were debarking from the plane after landing in New York, a reporter asked Romney how he was going to handle the security.

"Do you feel secure?" Romney asked as he revealed a wall of toothless gums.

"Yeah," uttered the reporter.

"It seems to be working," answered Romney.

The Hog Farm arrived at Woodstock a full week before the festival was to begin. While most of the commune's members helped put finishing touches on the stage and other facilities, Romney and a few other Hog Farmers planned security strategy with Wes Pomeroy. Pomeroy had been hired by Woodstock Ventures to head and organize a festival security force. He was a police officer himself and had a superb reputation as a crowd controller. He had handled security at the 1964 Republican Convention and took a deep interest in young people. Two of the most important decisions he made at Woodstock were not to allow any guns or weapons on the festival site, and to dress the off-duty police officers in low-profile uniforms. Pomeroy insisted they wear jeans and T-shirts with the Woodstock logo on the back of them. No badges were worn, and the idea that they were "peace officers" rather than police officers was to be obvious at all times.

Friday afternoon, August 15

The traffic problem had grown worse. Nothing was moving. Long lines of cars just sat there in the August sun. The police considered shutting down the Thruway and ordering those that were just arriving on the scene to turn around and go home. (Later on they did just that.) All roads leading to the festival

The road to Bethel.

were completely void of movement. The more impatient in the crowd drove their cars off to the side of the road and began walking to the site. Others quickly followed suit. And when parking space ran out along the side of the highways, people merely turned their engines off and left their cars in the middle of the road.

According to the New York State police, there were more than a million people on the road in the festival vicinity by late Friday afternoon. Of that number, at least forty percent never even got close to the festival site. Some, realizing the insanity of it all, turned around as soon as they hit the first signs of traffic. Others endured, in some cases spending over fourteen hours in the snarl. The only way to get from one point to another, aside from walking, was by helicopter. All weekend long the sky was dotted with police, Army, and Air Force choppers, plus an assortment of private ones that were hired by the promoters and the media.

Hours before the show was to commence that evening, the promoters declared the festival a free event. They had little choice. The fences that encircled the site had been knocked down and the continuous stream of people made it impossible to collect tickets. Once the fences went down, the promoters gave up all hope of selling tickets at the gate. The only sane thing to do was go with the flow; the flow of people, the flow of traffic, the flow of energy, and the flow of incredibly good vibrations despite all else.

Friday evening, August 15

The word had spread fast: The Sullivan County area was expected to be hit with a series of thunderstorms that could start as early as Friday evening. What about the music? Would the performers still take the stage if it rained? Rain or no rain, the promoters had already decided that the festival and the music would go on. Extra precautions were taken to make sure wires and cables were safely in place, and the lighting and sound fixtures on the towers were tightened since there also had been a prediction of high winds.

The warm silhouette of the Catskills sunset was partially blackened by approaching storm clouds off in the distance. But the threat of rain did not fade the festive spirit just as long as those in the crowd were sure the music would go on as scheduled. There were just too many people present to make a big issue about some rain. Only the promoters and stage people seemed to be aware of what a heavy rainstorm could do to the electrified rock music and the safety of those who performed it. They preferred, however, to think positively. They had done all they could to prepare for it; the only thing left to do was to wait for Mother Nature to strike—and begin the music.

A great roar went up from the crowd. Richie Havens emerged from the wings of the stage, strumming his worn acoustic guitar fast and powerful as always, and moved to the center microphone to begin the music. So after all the planning and all the hassles and all the money spent to make the festival a reality, the music began at the Woodstock Music and Art Fair.

Dressed in an African tunic, Richie Havens did not look like the urban folksinger that he was but rather like a tribal medicine man or soothsayer about to bestow a blessing of good fortune on the gathered masses. The folksinger recalled why he had been chosen to open the festival:

"The fact that those of us with acoustic instruments could be set up quickly was the only reason why we went on first. Actually, I was scheduled to play fifth on the billing, but since no one had made it up there on time, the promoters kept eyein' me up. Some of the rock bands were backstage but their equipment was somewhere else. Other bands' amps and things had arrived, but the actual musicians were stuck in the traffic jam. But it was good that Friday night was acoustic night because it relieved the tensions of the whole scene, ya know, the traffic, the crowds, the threat of rain. It made the festival start out on a mellow note.

"The music was already two and one half hours late, and everybody backstage is beginning to panic. Mike Lang comes up to me and says, 'Richie, please. Ya gotta go on now, man. You gotta open this thing. There's no one else. Richie, I'm beggin' ya, man.'

"So I look at the unbelievable amount of people out there and say, 'You're *crazy*! What do you want me to do, get killed?' Mike persisted, telling me that I had to do it, I had to do it.

"I turned and looked around and spotted Timmy Hardin standing a ways away, but listening to the whole thing and wondering what was going to come of it all. So I said, 'There's Hardin! He'll open up for you! He's your man!' I turned back to look at him and the cat split. Vanished just like that into thin air!

"Lang looks at me like the pressure of it all is starting to get the best of me. He was probably thinking, 'Wow, this dude is seeing things!' So he says to me, 'Look Richie, they're gonna go nuts out there if they don't get some music soon. You're the only one ready to go. You can do it, man. Just go out there strumming your ax.'

"I had played festivals before Woodstock so it wasn't like I was afraid of performing in front of so many people. But Woodstock was so much bigger and different from the rest. Anyway, I just walked out on the stage and did it."

Richie Havens ripped at his guitar and featured in his set two of his most popular and persuasive songs, "Handsome Johnny" and "Freedom." Havens drove his music hard and dexterously quick; he closed his eyes often and let the music take hold of his internal energy.

No one knew if the event could go on for three days as originally planned. New problems arose with the passing of each hour, the most serious being the continued arrival of more and more festivalgoers. There surely were not enough basic provisions on hand to accommodate a half-million people. Medical supplies were running dangerously low. People were already waiting in hour-long lines just to use the portable toilets. A two-hour wait was reported by those wishing to use the pay phones. There was even a forty-five-minute wait just to get some water. But a warm, congenial effervescence permeated the air and made it feel like the ordeal was all very worth it.

Arlo Guthrie and Joan Baez were two other big-name acts that performed on the first night. Guthrie had been a favorite with rock and folk audiences ever since he stepped out of his father's shadow and recorded his own "Alice's Restaurant," an eighteen-minute song that became a folk-music classic and was eventually made into a movie. His laid-back attitude came to epitomize the stoned-out hippie who let the world slip by without any resistance. At Woodstock Guthrie was flabbergasted by the size of the crowd he was playing to. He made repeated references to the latest estimate of the number of people at the festival and joked that the world never saw so many freaks in one place.

Joan Baez assumed her position at center stage looking profoundly solemn. She spoke of her husband, David Harris, who had been in prison for the last three weeks, and dedicated the song "Joe Hill" to him. Harris was an antiwar and antidraft activist who had gone to jail for his political beliefs. He was now in the midst of organizing a hunger strike with a few dozen inmates in protest of America's role in Vietnam and the drafting of young men into the armed forces. The highlight of the singer's set, however, was a chilling a cappella rendition of "Swing Low, Sweet Chariot." The old spiritual emphasized Baez's wide vocal range and symbolized the mood that permeated the crowd for three days.

Folksingers Tim Hardin, Bert Sommer, and Melanie also played on Friday night, along with the Incredible String Band, Sweetwater, and Ravi Shankar. Just about everyone who performed on Friday night had their set softened with rain. At first it struck as a downpour, like so many August storms in the Catskills do; then it tapered off and almost seemed to stop. But all of a sudden the pattern would resume, heavy at first and

Richie Havens and a cast of 400,000.
New York **Daily News**

then easing off to a steady drizzle. The lightning that had appeared in the distance earlier in the evening came ominously close during Shankar's set and threatened to strike one of the support towers. Luckily it was an empty threat.

The mud that resulted from the rain quickly turned most of the pasture into a sloppy quagmire when people began to trudge back to their tents and campsites. The more peole walked in it, the deeper and thicker the mud got. The severity of the problem was not realized until daylight broke on Saturday morning. People with radios passed the word that due to the rain and mud and the shortage of drinking water, the words "disaster area" were creeping into many of the news bulletins.

Saturday, August 16

It was there for the whole world to see. The *New York Times* had made the Woodstock music festival its headline story. A large aerial photo depicted the massive crowd and the festival site as the hub of the counterculture. Accounts filed by reporters accented and even exaggerated the hardships of camping in the mud, the problems with food and water supplies, the drug overdoses, and the disaster-area theme that people on the outside wanted to read about. What was not pointed out in any detail was that most of those at Woodstock thrived on the adventure and excitement of it all. Those who were participat-

In an editorial that appeared on Monday, August 18, *The New York Times* asked, "What kind of culture is it that can produce so colossal a mess?"

New York **Daily News**

The Woodstock Festival at two thousand feet.

ing in the greatest countercultural event of the decade—and perhaps even the century—privately considered themselves heroes and chosen crusaders. They felt the importance of the event every time a news helicopter flew daringly close to the sea of people or someone onstage told them how the whole world wanted to know what was happening at the festival site. When it was all over, they would relate to parents and friends how *they* managed to endure at Woodstock. The stories and escapades that were later told about the festival rivaled old soldiers' war stories in terms of the multitude of sensationalistic and colorful details. It was fashionable to say that one had been at Woodstock, but if all who claimed to have been there had actually attended, the crowd would have numbered in the millions.

By noon on Saturday it was not uncommon to see helicopters setting down close to the stage area to drop off supplies and cart away those who required medical attention. Actually, were it not for the shortage of medical supplies, the medical situation at Woodstock would have been under control. Dr. William Abruzzi, a physician from Wappingers Falls, New York, was in charge of medical personnel and responsible for coordinating an efficient program at the festival. Abruzzi had much experience at this sort of thing. In the past he had organized medical units and first-aid stations for mass antiwar demonstrations and civil-rights marches, and he possessed a firm grasp of what was required in order to handle drug-overdose victims and those suffering from bad trips. Abruzzi worked side by side with Hog Farm members on drug problems and also had at his disposal eighteen physicians, thirty-six nurses, and twenty-seven medical assistants to take care of the more complicated problems. Two emergency rooms were set up in trailers, and a large hospital tent was originally set up to accommodate the expected crowd. But the size of the crowd required that additional medical teams be flown in by an air force helicopter. Abruzzi also set up a large emergency area at neighboring Monticello High School to handle patients who were not actually inside the festival site.

Once it was deemed that food supplies were at the critical level and much of the water from the recently drilled wells had lost its purity in the rainstorms, townsfolk from Bethel and Monticello drew up plans to head off a crisis. A group of women from the local community clubs donated thousands of sandwiches to the Hog Farm's kitchen, to be given away free to hungry festivalgoers. The concession food stands run by Food For Love Inc. gave away soft drinks and milk as well as whatever food had not been destroyed by the rain; most of their supply of hamburgers and hot dogs had been consumed the first day. Many of the local merchants in the festival vicinity could have taken advantage of the situation by jacking up prices. Instead, many of them merely continued the neighborly policy of assisting festivalgoers with no money and supplying basic necessities for whatever price the young people could afford.

The rain that began late Friday evening continued for the rest of the weekend. So did the mud. These two problems, however, were rapidly becoming fundamental ingredients of the whole Woodstock phenomenon. Their presence added that extra dimension that helped transform Woodstock from just another summer rock festival into an *event*. The inclement conditions provided an opportunity for people to display their humanistic and communal regard for their neighbors at the festival site. The spirit of nonviolence and brotherhood was never in doubt, and the fact that this was all happening spontaneously added even more meaning to the event.

Rather than resist the rain and mud, some people in the crowd actually took advantage of it. The news magazines printed photos of young people splashing and sliding in the mud and shunning all clothes after becoming tired of wearing wet ones. But the rainy conditions endangered the lives of those in the crowd and up on the stage, though only a very few people actually knew it at the time.

Because of the amount of rain that had fallen, the dirt that covered the main electrical feeder cables had washed away, leaving them fully exposed to that part of the crowd that was seemingly in continuous motion. As Saturday night wore on, the insulation on the cables wore out and endangered not only those who walked on them but also those in the crowd who were wet and huddled close to the stage. The chief electrician spotted the dangerously thin level of insulation that remained on the cables and immediately informed Joel Rosenman. He told Rosenman that there was a strong chance of mass electrocution if all the power at the festival was not turned off instantly and the problem remedied. Rosenman had to make one of the biggest decisions at the festival. He could either turn off the power, which meant no music, no lights, and 400,000 kids sitting in the darkness with nothing to do—or risk frying half the crowd.

Rosenman had always feared what might happen if the music, for some reason, was not able to continue. What would the kids do? Would they reject the "beautiful people" attitude and go on a rampage, raising hell in Sullivan County? Or would they remain calm and understanding? Rosenman did not want to be responsible for this decision, but he knew he had no choice. Each second that passed brought catastrophe closer to the festival. Finally he did what any nervous, paranoid, and unsure promoter would have done in a similar situation: he went ahead and told the electrician to do what he had to do *without* cutting the juice! After he gave the order, Rosenman wanted to be someplace far away. Maybe India or the North Pole. Anywhere but on a dairy farm in New York State with the lives of so many well-behaved kids resting on his decision. He swallowed hard and hoped for the best. Meanwhile the music continued to blare from the stage. Rosenman paced the area behind the stage. He kept waiting for some giant orange and yellow flash to light up the sky. Time seemed to pass at an agonizingly slow pace. All of a sudden he noticed the electrician breaking through a crowd of people with a smile that covered two thirds of his face. Things had gone well. The electrician had run the power from the exposed lines to other lines that were still underground without incident or loss of power. Rosenman breathed a giant sigh of relief. Mission accomplished.

Saturday's music line up was much more ambitious and energetic than Friday's. Only one folk artist performed, the zany John B. Sebastian, who appeared on stage wearing a multi-colored tie-dyed shirt and a pair of pedal pushers, and dedicated one of his songs to a young mother who had given birth at the hospital tent. Otherwise the lineup was comprised of full-on, top-notch rockers: Canned Heat, Janis Joplin, Country Joe and the Fish, The Who, and the Grateful Dead. There were some lesser-known acts on the billing as well: A band from Boston called Quill, the Keef Hartley Band, and Sha Na Na, a group of college kids from New York City who performed a series of satirical interpretations of the life-style and music of the 1950s. Dressed in T-shirts, white socks, and leather jackets, with their hair slicked back, the group choreographed their way into the hearts of the Woodstock crowd.

Santana, the volatile Latin rock group that capitalized on the immense talents of founder and lead guitarist Carlos Santana and the vibrant beat of the congas and timbales, had the crowd up on its feet for most of their set. The group Mountain shelled festivalgoers with the piercing sounds of Leslie West's lead guitar. Both these acts used their successful shows at the festival as springboards to stardom in the following decade.

But *the* performance of the day, and quite possibly of the entire festival, was that of Sly and the Family Stone. Sylvester Stewart (Sly Stone) and his band had been revving audiences up all summer. Sly ran his life and his music at high speed, and used an audience's frenzy as fuel for his act. At Woodstock the dashing front man had a gathering of almost a half-million young people from which to garner strength.

Just a few hours before the sun was to rise, Sly Stone came onstage donned in an elegant white and mauve fringed outfit. The night's darkness dramatized both the performer and the excitement that surrounded the stage. Larry Graham's bass pulsated with the riff that opened one of Sly's biggest hits, "Dance to the Music." *"Dance! Get up! Dance to the music!"*

Sly Stone bellowed to the crowd. Backstage Janis Joplin and Grace Slick were dancing and clapping their hands. *"Get on up! Dance to the funky music!"*

Four hundred thousand souls were up on their feet. The Family Stone horn section emitted a volley of background rhythm as the clapping and shouting and bouncing of the crowd made the earth shake with cadence. "Dance to the Music" was in full swing, and Sly Stone was king of the world.

Without pausing, "Dance to the Music" gave way to "(I Wanna Take You) Higher." Sly's music showed its power as never before.

"What we would like to do is sing a song together. . . . We would like to sing a song called 'Higher,' and if we could have everyone join in, we'd appreciate it."

The crowd responded with a devastating cry of impatience and energy. "Wanna take you higher!"

"Higher!"

"Say *higher* and throw up the peace sign. It'll do you no harm. Wanna take you *higher!*"

"Higher!" The crowd boomed back in orgasmic force.

"Wanna take you higher!" Stone shot up the peace sign at full arm's length, and his fringed shirt flapped with the motion, suggesting that the performer had grown wings.

"Higher!" The audience echoed Stone's commands feverishly.

"Way up on the hill, *higher!*"

"Higher!"

"HIGHER."

"HIGHER . . ."

The drums rolled, the horns blared, and all of Woodstock was racing. The energy could have lit up New York City for a month!

"HIGHER!"

The Who followed Sly and the Family Stone. As the stage crew positioned the band's equipment, John Morris, one of the emcees of the festival and the person who had handled the booking chores for Woodstock Ventures, went to the microphone.

"This is the largest crowd of people ever assembled in the history of the world. But it's so dark out there we can't see you and you can't see each other. So when I say 'three,' I want every one of you to light a match."

The emcee paused a few seconds to allow people to locate

matches. The countdown began, and when Morris said the magic number, a breathtaking fiery light illuminated the night. The emotion and striking beauty of the scene was deeply touching. Whether this is the origin of the match-lighting ritual that has become so common on the concert circuit is unclear. What was clear, however, was that the moment marked the birth of a nation: the Woodstock Nation.

Peter Townshend, Roger Daltrey, Keith Moon, and John Entwistle took the stage at Woodstock as the sun was rising in the east. They performed brilliantly despite the fact that they had been dosed with acid backstage. (Townshend never forgot the incident and to this day voices his disgust with Woodstock and rock festivals in general.) In the film *Woodstock*, Michael Wadleigh caught the picturesque Roger Daltrey, stunning in his fringed outfit, as well as guitarist Townshend in perfect stride, and treated the world to an unforgettable split-screen segment of their performance. Wadleigh captured Daltrey's compelling stage presence and Townshend's windmilling guitar antics in poetic harmony. The Who's filmed performance turned out to be one of the movie's climactic moments.

The Woodstock crowd was largely apolitical (although they did show their concern over the Vietnam War during the Country Joe and the Fish set). But that did not stop Yippie leader Abbie Hoffman from pirating a microphone during The Who's set in an attempt to incite the crowd with political fervor. Hoffman appealed to the throng that it was wrong to celebrate when John Sinclair, a fellow political radical and manager of the band the MC5, was in jail for possession of two joints. But Hoffman had picked the wrong time to attempt arousal of the crowd. Peter Townshend, angered by the audacity of the radical, struck Hoffman with his guitar in the middle of a song and forced him to leave the stage.

It was not the first time Abbie Hoffman and members of the underground had forced a confrontation with the Woodstock image. In the book *Young Men with Unlimited Capital*, coauthor Joel Rosenman wrote about the first meeting he and John Roberts had with Hoffman some weeks prior to the festival. After receiving threatening phone calls from unidentified underground members, the promoters had agreed to meet with Hoffman, who promised to spike the festival's water supply with LSD if Woodstock Ventures did not donate $10,000 to the Yippie Party. No money was given to the radical group in an official sense, but the promoters did hand over funds to pay for setting up booths at Woodstock for various radical organizations.

Hoffman continued his efforts to manipulate the Woodstock hoopla toward a political end after the festival was over. He signed a contract with Random House to write a book on the event and its immediate significance for the counterculture movement in America. In *Woodstock Nation: A Talk-Rock Album*, he coined the phrase "Woodstock Nation" and prophesied a new spirit and energy for radicalism in the 1970s.

Sunday, August 17

"Good morning!" Wavy Gravy of the Hog Farm adjusted the microphone. "What we have in mind is breakfast in bed for 400,000. Now, it's gonna be good food, and we're gonna get it to ya. It's not just the Hog Farm either. It's everybody. We're all feedin' each other. We must be in heaven, man! There's always a little bit of heaven in a disaster area."

If it was truly a disaster area, one could not have picked a better one to be part of. By Sunday morning most crises that had threatened the festival were brought under control. Those festivalgoers who wanted to leave but had been prevented from doing so by the endless line of abandoned automobiles clogging the roads could now do so. State police had cleared most of the roads linking the festival with the Thruway. There was now a regular helicopter service transporting accident and drug-overdose victims who required serious medical attention. The phone lines that had come down during the rainstorms were repaired; young people could finally call home and alleviate parental fears that sons or daughters were helplessly trapped in a sea of mud and madness. Even the Port-O-Sans had been flushed out so that those tired of squatting in the woods could now sit in semicomfort in a sanitary closet without being overwhelmed by the fumes. The only major problem that still existed was the threat of more rain. And through it all, the music played on.

"All right friends," said Gracie Slick to those who were awake enough to comprehend what she was saying. "You have seen the heavy groups, now you will see morning maniac music, believe me. It's a new dawn!"

With that the Jefferson Airplane launched into "Volunteers" with enough might and alacrity to begin the third and final day

Robert Santelli

Growing up at Woodstock.

of the Woodstock festival in grand fashion. The Jefferson Airplane, like a few other San Francisco bands, had played almost every major festival since the inception of the concept in June of 1967. They were proven festival attractions, and in the two years since the Summer of Love, the Airplane had only increased their potency and charm.

But there were signs of philosophical alterations in the group's lyrical content. Some of the music from *Volunteers*, the band's most recent album at the time of Woodstock, indicated a deliberate step away from the notions proclaimed in the early Haight-Ashbury days. The peace and love theme from 1967 had withered away and was replaced by a more forceful, revolutionary tone. The Jefferson Airplane sought to represent this new attitude the same way the Rolling Stones ("Street Fighting Man") and a growing number of other rock bands were doing at the time: using expressive, inflammatory lyrics exhibited in a we're-not-going-to-take-any-more-bullshit attitude. And even though this image was not entirely relevant at Woodstock, it did serve to make the transformation from the generally passive resistance of the mid-sixties to an activist and ultimately militant stance of the early seventies a decidedly quick one.

Just as Joe Cocker was finishing up his resounding and symbolic version of "With a Little Help from My Friends," the final collection of rain clouds came over the horizon. From the darkness of the sky, it promised to be one of the worst downpours of the weekend. The now-familiar sound of thunder rumbled a few miles distant, and its threatening booms were picked up by the festival's sound system. There was nothing to do about the upcoming storm if one was in the middle of the crowd except get wet. Trying to blaze a path through the huge mass of people was a major chore that required balance, skill, and patience. Most people were just plain tired of the rain, however. They were tired of being cold and wearing wet clothes. They were tired of sitting in mud.

"Hey, if you think real hard, maybe we can stop the rain!" A voice from the stage tried to rally the spirits of the crowd as everyone prepared for the inevitable. The thunder grew louder and the winds swept across the festival site. A few seconds later the first drops of the approaching storm were felt.

"No rain! No rain! No rain! No rain! No rain!"

The crowd picked up the rhythmic chant begun on the stage. Soon everyone was shouting the defiant chant at the top of his lungs. It was the last great challenge; the last battle for the Woodstock crowd to win. They had beaten the odds and the claims of disaster with impressive shows of solidarity and brotherhood. They had survived the food and water shortages, the traffic, and even the mud, but victory over the inclement weather had thus far eluded them.

"No rain! No rain! No rain! No rain! No rain!"

But it was not to be. The rain came down in buckets. The crowd stubbornly kept chanting and raised their fists to the sky, but it did no good. The failure to stop the rain with the last, powerful, total, communal commitment of the festival revealed that the magic of the weekend was not absolute. The energy built up over the three days was not enough to wrest control over nature, even if many in the audience actually believed it *could* be accomplished.

The rain finally did subside, and after it had completely stopped, many people decided to leave for home. There was a steady and growing stream of people moving away from the stage and toward the roads that would take them back to the *other* world. By the time Crosby, Stills, Nash and Young took the stage late Sunday night, fewer than 100,000 people remained. Those devoted enough to stay until the very end heard the sounds of Alvin Lee and Ten Years After; Blood, Sweat and Tears; the Band; and Country Joe and the Fish among others. Many people waited until the Band performed to see if Bob Dylan would show up and play with his Woodstock neighbors as rumor had it. He didn't.

Woodstock was only Crosby, Stills, Nash and Young's second live appearance, but it gave the group instant success and stardom. The music of David Crosby (formerly of the Byrds), Stephen Stills (formerly of the Buffalo Springfield), Graham Nash (formerly of the Hollies), and Neil Young (also from the Buffalo Springfield) emphasized the natural, vibrant sound of acoustic guitars and four-part harmonies and was in direct contrast to the acid- and hard-rock styles of the day. Their music brought to mind the soothing, ethereal qualities of folk music, but they handled it with much more complexity and emotionalism than anything done in the early sixties at the height of the folk movement. The instrumental work was more elaborate and provocative, especially the lead guitar solos of Young and Stills.

The group's Woodstock set was begun with a shaky rendition of "Suite: Judy Blue Eyes," written by Stephen Stills for folksinger Judy Collins. The harmonies were a bit off and the guitars had problems staying in tune, but the trio (Neil Young had not yet appeared on stage) introduced a new brand of sensitivity and cognizance to rock. A half-hour into the set, Neil Young sauntered onstage and, along with close friend and occasional enemy Stephen Stills, performed an acoustic version of the old Springfield number "Mr. Soul."

Crosby, Stills, Nash and Young were not totally acoustic. In the second half of their set, the band settled into some definitive rock. Accompanied by Dallas Taylor on drums and Greg Reeves on bass, the quartet moved through most of the tunes from their debut album, along with some old Springfield numbers.

At 6:30 on Monday morning, the last performer took the

stage at Woodstock. The crowd had withered to a meager 25,000, a far cry from the half-million or so people of two days before. Strewn among the people was a field of garbage and abandoned belongings. Jimi Hendrix had been given the honor of closing the festival. The high priest of rock festivals was perhaps the most successful artist ever to play at the large events. His music summed up best what music and the masses could ultimately amount to. How appropriate it was to end the festival with a psychedelic version of "The Star Spangled Banner."

It was all over. By Monday afternoon only those who had volunteered to help clean up the garbage remained at the festival site. But Woodstock was, and would continue to be, a newsworthy item. The *New York Times*, which had given the festival intensive coverage for three days and had placed stories of the event on the front page, criticized Woodstock in an editorial on Monday, August 18. Entitled "Nightmare in the Catskills," the editorial asked, "What kind of culture is it that can produce so colossal a mess?" It also compared the zealousness of 300,000 fans to the impulses that "drive the lemmings to march to their deaths in the sea."[3] But in a highly unusual move, the following day the *Times* ran another editorial, "Morning After at Bethel," that softened considerably the verbal blows of the previous day and actually praised those who had participated in the event.

> . . . By adult standards, the occasion was clearly a disaster, an outrageous upset of all normal patterns. Yet the young people's conduct, in the end, earned them a salute from Monticello's police chief as the "most courteous, considerate, and well-behaved group of kids" he had ever dealt with.
>
> Perhaps it was just the communal discomfort, that whiff of danger, that they needed to feel united and at peace. For comrades-in-rock, like comrades in arms, need great days to remember and embroider. With Henry the Fifth they could say at Bethel, "He that outlives this day, and comes safe home, will stand a-tiptoe when this day is nam'd."[1]

Woodstock rapidly became more than just the largest rock festival ever produced. Overnight it assumed legendary proportions. Very little mention was made of the musical performances

except in the rock press. It was the crowd and the conditions that were important. Woodstock was labeled a giant tribal gathering that expressed the ideals and life-styles of the new generation. Others in the media considered the event in religious terms. Barry Farrell wrote in *Life* that "many minds seized upon the metaphor of religion that day: the people were the seekers, the rock stars their prophets and drugs pretty nearly their staff of life." Still there were others who considered Woodstock the ultimate symbolic display of just how massive and powerful rock music had become. Observers pointed out that rock music was the only thing that could have drawn together so many people under such trying conditions.

It was fortunate for the promoters of the festival that so much fuss was being made over Woodstock and that so much was being written about it. All the ink intensified the anticipation and impatience for the subsequent movie and albums that would result from the festival. Those young people who did not attend Woodstock but felt a spiritual bond with those who did needed to see the movie to confirm their belief in the power of the event. Those who were at Woodstock wanted to see the movie to recall memorable moments and see if their faces could be spotted in the crowd ("There! There I am! Did ya see me next to the guy with the orange T-shirt? I swear that was me!") as veritable proof that they were really part of the Woodstock legend.

The promoters claimed they had lost $1.3 million on the event. Such unexpected costs as helicopter rental fees and food and medical supplies helped raise their losses to such an outrageous figure. So they said. They also called attention to the fact that no tickets were sold at the festival site as originally planned because the fences were down before the music got started. They had no way of recouping their losses with the exception of the profits they would receive from the film and records. Those who were clever enough realized that the interest the media had generated over Woodstock would guarantee that enough money would be made from the movie and albums to at least wipe out the figures in the loss column. Speculation over future profits came to a head when it was reported that Albert Grossman, one of rock's most visionary front men,

---

The rain and the mud were all part of the Woodstock experience.
New York **Daily News**

wanted to buy into Woodstock Ventures and assume part of its million-dollar debt.

Michael Wadleigh and Bob Maurice had been contacted two months before the festival took place to film the event. The concluded deal stipulated that Woodstock Ventures would receive a portion of the profits from the film, but Wadleigh and Maurice would have to raise the money for the production of the film. They would also be responsible for finding a distributor. When Wadleigh had trouble locating one, he asked John Roberts for money to cover the costs of producing the film until a distributor could be found. Roberts decided to start being frugal at the wrong time and said he couldn't help him out. Eventually Wadleigh had to settle for a lean $100,000 contract with Warner Brothers. When the Woodstock craze finally leveled off, the movie had grossed some $17 million dollars for Warners.

The film opened in March 1970 and set house records in New York; Washington, D.C.; Dallas; Boston; and Los Angeles. Ticket prices hovered around the $5 mark. The high price of admission was based on the theory that since the three-hour extravaganza was similar to a rock concert, young people would not mind paying the large fee to see the movie.

The movie was a critical success as well as a financial one. Wadleigh and his twenty-five-person crew filmed not only the performances onstage but also the happenings in the crowd and at the campsites. When they were putting the film together, they used such visual effects as overlapping, split-screening, and double-framing to enhance the documentary. The high quality of the film was carried over to the lps that were released in 1970 (*Woodstock*) and 1971 (*Woodstock Two*). The albums, produced by Eric Blackstead, were made from over one hundred hours of tape that included all the performances and the stage announcements that were heard during the three days.

Immediately after the festival ended, a split in Woodstock Ventures ended the four-man partnership. John Roberts and Joel Rosenman sided against Artie Kornfeld and Michael Lang. It was revealed that intense bitterness had always existed between the two sets of men. Roberts and Rosenman felt that Kornfeld and Lang had done very little in the way of work to make the festival a reality. Roberts claimed that the two other promoters were more interested in securing publicity for themselves and had generally abused the status of being Woodstock promoters. On the other hand, Kornfeld and Lang accused

Roberts and Rosenman of trying to prevent them from receiving their rightful share of the profits. The bickering died down when Roberts and Rosenman consented to accept $31,250 apiece to leave Woodstock Ventures.

As for Max Yasgur, his friends in Bethel gave him a testimonial dinner and publicly thanked him for bringing the festival to Sullivan County and restoring some economic activity to the area. Yasgur appeared on many talk shows and became a sort of celebrity. In February of 1973, almost four years after Woodstock, Max Yasgur, at the age of fifty-three, died of a heart attack in Florida. In its obituary *Time* magazine labeled Yasgur the "patron saint of the counterculture."

The greatest summer in rock history ended when the last of the festivalgoers returned home from Bethel in mid-August and from the Labor Day weekend festivals held in Louisiana, Texas, and Washington. Across the Atlantic, English and European rock fans headed back to the mainland and the British Isles after participating in the Isle of Wight festival, where over 200,000 people had gathered for an English version of Woodstock. It was the only festival of the summer that could boast a performance by Bob Dylan.

The immense popularity of the summer rock festivals proved that the magnetic attraction to these events was much stronger than anyone had anticipated. Because of this, in October of 1969 a unique conference was held in the mountains of New Mexico. A collection of some sixty of the most influential leaders of the counterculture attended a "sympowowsium" on the future of rock festivals and other large-scale gatherings. Among those present were Ken Kesey—novelist, LSD advocate, and originator of the 1967 Trips Festival; Woodstock promoter Michael Lang; *Realist* editor Paul Krassner; Bill Hanley of Hanley Sound; and members of the Hog Farm.

The main theme of the conference was "What Comes After Woodstock?" The group was unanimous in its feeling that the rock festival was a potent force in the continuation of the counterculture and should be used to further advocate alternative life-styles, aside from presenting the newest sounds in rock music. Topics such as gate-crashing, drugs, rip-off promoters, and violence were discussed, but no course of action was agreed on. The group, however, did decide to gather information for a manual on how to produce a rock festival and to coordinate plans for a huge rock festival to be held on Cherokee holy land in Georgia, with profits from the event going to the Indians for the purchase of the land.

The conference could have played a major role in the future presentation of rock festivals, but due to a lack of leadership and an eventual parting of philosophical ways, the meeting turned out to be nothing more than a pleasant get-together of old friends. Perhaps if plans had been laid out and effectively carried through, 1970 would have been a much better year for rock festivals than it actually was.

PARTIAL LIST OF WOODSTOCK
PERFORMERS AND FEES[2]

These fees were the amounts performers were to have received according to *Variety*. Many performers, however, never got paid, whereas the Who, whose Woodstock contract was reproduced and included in the band's *Live at Leeds* album, received $12,500.

1. Jimi Hendrix $18,000
2. Blood, Sweat and Tears $15,000
3. Joan Baez $10,000
4. Creedence Clearwater Revival $10,000
5. The Band $7,500
6. Janis Joplin $7,500
7. Jefferson Airplane $7,500
8. Sly and the Family Stone $7,500
9. Canned Heat $6,500
10. The Who $6,250 (also reported at $11,200, but *Variety* claimed that number was inaccurate)
11. Richie Havens $6,000
12. Arlo Guthrie $5,000
13. Crosby, Stills, Nash and Young $5,000
14. Ravi Shankar $4,500
15. Johnny Winter $3,750
16. Ten Years After $3,250
17. Country Joe and the Fish $2,500
18. Grateful Dead $2,250
19. Incredible String Band $2,250
20. Mountain $2,000
21. Tim Hardin $2,000
22. Joe Cocker $1,375
23. Sweetwater $1,250
24. John B. Sebastian $1,000
25. Melanie $750
26. Santana $750
27. Sha Na Na $700
28. Keef Hartley $500
29. Quill $375
30. Paul Butterfield Blues Band Figures not available
31. Bert Sommer Figures not available

Iron Butterfly was to have received $5,000 plus an additional $5,000 for their light show. They never showed.

CHAPTER SIX

Altamont: The Plot Thickens

*If Jesus had been there,
he would have been crucified.*

—Mick Jagger
December 7, 1969

"Here they are, the Rolling Stones!"

The huge crowd rose to its feet. More than 300,000 cheers and whistles echoed in the darkness. The bright red-and-white stage lights crisscrossed the sea of people and then turned back to zero in on Mick Jagger, who was wearing a stirring black satin cape. His appearance forced many in the crowd to look twice. Was that really Mick Jagger, lead singer and principal spokesman for the world's greatest rock 'n' roll band, prancing around the stage? Or was it an underworld demon crested in man's image and prepared to blacken the soul and pilfer the innocence of the youthful Woodstock Nation?

Those who had waited nearly ten hours for the Rolling Stones to take the stage at the Altamont racetrack on Saturday, December 6, 1969, witnessed the beginning of the end of an era. Sitting on the rock-strewn piece of land amid rusted bottle-caps, broken glass, and old pieces of tin and metal, 300,000 people saw the rock festival concept become further blemished with bloodstains and violence. The spirit of Woodstock had been stifled. The mass celebration of youth with the sound of rock music would take on a different meaning after the news of Altamont spread. The Age of Aquarius was befouled with murder, and in the center of it all were the Rolling Stones.

The Stones were adamant in their decision not to begin playing until the sun was down and darkness had set in. It would mean almost an hour's delay, but the group did not seem overly concerned. They insisted that the atmosphere be perfect for their entrance. The crowd would wait, they reckoned. They had waited all day. The Stones figured the dramatic intensity of their appearance in the nocturnal setting would be worth it. And it was. When Mick Jagger, Mick Taylor, Bill Wyman, Charlie Watts, and Keith Richards finally took the stage, the Rolling Stone–starved audience responded with a barrage of excitement that was decibel-defying.

The Stones returned the powerful greeting with a rousing version of "Jumpin' Jack Flash." Chuck Berry's "Carol" quickly followed. Both songs sounded superb and promised that the Stones' performance that night would be one of the best of their American tour. Richards's guitar playing was sharp and calculated, and Jagger sang with his usual energy and force. All the excitement of seeing and hearing the Rolling Stones live ignited the crowd with an infectious ebullience. But as the set progressed, it became more and more difficult to locate Jagger on the stage. His voice could be heard by most in the crowd through the muffled sound system, but his body was swallowed up by the more than one hundred people who were also on the stage. Most of these were members of the Rolling Stones' security staff, the Hell's Angels. Jagger, who was used to moving around the stage, cleverly outfitting each step with some sort of sexual implication or gesture, was trapped in a small circle near center stage. Mick Taylor and Billy Wyman stood off to the side, barely recognizable. Charlie Watts fortified himself behind his drum kit. Only Keith Richards had room enough to display the emotional vigor that the Stones were noted for.

There was pushing and shoving on the stage and in the audience. Two Angels with sawed-off pool cues took swings at a man near the side of the stage. Another Angel was seen kicking a young man near the wall of amplifiers closest to Wyman. All day the people close to the stage fell victim to the brutal force and sadistic might of the Angels. They seemed to enjoy their cruelty as they mercilessly beat innocent people to bloody pulps. Chains flew in the air and knuckled fists landed swiftly on stunned faces. The Hell's Angels were in control the entire day and had no intention of lifting their reign of terror during the Stones' set.

Not thirty feet from the stage stood Meredith Hunter, an eighteen-year-old black man from Berkeley, California. He had left his home at 5:30 in the morning to get to the Altamont Speedway in Livermore and position himself as close to the stage as possible. All day Meredith Hunter, like others around him, had been pushed and sometimes manhandled by the Angels. By dusk most of those near the stage who had not retreated to a safer spot were weary veterans of the day's conflict. They should have realized that the Angels would probably mount their most belligerent offensive when the Rolling Stones appeared onstage. But the thrill of listening to the Stones up close smothered good sense. When the Stones came on, the mob pushed toward the stage, with Hunter in the center of the crowd.

The Rolling Stones were now halfway through "Sympathy for the Devil." Jagger emphasized certain lyrics and with seductive and tantalizing gestures doubled the potency of the song.

Jagger was remarkable at dictating the emotional response to each song the Stones played. Throughout the American tour that had begun a month earlier, Jagger had commanded attention to his every move. Every sway of the body was gratefully accepted and later, after the concert had ended, replayed over and over in the minds of those who had been to the show. But it was "Sympathy for the Devil" that summoned the most response at Altamont. During the song Jagger transformed himself into a Satanic messenger with a ritualized crescendo of energy. The audience begged for more. Mick Jagger, at that moment the most powerful man in rock, gave those at Altamont just what they wanted.

Then it happened—quickly. There was more pushing and shoving off to the side of the stage—nothing out of the ordinary, though, considering the circumstances. But this time there was a quick flash of metal—some glint caught by the stage lights. Something, according to the Angels, that *looked* like a gun. Within seconds gang members swarmed about, pouncing on the lanky figure who they *thought* held the object. Then, in the midst of the chaos, Meredith Hunter felt the cold steel of a silver switchblade jab into his back. Not once or even twice—but four, maybe five times. And he felt the unerring blows of more fists and boots as other Angels moved to finish him off.

Jagger witnessed the attack on Hunter with horror and dismay. He turned away from the scene and called for the band to stop playing. People near the front of the stage began screaming and shouting for a doctor. Panic and fear gripped those close to the fallen young man. Keith Richards moved toward the microphone.

"Cool it! Cool it out there!"

Mick Taylor, looking like a frightened young English schoolboy, backed away from the fray. Bill Wyman, until then standing motionless, was aroused by the violence and also moved back.

"Brothers and sisters, come on now. . . . Everybody just cool out! Everybody, come on now! Cool out!" Jagger pleaded with the Angels and the crowd, hoping that his influence would subdue the tension at the front of the stage.

"Are you all right?" Jagger, not fully aware of what had happened, cautiously leaned over the edge of the stage to get a better look at what had transpired. Angels surrounded the body on the ground.

Jagger signaled to resume playing, hoping that the music would quell the mean streak of the Angels and preclude any more violent eruptions. But it was in vain. Another fight, more pool cues, more chains landing on human flesh. Three more Angels jumped from the stage to assist in the beatings. A young man, apparently drunk or tripped out on acid, climbed the stage over to the side opposite where Jagger stood and immediately was hurled off. Like sharks in a feeding frenzy, the Hell's Angels were uncontrollable. Jagger cried out into the crowd.

"Why are we fighting? Brothers and sisters, why are we fight-

---

Mick Jagger and the Rolling Stones.
Courtesy of Cinema Five

ing?" Again the Stones stopped playing and again they started up. This time they did an instrumental, with Jagger looking wan and shell-shocked, trying to mollify the virulent Angels.

Meanwhile Meredith Hunter was on the ground, bloodied and fast approaching death. Knife wounds dotted his back, and there was a large opening on the left side of his head. His face was swollen from cue-stick lashes, and his clothes were ripped and bloody. Robert Hiatt, a medical student from the San Francisco Public Health Hospital, answered Jagger's request for a doctor. He was the first person with any first-aid knowledge to tend Hunter. But there was really nothing he could do for him. Judging by the way the blood was gushing out of one of Hunter's back wounds, Hiatt surmised that a major artery had been cut. If the bleeding was not stopped at once, Hunter would be dead in a matter of minutes.

A passageway was made through the crowd so that Hiatt could pass with Hunter in his arms. Hiatt ultimately made his way backstage and did what he could to keep Hunter alive. Because of the lack of emergency logistic planning, Hunter could not be quickly moved to a hospital. There wasn't even the essential medical equipment backstage to sustain Hunter until help arrived. Meredith Hunter was officially pronounced dead at the Alameda County coroner's office at 11:00 P.M. The official cause of death was severe hemorrhaging due to multiple wounds in the back and head.

After Hunter's body was removed from the front of the stage, the Rolling Stones did the only thing they could do: continue playing. Jagger realized that any cessation of the music might ignite a large-scale riot, resulting in scores of wounded and dead. The Rolling Stones even had ample reason to fear for their own lives. All day certain Angels had made sarcastic remarks and had scoffed at Jagger's mannerisms. They had labeled him a fag and resented all the attention he received. Jagger knew that his "bodyguards" could turn on him at any moment and that his fate would be entirely in their hands.

Many members of the huge crowd did not know what had occurred. Some were sitting as far as a quarter-mile away from the stage, and the lack of adequate lighting made visibility even worse. They knew *something* had happened but had no idea that a man had been murdered. Rolling Stones fans were used to physical and emotional eruptions when the band performed in concert; most incidents, however, were usually snuffed before major problems arose.

"Stray Cat Blues," "Love in Vain," "Midnight Rambler," and the first public presentation of "Brown Sugar" followed Hunter's exit. Then, during "Under My Thumb," the fighting resumed. This time the Angels were incited by fans trying to climb on the stage to get closer to Jagger. The bikers responded by violently kicking and throwing people off the sides of the platform. Again the blood flowed and reddened welts marked the victims. No one in the audience attempted to curtail the violence, and the Angels beat people at will. There were over 300,000 festival-goers at Altamont, compared to maybe 200 Angels. One hastily planned charge and the Angels would have been easily overwhelmed. And yet for the entire day, they controlled the stage area entirely. They were the masters.

The Stones continued their set with "Gimme Shelter," "Little Queenie," "Satisfaction," and Honky Tonk Woman," and ended with "Street Fighting Man." Most of the tunes played at Altamont were the ones they had done in the previous shows of the whirlwind tour that had begun in mid-November. *Rolling Stone* magazine reported, "It's just amazing. There could be no worse circumstances for making music, and the Stones were playing their asses off."

A few minutes after the Stones left the stage, they boarded a waiting helicopter that took the band to San Francisco Airport in time to catch their flight back to London. Both in the helicopter and on the plane the Stones spoke little. It was a day they would never forget, and they couldn't help but think that they were at least partially responsible for the bloodshed and violence that had occurred. At the airport a reporter approached the ragged Jagger and asked him to comment on the scene he had just left.

"I know San Francisco by reputation," he said. "It was supposed to be lovely here, not uptight. What's happened? What's gone wrong?"

The next day, Sunday, December 7, the accounts of Altamont covered the front pages of the San Francisco newspapers. Many of the correspondents present at Altamont had not stayed for the Stones' set owing to deadlines and therefore did not report on the stabbing of Hunter and the violence near the stage during the Stones' performance. It was prematurely assumed that Altamont was another Woodstock, with minor— *only minor*—altercations. There were 300,000 people gathered for the sole purpose of listening to rock music. There were plenty of drugs: all colors, all brands, and all flavors. There were people walking around nude. And there was a festival atmosphere. Why not tag it another Woodstock, thought the media.

The glory lasted for one day. When the reports came in about the death of Hunter and the behavior of the Angels, the Woodstock image of Altamont was shattered. Even the national media had hoped for another Woodstock on which to capitalize. Photos of young hippies partially clothed or bathing in the nude and stories about how the youth culture celebrated its sovereignty sold magazines and newspapers. But it wasn't to be this time. Confronted by the destruction of the Woodstock myth, hardly any print was given to what had really gone on at Altamont. *Rolling Stone* was one of the few periodicals to give it full coverage and accurately report on the violence. *Life,* which had intended to do a spread similar to their Woodstock one of only a few months ago, did nothing. The *New York Times* did a short piece on the concert, but it was not a front-page story as the editors originally hoped for.

The original idea for a free Rolling Stones concert in America was prompted by the success of a free show the Stones did in London's Hyde Park in July 1969. Altamont, strictly speaking, was not intended to be a rock festival. But because it took place outside and away from the city and because it attracted such a large crowd, the term "concert" quickly succumbed to "festival." America was festival-crazy in 1969, and any large concert or youth-oriented event that included music was apt to be labeled a rock festival by the press as well as by the promoters who staged the event.

In June of 1969, Brian Jones, the rhythm guitarist and an original member of the Stones, decided to leave the band. Since 1967 it had been publicly known that Jones had a drug problem. He also had trouble coping with the huge success of the Rolling Stones. Jones was in and out of hospitals and, like Jagger and Richards, was busted for possession of drugs. His departure from the Stones was designed to alleviate the pressures and give Jones time to regain his health. One month later, on July 5, Brian Jones, age twenty-five, was found dead in his swimming pool. An autopsy revealed a large amount of barbiturates in his system.

Mick Jagger and the rest of the Rolling Stones quickly formulated plans to do a free memorial concert in Jones's honor. The concert, taking place in Hyde Park just two days after his death, attracted more than 250,000 fans. Jagger opened the concert by reading from Shelley's elegy "Adonis," and then released one thousand white butterflies in memoriam to the dead guitarist. No trouble was reported, the music was outstanding, and the press favorably commented that the peacefulness of the event was a tribute to the younger generation. Various members of some of London's motorcycle clubs acted as a security force. The scene was unusually low-keyed for a Rolling Stones performance.

There had been talk of doing a concert in Hyde Park ever since the Rolling Stones had heard an idea proposed by Ken Kesey and members of the Merry Pranksters and Hell's Angels in late 1968. Kesey and the rest had asked the Stones if they might be interested in doing a free concert in the Bay Area. San Francisco, they reminded them, had always been a favorite city of the band. Besides, they had publicly expressed interest in visiting the Haight-Ashbury section of the city. The Stones promised to keep the idea up front when they began planning their American tour, but first they wanted to try out the idea in England. Brian Jones's death was the perfect time to do the free concert. After the success and critical acclaim of the Hyde Park tribute, a free show in America seemed possible and even attractive.

The Stones arrived in early November in Los Angeles to prepare for their first U.S. tour in more than three years. While they were in Los Angeles, Rock Sculley, former manager of the Grateful Dead, approached the band to find out if any more thought had been given to the free concert idea. He had checked the Stones' tour itinerary and found nothing that mentioned a free concert in the Bay Area. After meeting with Jagger and Richards, Sculley had been instructed by the two to confer with Sam Cutler, the Stones' tour manager, about the plans. Cutler informed Sculley that the idea was still very much aive, but he confessed that no actual planning had been done up to that point. Sculley and Cutler agreed to begin work on the concert now that the Rolling Stones entourage was in America. Sculley proposed that the best place for the Stones to play would be at Bill Graham's Fillmore West. Without publicizing the event, the Stones could just show up and play. The plans were left with the Fillmore as the concert site until the Stones decided it was too small. The band wanted to reach a much larger audience and also to capture some of the limelight that such rock events as Woodstock, the Atlanta Pop Festival, and the

Backstage at the Los Angeles Forum.
Left to right: Keith Richards,
Mick Taylor, Bill Wyman, and Mick Jagger.
Charlie Watts's image appears in the mirror.
Courtesy of Cinema Five

Three weeks prior to Altamont: the Rolling Stones *live* in Boston.

Texas International Pop Festival were still receiving from the past summer.

A request for the use of Golden Gate Park was presented to the City Parks and Recreation Department. Rock Sculley, friend Emmett Grogan, and members of the Rolling Stones entourage sludged through the quagmire of red tape that inevitably resulted when one applied for a park permit. They impatiently waited for a reply while the Stones performed at the West Palm Beach Rock Festival in Florida. Grogan came up with an idea that would solve the problem of security. He proposed that the Rolling Stones hire the local chapters of the Hell's Angels to provide a motorized escort into and out of Golden Gate Park. Everyone had been concerned about how the Stones would manage to get to the stage in the park with an estimated 250,000 people jamming every inch of the way. The idea sounded like a good one. The Angels had been used as security men for the Human Be-In in January 1967. They had been present, although not in large numbers, at the Monterey Pop Festival in the summer of the same year, and just six months prior to the date of the free concert, English bikers had assisted with security measures at the Stones' free concert in Hyde Park. It was also brought up that the Angels were influential in the original proposal by Kesey and friends that the Stones do a free concert in the Bay Area. They deserved a right to participate, and besides, everyone respected the colors of an Angel.

The escort through Golden Gate Park was not necessary. The city turned down the request. The expectation of 200,000 kids in the park frightened the City Parks and Recreation Department. The largest gathering for a rock performance prior to the proposal was at a free concert given by the Grateful Dead and Jefferson Airplane that drew 50,000 people. There was also a significant amount of bitterness in the city government concerning the cancelation of the Wild West Show. This was to have been a six-day celebration of the arts in San Francisco that was put to rest by political haggling and repeated threats of violence. The atmosphere at the time of the Stones' request was still too heavy with ill feelings, and thus the proposal was rejected. The City Parks and Recreation Department was kind enough to suggest the possibility of using one of the vacant federal forts in the Bay Area, but Sculley and Grogan did not see any of these as logical settings. As of November 30, no site had been approved. The concert was only a week away.

Five people were prominent in the search for a concert site. Chip Monck, the stage manager from Woodstock who had been hired by the Stones to handle the stage chores for the American tour and was responsible for building a stage at the site—if and when one was found—was one of these people. Sam Cutler, the Rolling Stones' tour manager, was another. He was responsible for the overall supervision of the free concert. Jo Bergman, Mick Jagger's personal secretary, handled everything from publicity to secretarial duties. Rock Sculley and Emmett Grogan, friends of the Stones and advocates of the free concert idea, rounded out the team. Their job was to sweep the Bay Area for potential sites.

After Grogan, Sculley, and Cutler had checked out and rejected three possible sites, Sears Point Raceway, located just north of San Francisco and offering a natural amphitheater of sorts, was agreed on as the best possible choice. Jagger and Richards were contacted and gave their approval; and Chip Monck, his stage crew, and some Bay Area carpenters went immediately to the racetrack to begin construction of the stage.

With Monck's experience the stage was built in less than forty-eight hours. The crew was putting the finishing touches on the stage when news came to halt all construction. Sears Point Raceway would not be the site of the concert after all.

Filmways Corporation was the owner of the Sears Point Raceway. They also owned Concert Associates, the group that had produced the Stones' Los Angeles concerts. Filmways demanded that the Rolling Stones pay $100,000 in rental fees for use of the raceway property or sign over the distribution rights of the film that was to be made of the concert. The Stones were furious over the demands. Filmways Corporation felt it had evened things up with the band. Back in November, after tickets were snapped up voraciously for the Stones' Forum shows, Concert Associates had pleaded with the Stones to add a third performance. The Stones had refused, and Concert Associates saw a large potential profit disappear with the wind. Neither side would budge on the Sears Point issue, and the plans for the free concert came to a grinding halt. At an afternoon press conference on December 4, Sam Cutler announced the cancelation of Sears Point as a concert site but expressed optimism that an alternative site would be found before Saturday, December 6.

Things looked grim until Dick Carter of Altamont Speedway came forward with a proposal. He told Cutler and Scully that the Rolling Stones could use his raceway facilities at no charge. All he requested was that the Stones pay for the clean-up and garbage removal and for an insurance policy that would cover damages or legal suits. Time was running short and no other location offered itself as a possibility. Sam Cutler and Rock Sculley agreed on Altamont and sent word to Jagger and Richards, who were in Muscle Shoals, Alabama, sifting through tapes of the band's live performances for use on the next Stones' live lp. *Get Your Ya-Yas Out!* Without even inspecting the premises, Cutler, after securing an okay from the band, signed a contract with Carter. Chip Monck and the stage crew went back to Sears Point Thursday evening (December 4) to dismantle the stage and began transporting the equipment to Livermore, home of the Altamont racetrack.

The facilities at Altamont shocked Sculley and Cutler when they viewed them for the first time on Friday afternoon. The grounds were a mess and certainly in no shape to accommodate a couple of hundred thousand kids. The raceway also had a barren, desolate, eerie feeling about it. It just didn't look or feel right. Someone mentioned in jest that it was an ideal location for a Hollywood war scene. There was little time to joke, however.

It was obvious why Carter had volunteered the use of Altamont as the Rolling Stones' free concert site. The raceway had seen its best days. Demolition derbies were the only activities the place was good for, and they did not attract enough paying customers to keep Altamont in the profit margin. Carter knew that with the Rolling Stones playing at Altamont and a movie made of the concert, the raceway was sure to receive valuable exposure and publicity. Carter had visions of Altamont becoming a permanent outdoor site for huge concerts and festivals. He had read about other racetracks in Atlantic City, Miami, and Atlanta that had been used successfully for rock festivals and made handsome profits. The Rolling Stones' concert was Altamont's big chance for a rebirth and a new claim to fame.

Sculley and Cutler had twenty-four hours in which to prepare for the concert. They realized that security, medical personnel, food and water supplies, and communications would be minimal at best. There was no knowledge as to the number of people that might attend, since no tickets were sold. The biggest problem was making sure that the stage was built and the sound and lighting equipment were ready to go. They shuddered to think what 200,000 or so kids would do in a place like Altamont with no entertainment.

Another problem was the performers themselves. The concert was supposed to begin at 10 A.M. on Saturday, but Jagger and Richards were still in Alabama. No helicopters had been hired to transport the Stones and the other bands that were to play to and from the concert site.

Along with the Rolling Stones, the other bands scheduled to perform were the Grateful Dead; the Jefferson Airplane; Santana; the Flying Burrito Brothers; and Crosby, Stills, Nash and Young. These bands had previously been asked to perform if and when the free concert took place. The Stones knew they had tremendous drawing power in the Bay Area, and they wanted as many people to show up as possible. If only the Stones were to play, there was a slight chance people might think twice about driving a considerable distance to hear a two-hour Stones set and then drive home bucking the murderous traffic that was sure to occur. The Stones also wanted that festival atmosphere, and, therefore, needed more than one group to perform.

The Alameda County Sheriff's Department was notified of the hastily constructed plans for the concert. They were warned that traffic would be very heavy heading east from the Bay Area. There wasn't enough time to arrange for police security at Altamont; thus the entire job fell in the laps of the Hell's Angels. Cutler hired them for $500 worth of beer.

The Medical Committee for Human Rights and the Red Cross volunteered their services, but, again due to the lack of time, only nine doctors and some fifty nurses and medical assistants could be rounded up on such short notice. Supplies would be severely limited if the crowd swelled past the 100,000 mark. As it turned out, more than 300,000 kids showed up. There would be only two diesel generators available to supply the energy necessary to power the lights and sound system. If either one failed there would not be enough power to continue the show, and if they blew during the evening portion of the concert, 300,000 people would be left with only the moon's light to make their way back to their cars.

The Altamont concert should never have occurred. It had taken months of planning for Woodstock to get off the ground, and even that wasn't enough time for it to run hassle free. At Altamont the Rolling Stones attempted to bring it all together in less than twenty-four hours. It was a noble idea, but not a safe one. If any serious incidents did occur, the festival organizers could only blame themseves.

The San Francisco rock radio stations had been busy all day Friday announcing the new concert site at Altamont and passing along directions on how to get there. By Friday evening the surrounding hills near the racetrack were transformed into a massive campsite. Campfires sparkled in the night; a pretty backdrop for the stage crew that worked frantically through the night to complete construction of the stage. The general mood *appeared* to be festive, but there were hints that a different aura would be present at Altamont than was at Woodstock or any of the other festivals in 1969. Drugs had always played an important role at rock festivals. Marijuana, hashish, and acid, however, were the only drugs used in large quantities. At Altamont, even as early as Friday night, there was a noticeable increase in the use of alcohol and some of the harder hallucinogens such as STP. The combination would cause serious complications the following day. It promised to be a long Saturday for those who worked at the medical tents.

December 6, 7:30 A.M. The sun had risen above the bald hills, and for miles a continuous stretch of automobiles could be seen facing in the direction of Altamont. Every so often a news helicopter would zoom down for some close-up shots of the crowd to be used on the Saturday evening news broadcast. It looked as if San Francisco, Berkeley, and Oakland had sent their youth populations to Altamont to celebrate the conclusion of a tumultuous decade. The towns of Livermore, Tracey, and Pleasanton were already swarming with hungry young people looking for a place to get some breakfast and bleary-eyed campers in search of ice for the chest that harbored the day's supply of beer and wine.

As the morning wore on, many people simply parked their cars off to the side of the road and began to walk to the concert grounds, fearing that they would be stuck in the traffic jam and miss the Stones' performance. For many it was a seven-mile hike over hilly terrain. The long line of people that was rapidly forming looked like refugees fleeing an advancing enemy. Fans who brought young children with them soon found themselves hoisting the youngest one on an adult's shoulder. An unusual number of pregnant women made the journey to the stage area; at least three of them gave birth that day. On one of the hills close to the racetrack, a group of Berkeley Hare Krishnas were chanting and singing in the monotonous fashion they are notorious for. Not far past them, drug dealers hawked their goods.

The Angels arrived in small groups. They expertly maneuvered their shiny choppers between and around the long line of traffic. When they got to the stage area, they parked their bikes off to the side of the structure. Almost at once they began drinking beer and sipping wine spiked with acid.

By 11 A.M. there wasn't a free square foot of space within seventy-five yards of the stage. Blankets and picnic spreads seemed to cover every inch of ground. Many sat bare-chested, drinking wine and passing joints in the sun. More audacious souls stripped naked, drawing the usual stares, compliments, or bursts of laughter, depending on the appearance of the unveiled body. The first-aid tents were already handling cases of overdoses, and those who had dropped impure acid were coming in regularly. It was announced later that much of the

Paul Kantner, guitarist of the Jefferson Airplane, surveys crowd situation at Altamont.

acid circulated was bad and should not be taken. For many the warning came too late.

The first hint of the violence to come occurred sometime after 11:30 A.M. Down by the stage someone insulted an Angel and was promptly punched and kicked by the biker and an assortment of his buddies until he fell on the ground and begged for mercy. Another fight broke out some thirty yards away when an Angel rode over a blanket of food with his motorcycle. A startled picnicker objected, and the husky, bearded biker responded by hitting him across the legs with a rusty chain. Clearly, something sinister was in the air.

Santana was the first band to perform on the Altamont stage. They opened with a blast of high-energy Latin-rock just minutes before noon. Most of the material that comprised the forty-five minute set was from their debut album, *Santana*. The commercially successful lp had been released in August of 1969 at the height of the Woodstock craze. "Evil Ways," "Soul Sacrifice," and "Jingo" had had the massive crowd at Woodstock grooving to their powerfully accented rhythms. Santana's triumph there propelled the band into the ranks of stardom within a matter of months. By December they were certified rock stars and eager to play in front of a hometown crowd at Altamont.

Santana performed basically the same tunes at Altamont as they had at Woodstock, but with different results. Now the energy of the music and its quick tempo incited tempers, and instead of producing togetherness, the music fed the hostility of the Hell's Angels. Twice Santana's set was marred by violence as Angels battled with ecstatic fans who attempted to climb onto the stage. During the second brawl Carlos Santana motioned to his band to stop playing. He pleaded in vain with the people up front not to come near the stage.

In order for the reader to acquire a balanced understanding of the situation, two very important points must be stressed here. In 1969 Chip Monck was probably the best stage manager in all of rock. He had had a hand in the success of most of the major festivals up to the time of Altamont, including Woodstock. He had been hired by the Stones to handle the staging because of his excellent reputation and vast amount of experience. Had he been given more time, it is safe to assume that he would have built the Altamont stage much higher than he did. Forced, however, to work under pressing conditions in a limited time period, the best Monck could do was construct a stage that was only seven feet high. It was a stage that could easily be climbed by overzealous fans; the minimum height should have been twelve feet. Monck, with all his experience in this sort of thing, knew that the lack of height could pose problems. Building the lower stage was an egregious mistake and a major reason for the violence at Altamont.

Another major factor that contributed to the brutality at Altamont was the presence of the Hell's Angels. The Angels had been hired to act as a security force—a buffer between the bands onstage and the crowd. It was their job to prevent people from assaulting the stage and endangering the safety of the performers. With the size of the stage being what it was and the large number of people present, this promised to be no small chore. One must realize that the Angels were *not* policemen. They had no formal experience in crowd control, nor were they knowledgeable in the techniques of security. Moreover, they were hardly motivated toward maintaining peace. The Angels traditionally practiced little self-discipline or self-control. In most cases they had a minimal regard for law and order and acted on emotion and pride rather than on common sense. They should have been the *last* people hired to protect the stage and performers.

As soon as Santana commenced with their music, excited fans rushed to the front of the stage. When they realized how easy it was to climb on the stage and get even closer to the band, some of them did just that. They were met by groups of Angels doing their job in the only way they knew how: using brutal force in often uncontrollable fashion. The Hell's Angels cannot be solely blamed for the violence at Altamont, although, at the time, many people felt otherwise. It is true that, as the day wore on, the Angels often attacked the crowd unprovoked for the sheer pleasure of beating a body. But had they not been obligated to be near the stage, much of the violence would have been avoided.

Sam Cutler, who had hired the Angels as a security force, cannot be blamed entirely, either. Having used English bikers at the Rolling Stones' Hyde Park concert in London, Cutler wrongfully surmised that the Hell's Angels could be used as effectively as their seemingly pacified English brothers. Cutler was downright ignorant of the reputation and customs of the Angels around the Bay Area. He should have looked into the proposal in much greater depth. It is interesting to note, on the other hand, that no one advised him *not* to hire the Angels. Grogan and Sculley were both aware of the violence of which the Angels were capable but said nothing that might have made Cutler choose another course. If anything, Grogan and Sculley advocated the use of the Angels at Altamont.

Even if the Angels had not been asked to act as a security force, they probably would have shown up at Altamont anyway. Angels were usually found at Grateful Dead concerts, and the Dead were scheduled to perform sometime during the day. But chances are that so many of them would never have been so close to the stage.

Santana had intended on playing for more than forty-five minutes but cut their set short, finding it difficult to perform for the unruly crowd. The Jefferson Airplane were on next and met with the same fate. The Airplane had flown in from Florida the night before, after having played the West Palm Beach Rock Festival with the Rolling Stones and later spending a few restful days in the Miami sun. According to Ralph Gleason, who reported in the San Francisco *Chronicle*, "Mick (Jagger) wasn't sure he wanted them on the show since they outplayed the

Stones at West Palm Beach. He eventually insisted there be several groups between the Airplane and Stones' performance."

The Airplane began with "We Can Be Together." The song was deliberately done at the top of the set with the hope that its lyrical message might tone down the mood, and for a while it looked as if the song's temperament were achieving the desired effect. Then the Airplane broke into "The Other Side of This Life." The powerful nature of the song, combined with Grace Slick's efficacious voice, got the crowd to its feet, and the pushing toward the stage began once more. Two Hell's Angels were pushed, one briefly to the ground. Fellow members quickly retaliated by jumping those closest and hammering them with punches and kicks. Marty Balin, the spirited lead singer of the Airplane who shared the duties with Slick, moved to the side of the stage, saw a member of the crowd succumbing to numerous blows in the stomach and stepped in to prevent further beating. Within seconds Balin took a punch to the head and the groin and was knocked unconscious. This marked the only instance during the entire day in which someone had physically stood up to the malicious actions of the Angels. There wasn't a better opportunity for the fans to rise up and quell the violence induced by the Angels. Instead of rebelling, though, they watched the fight with shocked expressions. No one lifted a finger. Bill Thompson, the Airplane's manager, had to come down from the stage and assist Balin to his feet.

Guitarist Paul Kantner quickly motioned for the Airplane to stop playing. Like Carlos Santana before him, he pleaded with the Angels to cease their brutality, but the microphone he used was confiscated—by an Angel. At this point the stunned crowd began to display some anger and set off a barrage of boos. Another Angel walked up to Kantner and nearly decked him.

The stage was finally cleared of Angels after about ten minutes, and the Airplane finished their set under strained conditions. They performed "Somebody To Love," "Do Away With People," and "Volunteers," and the set was over.

Fearing that if the music stopped for a considerable length of time, the Angels would grow restless and provide their own entertainment, the Flying Burrito Brothers had their equipment quickly readied for their set. The Burritos did not offer a brand of music that was hard-edged and aggressive as that of Santana and the Jefferson Airplane. Their mellow sound of countrified rock temporarily soothed emotions, and no fights erupted during their performance. They were careful not to play anything that would instigate a surge by the crowd toward the stage area. For a while it seemed as though the remainder of the afternoon would be free of conflict.

Things did not look optimistic at the hospital tents, however. Aside from the normal problems that one expected at a gathering of this size, a growing number of kids were experiencing bad acid trips. These people needed sensitive care, but the lack of trained personnel in this sort of thing made whatever attention they got sporadic and superficial. There had been much mixing of wine and impure acid, and festivalgoers who thought they were taking a few mouthfuls of red wine to quench their thirst found themselves in the midst of an unexpected and unwanted hallucinogenic trip a short time later. Members of the film crew assigned to the Maysles Brothers, the group hired to film the event, unknowingly drank some wine spiked with LSD and wound up as patients at the Red Cross tent. *Rolling Stone* magazine reported an unusual case in which a young Oakland man insisted on being driven in an ambulance to the nearest maternity ward, screaming that he was just minutes away from giving birth. Bewildered onlookers watched the crazed fellow as he proceeded to strip, and then, before anyone could stop him, he jumped off a freeway overpass. Miraculously, he was not killed.

At the day's end more than 780 people were unofficially reported to have experienced bad trips and to have required medical attention. But the most serious casualties were those brought in from the stage area. A woman nearly died after she had been hit in the head with an unopened bottle of beer and suffered a serious skull fracture. Others came in needing stitches to close wounds incurred by blows from club-wielding Angels.

Everyone hoped that the music of Crosby, Stills, Nash and Young would continue the peace that had settled in during the Flying Burrito Brothers' set. But hope was short-lived as some Angels delivered an assault on a young man under the influence of either alcohol or LSD. This person had walked up to an Angel's bike that was parked alongside the stage and kicked it, apparently demonstrating his anger over the way the Angels had been treating the crowd. The owner of the huge chopper wasn't in the vicinity, but a group of Angels sitting on the side of the stage sharing some wine saw what he did. The intoxicated man had started to stagger back to his place in the crowd when four Angels jumped and kicked him until it looked as

Wine spiked with LSD made the rounds at Altamont.

if he might be dead. The Angels peered down at him, convinced that he had received his rightful punishment, and sauntered back to their seats on the stage. Friends of the victim carried him to the hospital tent.

Another round of violence occurred when the Angels decided to beat an immensely obese young man who had taken all his clothes off. To some of the Hell's Angels, he was an ugly mass of flesh who deserved to be beaten, and they joyfully set about clubbing him near the spot where Meredith Hunter would be fatally stabbed a few hours later. In a way, the grotesqueness of his nude body and the pictures of him that were printed in the newspapers and magazines symbolized the gruesome and sordid atmosphere that prevailed at Altamont. Grossly overweight, with womanly breasts and a muddled countenance, he wasn't demonstrative of the pictures of youth and beauty that had been expounded by the press after the Woodstock story made international headlines. Then *Life* and *Time* printed photos of seminude girls with wholesome bodies bathing with their weekend mates in a lake of idyllic purity. At Altamont an entirely different glimpse of the counterculture was brought to the surface.

While the other groups were doing their best onstage to stifle the violence and perform at the same time, the Rolling Stones were listening to unpleasant reports at their hotel. A debate as to whether they should go to Altamont ensued, but it was evident that things would really turn bad if they decided not to show up and play. The Grateful Dead were to follow Crosby, Stills, Nash and Young, and then it would be the Rolling Stones. If the violence continued the Dead decided they would not take the stage, but the Stones had no choice. They simply had to go on, violence or no violence.

Around three P.M. the helicopter landed behind the stage and near the set of trailers brought in for the bands' comfort. As the Rolling Stones stepped from the craft and into the crowd that had rushed to greet them, they were immediately flanked by the private security guards they had brought with them from New York. Hell's Angels also stood nearby. Not quite two hundred feet from the helicopter landing pad, a man in his early twenties with a sinister look in his eyes broke through the crowd.

"I'm gonna kill you! I hate you! I'll kill you!"

The man ran toward Jagger and in one swift motion broke through the security-guard ranks and punched Jagger squarely in the jaw. The guards and Angels quickly subdued the man while the Stones were herded off to a trailer where they were to wait until it was time to perform. Jagger was unhurt but shaken. Within five minutes of his arrival at Altamont, Mick Jagger was physically introduced to the monster he had helped create.

Throughout the day reporters and photographers were able to record the activities, with only a few of them being seriously hassled by the Angels. A couple of cameras were smashed, but no one was beaten. It was the Maysles Brothers, however, who had free reign of the stage area and were able to capture the complete story for the world to see in the form of the film documentary *Gimme Shelter*.

The Rolling Stone organization had contracted Albert and David Maysles to shoot footage of their free concert. The brothers had been involved with previous culture-oriented documentary films, the most noted being a television special on the Beatles that was filmed during the group's 1964 American tour. Albert Maysles, who had shot the footage of Ravi Shankar and other performers at Monterey in 1967, was no stranger to the art of outdoor concert photography. The film crew at Altamont had Hell's Angels for bodyguards and therefore encountered no resistance from other members of the bike club as they shot reel after reel of the Stones, the crowd, and the fatal stabbing of Meredith Hunter.

The crew used three cameras to capture, in remarkable clarity, the entire sequence of Hunter's death. The Alameda County Sheriff's Office later subpoenaed all the film that was shot by the Maysles Brothers at Altamont as evidence in the investigation of the Hunter stabbing. In vivid color one could clearly see Hunter being stabbed repeatedly by an Angel whose face was strikingly visible. Identified later as Alan Passaro, a member of the Oakland chapter of Hell's Angels, he was indicted for the murder of Meredith Hunter. At the time of the murder, Passaro was out on bail awaiting trial for charges of grand theft.

The trial that followed Altamont was an unusual one. The subpoenaed film showed Passaro stabbing Hunter, but the jury felt it was "justifiable homicide" since it was also revealed that Hunter possessed a pistollike object in his right hand. The Angel argued that it was necessary to subdue Hunter because he had pointed the weapon at members of the Rolling Stones. The film also showed that Meredith Hunter had twice attempted to scale the stage in defiance of the Angels that guarded it. Passaro was acquitted of the murder charges.

The gun Meredith Hunter allegedly had in his hand at the time of the stabbing was never found. It was either picked up by an Angel or a bystander, or else Hunter never possessed one in the first place. Of the thirty or forty people standing near Hunter when he was killed, only one could be persuaded to testify in the prosecution's behalf. Many of the witnesses feared reprisals by the Angels if their testimony helped send a club member to prison.

The list of casualties at Altamont did not conclude with Hunter and those who had been beaten throughout the day. Before the night was over two young people who had camped out along the edge of the road that led back to San Francisco were killed instantly when a hit-and-run driver ran over both

Members of the Angels turn a Stones' fan into an Altamont casualty.

Courtesy of Cinema Five

Mick Jagger looks on as Angels confront members of the audience.

of them. The driver was never apprehended. Another body was found in a local irrigation canal. Friends of the victim told police that he had been tripping on LSD and had decided to slide down a tributary cement canal into rapidly churning waters. When he hit the main artery of the canal, he went under, only to be found dead some miles downstream.

So it ended with four people dead and numerous people severely beaten. The Rolling Stones had fulfilled their promise of a free concert, but at the ultimate expense of the Woodstock spirit. Altamont was a substantial setback for the youth culture as well as for the promoters who had hoped to stage similar events in the summer of 1970. The Woodstock Nation was made up of good as well as bad—a startling new discovery for the young idealists. The desire to lead America and the rest of the world on a voyage that emphasized peace and love of one's brother was a gallant one in troubled times. But Altamont revealed that it would not be as easily accomplished as the success at Woodstock had indicated. Rock music was the medium by which the Woodstock Nation galvanized its strength and spread forth its messages of peace and communal harmony. Somewhere along the line it was either forgotten or deliberately set aside that there was also an ingredient in the music that brought out the raw, aggressive tendencies in people.

It was fitting in an odd way that Altamont was the offspring of the Rolling Stones. They, more than any other band, represented the power of rock in its most arrogant form, and it was the Stones who consistently emphasized its arrogance. The press incessantly contrasted the band with the Beatles when both groups were vying for international prestige. Many things were said, both good and bad, about the life-style and attitudes of the Rolling Stones. One thing was certain, however: When they plugged in, the Stones set forth an avalanche of power and emotion that, in 1969, was rarely reproduced.

The Rolling Stones, the Hell's Angels, and, to some extent, the Grateful Dead, took most of the rap for Altamont. The Stones didn't do much in the way of commenting on the episode. They preferred to put Altamont behind them and let the film *Gimme Shelter* speak for them. The Grateful Dead indicated their views on the event with the recording of "The New Speedway Boogie," a song written by the prolific Robert Hunter and found on their album *Workingman's Dead*.

"The New Speedway Boogie" is an interesting reflection of

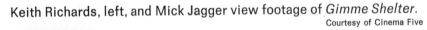

Keith Richards, left, and Mick Jagger view footage of *Gimme Shelter.*
Courtesy of Cinema Five

Altamont. By declining to perform that day, the Dead removed themselves from the direct fire, for their music did not incite violence that day. Robert Hunter wrote in the song:

> I spent a little time on the mountain,
> Spent a little time on the hill,
> Like some say, better run away,
> Others say better stand still.[1]

The Hell's Angels had their own explanation of why things had gone sour at Altamont. Sonny Barger, president of the Angels, was interviewed on KSAN-FM, a San Francisco radio station the day after the debacle. Barger had called in, asking to be put on the air to explain the Angels' version of what had happened.

> We were told if we showed up, we could sit on the stage and drink some beer that the Stones' manager had bought us, ya know. And I'm bum kicked about the whole thing. I didn't like what happened there. We were told we were supposed to sit on the stage and keep people off and a little back, if we could. We parked where we were told we were supposed to park. Mostly, a little bit to the side of the stage so that people who were there earlier didn't have to move back too far.
>
> Now I don't know if you think we pay $50 for them things [motorcycles] or steal them, or pay a lot for them or what. But most people that's got a good Harley chopper got a few grand invested in it. Ain't nobody gonna kick my motorcycle. And they might think because they're in a crowd of 300,000 people that they can do it and get away with it. But when you're standing there looking at something that's your life, and everything you got is invested in that thing, and you love that thing better than you love anything in the world, and you see a guy kick it, you know who he is. And if you got to go through fifty people to get him, you're gonna get to him.

The controversy of Altamont was carried over into the new decade. *Gimme Shelter* and *Woodstock*, both released in 1970, disclosed contrasting views of rock festivals in movie theaters across the country. The glory of Woodstock shone as the documentary of the festival brought heaps of praise on the performers, the crowd, and Michael Wadleigh's film crew. A feeling of joy and exuberance filled those who went to see the movie. The triumph of Woodstock was there for all to see. *Gimme Shelter* was another story. The documentary of Altamont also received critical acclaim, but a somber and melancholy reaction to the film persisted despite the striking performance of the Rolling Stones.

Careful viewing of both films reveals the strength of Woodstock and the weakness of Altamont. One particular difference between the two events is obvious. Time and time again the stage microphone at Woodstock was effectively used to aid, instruct, and advise the crowd. Personal messages from home, announcements as to the availability of free food, and warnings of the oncoming thunderstorms greatly facilitated the relaxation of tension at Woodstock. The stage became the central nervous system of the festival. It provided people like Wavy Gravy and Chip Monck with the opportunity to assume leadership and take control when direction and control were desperately needed. In contrast, the Altamont stage was a war zone, a place to avoid if possible.

For a while it seemed as if Altamont would signal the demise of the ceremonious rock festival and sap the energy of youth's desire for them, but things didn't turn out quite that way. While many more ordinances and laws were adopted to ban or curtail rock festivals as city councils and state legislatures pointed with alarm to Altamont, the more ambitious promoters found loopholes in the laws or disregarded them entirely in their quest for the big money that could still be made from the festival idea. Similarly, the youth of the nation was hardly thwarted by the warnings that Altamont seemed to issue forth, and as the sixties became the seventies, the thrill of rock festivals was pursued with a new—although slightly altered—fervor.

CHAPTER SEVEN

Dreams Deferred (1969-1971)

It's the people that make the festival.
We don't need no music, man.

—Festivalgoers at Powder Ridge,
  July 30, 1970.

By the outset of the new decade, over two million people had participated in at least one rock festival and could rightfully claim to be citizens of the Woodstock Nation. The violence and tragedy of Altamont was either forgotten or deliberately pushed under the rug by the time winter succumbed to the warm weather of spring in 1970. Forgotten by the young festivalgoers, rock fans, and promoters who staged them, that is. The lawmakers and concerned members of "straight" society forgot nothing. They still remembered the gate-crashing incidents and the riots they had read about in Denver and Newport, Rhode Island. They remembered pictures of the 400,000 long-haired young people who had overrun the small town of Bethel, New York, and had the New York State Thruway closed down. They remembered hearing of the murder at Altamont. And they planned to do something about the situation in 1970.

Many Americans in 1970 came to view the rock festival as a harbinger of moral collapse, drug addiction, and general social chaos. It was one more evil that needed to be expunged if the nation was to resume its forward progress. Opponents of rock festivals found two powerful weapons to eliminate any plans of large-scale rock events in their immediate vicinities.

The most potent and often used technique was the court injunction. The injunction legally banned the staging of a festival. If the promoter(s) refused to obey the order, he, she, or they would be cited for contempt of court, fined, and even sent to jail. Getting a court injunction, however, was not always easy. But even the threat of an injunction was sometimes enough to make a promoter wary of investing time and money in a dubious venture. Using it as a bluff, many town and city councils successfully warded off would-be festivals in their city limits.

The second antifestival weapon was the strict enforcement of health and sanitary regulations. Local authorities would pass ordinances that were indirectly designed to curtail rock events the size of festivals. The often detailed and laborious regulations made staging a festival such a hassle that promoters found it easier to search elsewhere for a festival site.

Both methods were used often, and numerous festival plans were effectively destroyed by local authorities who vehemently opposed such an event in their domain. In Tampa, Florida, for example, plans for a rock festival were nixed when the city council refused to lower a $100,000 performance bond required of promoters under a newly signed law. In Atlantic City, New Jersey, plans for a second Atlantic City Pop Festival came to a halt when Hamilton Township authorities passed an ordinance that banned large gatherings of people for music-oriented events. A special zoning ordinance prohibited a festival from taking place in Orlando, Florida; and in New York, the state Public Health Council and the legislature issued the "Woodstock" or mass-gathering law that applied to crowds of 5,000 or more people brought together for more than twenty-four hours.

The act gave an issuing permit officer the power and responsibility to make certain that a promoter had a maintenance staff large enough to insure proper operation of all sanitary facilities and had properly filed for a performance bond of $50,000 plus $5,000 for each 5,000 persons likely to attend.[1]

But there's an old adage that says, "Where there's a will, there's a way." And there was indeed a strong desire among young people, promoters, performers, and record-company executives to see the rock festival concept survive. Festival fever had increased significantly since the summer of 1969. Rock fans hoped that at least one of the festivals planned for 1970 would be a repeat of Woodstock, and they gave their unbounded enthusiasm and dollars to support any festival that seemed like it would be the *big* one.

Young people were so eager to participate in rock festivals in 1970 that a mysterious festival called the Great Florida Easter Rock Festival took in some $200,000 in advance ticket sales at $10 a head without acknowledging where the festival would be held or who was to perform at it. The promoter told ticket buyers that the location would be announced a day or two before the festival was to begin. This, he insisted, was necessary to avoid legal confrontations with the authorities, who would undoubtedly have prevented him from staging any rock festival in Florida. Officials all over Florida frantically searched for any signs of suspicious activities that seemed like a rock festival site was being prepared. Ordinances were quickly passed to ban such an event. Finally state officials found a way to end the panic and stifle the promoter's attempts at staging the secret festival. Laurence Correll, the impresario, was charged with violating the state of Florida's false advertising and fictitious trade name laws and was arrested. Correll, who had had every intention of staging the event, was also forced to make arrangements to return the money he had collected from the advance ticket sales.

Lured by the possible accumulation of large profits, many promoters with little or no experience in music production joined the ranks of those who planned on staging events in the 1970–1973 era. And each promoter artfully advertised his event to be "another Woodstock." There was much truth to claims by counterculture leaders that the festival concept was being raped of its innocence and social significance by those who were interested only in the profit motive. But these leaders were often no better than the people they were accusing. Abbie Hoffman in 1970 called what these promoters were attempting vanguard capitalism and urged revolutionary and leftist organizations to do whatever was necessary to end such schemes. A festival promoter who had planned an event for the summer in New York State was introduced to the countercultural "offensive" when Hoffman and the Yippies demanded 50 percent of his profits. The promoters who produced the Randall's Island festival in New York City ran into similar problems.

Tugging at the future of rock festivals from another end were the film entrepreneurs and the record-company executives. Film producers and directors were drunk with enthusiasm after they saw the box-office success of *Woodstock* and, later, *Gimme Shelter*. No festival plans were complete until promoters had lined up a film crew and distributor to insure future profits from the event in the form of a movie. The record companies, wanting desperately to continue using festivals as giant showcases for new talent, were also dizzy over the popularity and critical acclaim of the Woodstock albums. They hurried plans to record the music at the major upcoming festivals for eventual lps.

Rock festivals were one of the major reasons so many rock artists became rich overnight. Whereas at Woodstock promoters had paid somewhere around $15,000 for top-name acts, just one year later big groups such as Sly and the Family Stone; Crosby, Stills, Nash and Young; and Led Zeppelin were demanding and receiving as much as $50,000 for a single festival appearance. Their lust for a share of the big money was carried over into indoor concert negotiations. The big-name groups kept their festival price tags in mind when discussing their fees with promoters. Concert tickets in 1970 jumped as high as $8 per seat in some cases.

The situation forced promoters to rent arenas like Madison Square Garden and the Los Angeles Forum with more and more frequency, since large seating capacity could guarantee a sizeable profit for the promoters of the concerts. Because of this unhealthy situation, small concert halls like the Fillmore East and Fillmore West were eventually forced to close down. Their limited seating (3,000–5,000) would not generate enough revenue to clear a profit. Bill Graham, the owner of both Fillmore halls, ran a letter in the music trade publications demanding that rock groups come to their senses and cut back on the lavish and greedy fees they charged for their services.[2]

He asked the bands to reduce their price tags for the sake of the ultimate survival of the music form.

One of the most ambitious events planned for the summer of 1969 was a community celebration of the arts in San Francisco called the Wild West. The three-day affair was not to be a rock festival in the strict or traditional sense of the term, but it would have featured a series of rock concerts held at Kezar Stadium in conjunction with other community activities. Such star local performers as the Grateful Dead, Janis Joplin, Quicksilver Messenger Service, the Jefferson Airplane, Country Joe and the Fish, Santana, Sly and the Family Stone, and the Steve Miller Band, among others, had promised to participate in the event. The importance of the Wild West, as far as the history of rock festivals is concerned, lies in the way plans for the event were destroyed; the Wild West was one of the first large-scale happenings to fall under the sword of political radicalism. It was an indication of what was to come.

The idea for Wild West had originated with Ron Polte, then the manager of the Quicksilver Messenger Service. Polte had passed word among his friends in local rock circles that the city and its people should be thanked in a festive sort of way for all the support given to the rock scene over the past four years. Polte contacted Bill Graham and Chet Helms, the two most powerful men in the San Francisco rock-music business. Both thought the idea was outstanding. They promised to discuss it with their friends and associates and report on the feedback.

The promoters presented the idea to other influential people in the community until somewhere down the line it was brought up that the celebration should include *all* the arts in San Francisco, not just the rock community. A total city happening, for all ages and for all tastes, would make the event historical and memorable. Local painters, dancers, poets, classical and jazz musicians, and acting groups, along with rock performers, would all play a part in the festival. It would be a three-day celebration of San Francisco: Her arts and her cultural accomplishments would be on display for the rest of the country to see.

The plans for Wild West were officially announced after the formation of the San Francisco Music Council (the name Wild West had no special significance other than to disassociate the event from the other commercial ventures of the summer).

This group, made up almost exclusively of members of the rock scene, included Tom Donahue and Bill Graham, local rock impresarios; Ralph Gleason of the San Francisco *Chronicle*; Jan Wenner, editor of *Rolling Stone*; Barry Oliver, for fourteen years the director of the Berkeley Folk Festival; and Ron Polte, Rock Sculley and Bill Thompson, managers of the Quicksilver Messenger Service, the Grateful Dead, and the Jefferson Airplane respectively. The council nominated Oliver as director of the festival, since he was the one with the most experience in the production of large music and cultural events. It was agreed to pay Oliver $500 per week to organize and oversee Wild West, which was planned for the weekend of August 22.

Bill Graham and Chet Helms both agreed to hold benefit concerts to raise money to set organizational wheels turning. At the Fillmore West Graham presented the Jefferson Airplane, the Ace of Cups, and a few local, lesser-name bands to raise a portion of the needed revenue. Helms's show featured Joan Baez at the Family Dog. Both shows were financial successes, but more importantly, they initiated a Wild West fever. When would it be held? Who would perform at it? Where would it take place? Not since the Human Be-In in January of '67 had there been so much excitement concerning an inner-city hip happening.

It was decided that the event should encompass the entire acreage of Golden Gate Park. Speedway Meadows, the polo and soccer fields, and Kezar Stadium would be the main staging areas. More than 200,000 were expected to participate in the weekend's festivities, watching and listening to classical music concerts, Shakespearean plays, puppet shows, poetry recitals, folk music, ethnic dancing, and, of course, Bay Area rock.

By the end of July the entire city was buzzing with anticipation and excitement. A newsletter entitled "Any Day Now" was printed up and circulated by the San Francisco Music Council. It defined the goals and explained the concept behind Wild West. "The Wild West is the conglomeration of Bay Area artists in concert with nature, themselves and the people of San Francisco. The three-day celebration of creativity planned for the August 22nd weekend will be the most important artistic event of the decade."[3] The newsletter also told of Paul Crowley's proposed light show to open the festival: a bouncing and bending of light beams off the city's large office buildings to the pulsating beat of a Moog synthesizer, as well as a replica of an eighty-foot bar of Ivory soap designed by Bay Area artists to demonstrate the need for cleaner waters. The newsletter also hinted that Bay Area filmmakers might film the event and turn it into a full-length documentary for national release.

The Wild West sounded like a true, even utopian, communal artistic celebration. It was thought that if any city in 1969 could pull off something so large and complex and so contemporary in design, it was San Francisco. For the city possessed the necessary resources and cultural inspiration to make the weekend a thorough success. The successful staging of the event also promised to force a reevaluation of the current rock festival scene. Wild West was planned as a nonprofit, mostly free affair; the only activities carrying an admission charge would be the concerts at Kezar Stadium, where tickets would cost three dollars apiece. Some members of the rock world hoped that the Wild West would initiate a rebirth of nonprofit rock music festivals across the country. The council deliberately shunned offers from record companies for financial support in order to remain free of commercial interference.

The San Francisco Music Council called a general meeting at the Glide Memorial Church on July 28 to finalize community plans. The council expected only token resistance to the festival plans. What more could a city ask for than a free weekend in the park listening to homespun music and grooving on the wealth of good vibrations that were certain to be everywhere? Unfortunately, some of San Francisco's political radicals and street people did not see it that way. They viewed the Wild West affair as cultural thievery and a gigantic rip-off by profiteers and rock promoters of the community's artistic expression, indeed its very soul. The Haight Commune, a loosely aligned and hastily formed group of radical organizations, labeled the festival a plot to undermine the dignity of San Francisco's working class by selling back to them something that was inherently theirs to begin with. The Haight Commune consisted mainly of the San Francisco Mime Troupe and black and Chicano groups from the Fillmore district. They also had the support of the Berkeley *Tribe* and *Dock of the Bay*, two influential underground newspapers.

The Music Council and the Haight Commune clashed at the Glide Church meeting. The commune informed the council that it would organize a general strike against the festival if changes were not made in its format. The meeting was cursed with hostility, bad tempers, threats, and political innuendos. Oliver was unable to control the encounter and really had no idea of how to go about soothing the anger of these people and making them understand that the festival was not a community rip-off. The Haight Commune wanted to know why Oliver was getting $500 a week if the festival was nonprofit. What were Bill Graham and Tom Donahue doing on the council? Who appointed them? Hadn't they made enough money from the people of San Francisco already? What about the ticket prices? If it was a "free" festival, how could they charge $3 for the concerts at Kezar?

Words flew back and forth with increasing velocity. The radicals demanded that the Music Council include community members and reduce ticket prices to a $1 donation. Bill Graham could not hold in his feelings any longer. Not known as a patient or soft-spoken man, Graham entered into a heated shouting match with a black community leader over the true meaning behind the festival. In his most persuasive street language, Graham told the black leader and everyone else in the church that their claims of exploitation were only a backdrop for their ingratitude. As for him soaking the community for entertainment dollars, well, they wouldn't have to worry about that anymore because he was moving his Fillmore operation east to New York City. Nobody was going to tell him that he earned his money in a less than ethical way. He owned a beautiful house and some beautiful cars and all because he worked hard for them. Anyone who thought different could go to hell. End of meeting.

Things looked grim for the staging of Wild West. The Music Council was in disarray, and during the next couple of weeks Oliver received death threats. Radicals promised violent confrontations if festival plans were carried out. The police didn't want to battle radicals in Golden Gate Park with 200,000 festivalgoers standing around. Performers felt a certain allegiance to the community and did not know whether to show support for the festival or side with radical community leaders.

One of the biggest gripes in the community concerning Wild West was the ticket prices. No one seemed to understand that it took some money to run even a nonprofit event. Advocates of the festival pointed to the Monterey Pop Festival, a nonprofit festival that charged admission to clear overhead costs. Advocates of the strike against the festival pointed out that a free festival meant a free festival.

On August 2 the San Francisco Music Council printed up copies of its working budget in an attempt to make community leaders understand why an admission price was so essential. According to the budget, the cost of producing the festival was approximately $157,000. Of that money $39,000 went to salaries; $12,000 to rental of the Golden Gate facilities; $12,000 to security measures; and $10,000 for each sound system to be used at the festival.

It didn't do much good. Perhaps if the mayor and city council had come out and fully endorsed the festival as the true city celebration it was meant to be, and the artists that were to perform spoke with enthusiasm and even made personal appearances to bolster support for the event (most of the rock bands were on the road at the time), and if the Musicians Union and Chamber of Commerce had backed it wholeheartedly, the anger and resentment of the radical element would have been quelled.

On August 14, one week before the event was to have taken place, Director Barry Oliver announced the termination of plans for Wild West because of the fear of violence. The cancelation might have stirred up a heated reaction within the rock community and profestival countercultural groups had it not been for the news of Woodstock. Woodstock was an event; a historical happening and a triumph of the masses. The Wild West was a nonevent; a nonhappening. Hip people in San Francisco were more interested in what was going on in the village of Bethel some three thousand miles away.

The following summer a Connecticut rock festival billed as a continuation of Woodstock received almost as much prefestival coverage as the huge New York State festival had in 1969. The Powder Ridge Festival was scheduled to be a three-day affair located on the outskirts of the town of Middlefield, at the Powder Ridge Ski Resort. The ski area's three hundred acres of sloping hills were leased to Middleton Arts International for the last weekend in July.

Powder Ridge represented an opportunity for those in the Northeast who had missed Woodstock to experience the excitement and ebullience of what the media called a countercultural extravaganza of music, drugs, and out and out nudity. For those who were present at Woodstock, Powder Ridge was a chance to relive the glories and fun of attending such large rock events. The promoters promised at least eighteen top-notch acts such as Sly and the Family Stone, Led Zeppelin, Janis Joplin, Chuck Berry, and other artists who had performed at Woodstock.

Advance tickets sold fast. Two weeks prior to the festival promoters had already grossed over $500,000. They might have accumulated double that figure if a group of Middlefield locals had not decided to halt festival plans before it was too late.

The four thousand residents of Middlefield had read with trepidation and dismay of what had happened to Bethel and the surrounding villages during the Woodstock invasion the previous August. The traffic, the drugs, the hordes of long-haired kids who trespassed on private property, and the general unsettling of a peaceful environment all added up to a disturbing situation for the typically conservative community. They wanted nothing to do with those young people who expressed alien values and advanced social notions of anarchy and revolution. No, not in Middlefield. There was no room for a rock festival in a community that was proud of its three Vietnam War veterans and its girl scout troop and its reputation as a town that exhibited a decent moral tradition and a healthy, American atmosphere in which young people could grow into respectable adults. Middlefield simply did not want a rock festival to occur within its boundaries.

The local elected authorities, on advice from the municipal lawyer, filed a request with the state's judicial department for a court injunction against the rock festival. Twice Middlefield rejected the application for a permit to stage a rock festival at the ski resort, and still the promoters advertised the event as being "on." Three days before the festival weekend, the State Superior Court ruled that the Powder Ridge Rock Festival would create monumental traffic jams and endanger the lives of festivalgoers, as the roads leading up to the ski resort were extremely narrow and hazardous. A court order was therefore issued prohibiting the festival from taking place.

Almost at once the promoters filed for an appeal and promised to limit the number of festivalgoers to twenty thousand if the court injunction was dissolved (they had originally expected close to 100,000 people to attend and by July 27 had sold over 18,000 tickets at $20 apiece). The festival's future was indeed cloudy, but young people nevertheless began pouring into Middlefield, confident that the festival would somehow manage to take place. As early as Wednesday, July 28, more than eight thousand festivalgoers were already camped out on the slopes waiting for the weekend's festivities.

State Superior Court Judge Aaron Palmer denied the request by promoters for a reverse decision on the injunction and

This ineffective notice, posted by the State Highway Department of Connecticut, warned festivalgoers traveling through New Haven that the festival was off.

appointed Vincent Scamporino, the state's attorney for Middlesex County, of which Middlefield was a part, to use whatever means necessary to enforce the court order. Scamporino immediately ordered Connecticut state troopers to put up signs on all roads leading to Middlefield stating that the rock festival was called off. Press releases were issued indicating the state's decision to deny an appeal effort, and the residents of Middlefield relaxed.

The media had been following the events closely. Metropolitan rock radio stations reported regularly on the developments and advised those with tickets to adopt a wait-and-see attitude. The *New York Times* and the *Daily News* ran stories on the legal proceedings and also told of the many young people who were ignoring warnings from Connecticut state officials and going to Powder Ridge anyway. The eight thousand who had been at the festival site on Wednesday had swelled to over twenty thousand by early Friday. There were no signs that the kids were abiding by the court's ruling. Thus Scamporino ordered the state police to close all roads leading to Middlefield to all but local residents. He further stated that any bands that performed at

Powder Ridge would be charged with contempt of court and subjected to fines, imprisonment, or both.

No one at the Powder Ridge ski resort knew exactly what was going on. The promoters of the event were not to be found, and the responsibility for persuading the kids to leave was left to the owners of the resort area. The festivalgoers had heard about injunctions before but were confident things would be worked out. Very few left the site, and throughout the night more and more people were turning up, slipping through police blockades by walking to the festival area. By Friday afternoon, July 30, close to fifty thousand had set up camp and patiently awaited the commencement of the music.

There was talk that the state police were going to move in and forcibly clear the ski resort. But instead of taking such drastic action, Scamporino wisely permitted those who were already at the site to remain until they were convinced that no festival was going to take place. To speed things up local authorities were ordered to turn off the electrical power at the resort. Food and sanitary supplies were also curtailed. Meanwhile, radio stations reported that the festival was officially dead, and those with tickets or with the intention of buying tickets should not bother to come to Middlefield.

What followed became known as "the people's free festival of life." Fifty thousand young people camped out on a few gentle ski slopes with nothing to do but wait. Wait for what? Some had hoped that the rock performers would show up and play for free. Others were more realistic. But there were fifty thousand kids in one place. All of them together; there for one reason. The cops were on the outside, and they were on the inside. If they planned a clearing of the site, they would have done it by now, many reckoned. Aggressive festivalgoers urged everyone to stay and make the best of the situation. Throughout the area amateur musicians were jamming for any one interested in listening. "We'll have our own festival!" the campers decided. The spirit of Woodstock lives!

On Friday, July 30, just before dusk, Louis Zemel, one of the ski resort owners, took the previously built stage, bullhorn in hand, and tried to persuade the young people to go home since the festival was now an impossibility. Amid shouts, catcalls, and boos, he described the implications of the court order that pro-

---

Making use of the Powder Ridge ski lift.
UPI

hibited the occurrence of the event. He told the crowd that it was not his fault the festival was dead. The promoters were the ones who had caused the mess, and the townspeople, well, they were just not sure they wanted so many young people roaming their community. There were shouts that the festivalgoers planned to stay at the ski resort for the remainder of the summer. Cries of support came from the crowd. Someone yelled to the resort owner that elections would be held for Powder Ridge's first "freak mayor" tomorrow morning. Zemel left the stage unsure of his next move.

Dr. William Abruzzi, the physician who was to be in charge of the medical facilities at Powder Ridge and who was known by many as "the Woodstock doctor" for his role at that festival, took the stage next. When he introduced himself, the crowd rose to their feet.

"We intend to run a medical facility as long as you need us. We will keep this thing going. We'll have a medical facility, and we will keep the music going as long as we aren't carried out by people in blue uniforms."

A spirit of defiance and brotherhood swept through the crowd. Stick together, man, and we'll make our own festival and our own music. The word was solidarity.

But maybe there was going to be a real festival after all. A deal had been struck with a couple of Mister Softee ice cream vendors. In exchange for power generated from their trucks, they would be permitted to sell their ice cream to "the people." Melanie, the only signed performer to show up at Powder Ridge, wanted to play for the crowd. After Bill Hanley of Hanley Sound instructed his people to ready the stage for her performance, he was arrested and charged with contempt of court. But Melanie played, to the delight of those gathered on the main slope. She sang of the beautiful people gathered at Powder Ridge, and the crowd applauded with heightened enthusiasm. In between songs she told of how she was proud to play her music under such pressing conditions. Rumors spread through the crowd that Sly and the Family Stone were backstage and preparing to go on. The excitement grew and people nudged closer to the front of the stage. But after Melanie had sung every song she knew, only a couple of local bands took the stage. Still it was music, and it gave many hope that more performers would show up on the following two days. (Melanie, by the way, was never arrested for playing at Powder Ridge;

even though she was a signed performer, she was never paid, and the state doubted whether they had a case against her.)

No other artists risked a run-in with the law, however. The only other music heard throughout the weekend was the sound of car stereo systems and the makeshift noise of acoustic guitars, harmonicas, tambourines, and stoned-out campers singing in the night. Because of the prolific use of so many drugs, the scene was incredible and ugly at the same time. Near the pond, young people gathered to swim nude and wash their clothes and eating utensils until it became so polluted that people actually got sick from the water.

By Saturday afternoon Powder Ridge had become less of a music festival and more of an enormous drug orgy. Every manufactured chemical concoction and natural ingredient known to alter consciousness seemed to be present. In the camping area walkways became known as Acid Alley, High Street, and Pot Boulevard. More drugs were sold out in the open at Powder Ridge than at any previous festival, and more people per capita used them, especially such chemical psychedelic ones as LSD, speed and STP.

On Sunday a group of dealers held an auction attended by over two hundred festivalgoers.

"What do I hear for this unmatched ounce of the best marijuana Colombia has to offer?"

"Who has the true psychedelic mind that can handle grooving to the colors and fascinations of this pure, organic mescaline?"

"Name your product and name your price. We got reds, uppers, downers, speed, acid and specially priced peyote buttons. Don't be bashful. . . . Name your product and name your price!"

"Hey, man, how much for a hit of acid, man?"

"Seventy-five cents, but since it's Sunday and I'm checkin' out of here, I'll give you two tabs for a buck."

"Right on, man."

Bulletin boards listed prices. Hawkers stuck cardboard placards with a listing of their drugs for sale around their necks. What they didn't list, though, were notices that much of the acid being sold was impure and resulted in bad trips and freak-outs. Dr. Abruzzi told reporters afterward that the lack of music was the dominant reason so many young people resorted to drugs at Powder Ridge. He mentioned that when Melanie played, the number of kids who needed medical attention because of overdoses or bad trips was less than 50. Later on in

Capitalism at Powder Ridge.

David Gahr

the weekend he and his team were treating almost that number every hour. At one instance the medical tent had over 150 kids suffering from bad trips.

The freak-out problem would not have been so severe if much of the acid hadn't been laced with strychnine or mescaline. Furthermore, there was no centralized means of making the young people aware of the situation other than word of mouth. Had there been a coordinated communications system, many festivalgoers might not have attempted questionable drugs and the bad-trip predicament would have been reduced. But such an effort was exceedingly difficult without continuous electricity to power the sound system.

The Powder Ridge Ski Resort remained in youthful hands until most of the festivalgoers grew tired of turning on. After Sunday evening the exodus from the slope began in earnest. Some, however, did not make it as planned. State police checked cars on the way out and ultimately arrested 237 people on drug charges.

The big issue that remained after the Zemel brothers finally regained control of their resort was the refunding to ticket holders of the twenty dollars they had shelled out for admission to the festival. Spokesmen for the Middleton Arts group told the press that refunds were not necessary since the promoters had just signed an agreement with Yankee Stadium officials granting them permission to stage a two-day concert there. The deal fell through, and the promoters searched for another possible site.

They next contacted officials at Robert F. Kennedy Stadium in Washington, D.C. Before any lease was finalized the promoters stated that 20,000 of the stadium's 45,000 seats would be used for those with Powder Ridge tickets. The remaining seats were to be sold to other rock fans for $10 per ticket. There was no logic in the fairness, since Powder Ridge ticket holders had spent twenty dollars for their tickets, while others would have to pay only half that amount to see the same show.

When Middleton Arts was denied use of RFK Stadium, the promoters tried to lease a one-thousand-acre mountain site in Laurel Spring, North Carolina. But Allegheny County officials emphatically issued an order stating that no rock event was going to be held *anywhere* in the county. Meanwhile the Internal Revenue Service filed a $204,000 tax levy against the Powder Ridge group, and chief promoter Raymond Filiberti was indicted by a grand jury on perjury charges. The press strongly hinted of a possible Mafia link with Filiberti and the others in Middleton Arts, but no connections were ever confirmed. An interesting aspect of the situation was that no money was ever refunded to Powder Ridge ticket holders, and someone—no one ever learned exactly who—was a half-million dollars richer.

The Powder Ridge event didn't seem quite so bad after the abortive attempt to stage the Celebration of Life festival in the summer of 1971. The largest rock festival calamity occurred on the banks of Louisiana's Atchafalaya River after it was proclaimed the festival that would renew the Woodstock Nation's faith in itself and its future. The promoters billed the event as the true "resurrection of the rock festival." Celebration of Life lasted only four of the scheduled eight days, and when it was over, five people were dead, many were in hospitals nursing wounds inflicted by marauding motorcycle gangs, and hundreds had been arrested and thrown into jail.

The Celebration of Life was doomed from the very beginning. Before folksinger and Woodstock veteran John Sebastian had strummed the opening notes of the abbreviated event on Thursday, June 24, the festival's location had been changed three times in little over a week. Confusion, chaos, and uncertainty had effectively obliterated all efforts toward organization and order. The festival was on, then it was off. Then it was on again. Police officials and politicians bickered about the proper course of action. Performers didn't know whether to fly into Louisiana or Mississippi. Only the drug dealers seemed to have a grip on the situation.

The festival, scheduled for June 21 through June 28, was first set to occur in Laplace, Louisiana, on a stretch of lakefront property owned by members of a prominent New Orleans family. The festival promoters had a verbal agreement with the Guste family that the musical event could be staged on the six-hundred-acre Frenier Beach located on Lake Pontchartrain. But when Laplace residents found out about the rock festival, they pressured the owners of the property to rescind the agreement. The Guste family told Steve Kapelow, the spokesman for the Celebration of Life promoters, that they did not possess adequate insurance coverage for the festival to occur at Frenier Beach.

Kapelow claimed that fifty thousand tickets had been sold, and already people were converging on nearby New Orleans. It was impossible, he insisted, to halt festival plans at such a late

Fabio Battaglia

John Sebastian was one of the few artists to perform at Celebration of Life.

date. The Guste family stuck to their demand and requested that members of the festival's stage crew leave the property at once. Local authorities and sheriff's deputies set up roadblocks on all roads leading to Laplace and directed early arrivals away from the proposed site. Local campgrounds quickly filled up with those awaiting word on where the festival was to take place. Others went to New Orleans and received food and lodging from the Mardi Gras Coalition, a volunteer group designed to aid stranded young people.

Kapelow and the other promoters frantically searched for another site. The festival was set to begin in less than a week. A landowner in Lamar County, Mississippi, offered his property to the promoters, but before any plans could be worked out, a court order was issued that banned the Celebration of Life from moving into the area. Kapelow filed for an appeal, but the local judge, as expected, denied the request.

Kapelow and two other coordinators of Celebration of Life, Bo Emery and John Walker, went back to searching for sites in Louisiana. Several landowners contacted the promoters, offering them leases on private plots, but none looked promising enough to accommodate the expected 100,000 young people for over a week. Finally, on Thursday, June 17, an agreement was reached with a Baton Rouge attorney who owned a plantation in the small town of McCrea, Louisiana, located forty miles north of the state capital. At a news conference that evening, spokesmen for the festival told the press that the Cypress Point Plantation, a five-hundred-acre plot of land situated in a lush, green, damp environment and surrounded on three sides by the Atchafalaya River, was leased for $20,000 for the week of June 21. The festival was on, and people would be permitted on the site beginning Sunday morning, June 20.

It was obvious that the festival would need much luck to succeed. No festival the size of Celebration of Life had ever triumphed with only three days of site preparation; all one had to do was glance back to Altamont in December 1969. It took months and a budget of close to a million dollars to produce a successful festival of this size and scope.

The promoters had previously announced a hard-to-believe lineup that included seventy acts, many of which had never been contacted and certainly were not bound to perform by contractual agreements. The philosophy of the Celebration of Life, like that of many other festivals, was to hype the performer lineup and sell advance tickets by the sheer magnitude of it, and then assume production and talent fees as the ticket money rolled in. This technique afforded promoters an opportunity to spend a minimum amount of time and money on a festival project; just in case the festival plans fell through, they would not be badly hurt. The ones who would bear the brunt of inconvenience and lose time and money would be the festivalgoers who bought advance tickets.

One of the reasons the promoters settled on the Cypress Point Plantation as the site of the festival was due to a feeling that very little opposition would be made against the event in such an out-of-the-way place. This turned out to be a faulty assumption. The festival chaos had been front-page news in Louisiana for the past week, and the tide of resentment to rock fests had swept across even the smallest of townships. Not twenty-four hours after the Cypress Point site had been officially announced, the governing body of the Point Coupee Parish went into an emergency session and adopted an ordinance that banned the Celebration of Life. The ordinance, passed by unanimous approval, was based on an antirock festival state law that gave Louisiana counties the power to issue permits for mass gatherings and regulate the events in the interest of public safety and health. This law was enacted when the Louisiana legislature sought to block a small rock festival in Livingston Parish in the summer of 1970. The festival, which attracted ten thousand young people, was ultimately held, but the law went on the books to prevent future rock festivals.

The law required promoters to apply for a festival permit and to guarantee adequate water supplies and sanitary facilities. At the time officials sought to check on these things, workers at the plantation had not completed plans for either, since they had been on the festival site less than two days. Point Coupee authorities informed the promoters that because minimum health measures had not been insured, the ban on the festival would be enforced. They pointed out that the ordinance called for a maximum fine of $450 and a five-month jail sentence for those disobeying the ordinance, and that this applied not only to the promoters, but also to festivalgoers who remained on the site. At a press conference the local officials of Point Coupee Parish asked the governor and the National Guard for assistance in upholding the ordinance.

News of the ban came too late for many. By Saturday afternoon, June 19, the roads leading to McCrea were jammed as cars and people were halted a few miles outside Cypress Point. Although Louisiana state police had set up roadblocks and told festivalgoers that the event was off, many had traveled long distances and were not swayed by these claims. Thousands of young people set up camp along the roadsides, waiting for a more definite statement concerning the premature death of the event.

The sultry, sticky temperature in the Atchafalaya River region became unbearable when the sun swung directly overhead on the traffic jam and the makeshift campsites. The humid conditions aggravated the boredom of those who had been patiently awaiting further word on the festival's future. Clothes irritatingly stuck to the skin, and beads of sweat never seemed to leave the foreheads of those who were just sitting and waiting. Clothes were shed by many, but this time it was to escape the heat much more than it was to carry on the tradition of disrobing at rock festivals. Those who were brave enough to chance swimming in the swift currents of the Atchafalaya River cooled off quickly as the fast-moving water brought body temperatures down to a tolerable level. Most, however, were content to wet their feet and sunbathe on the river's muddy banks.

For those not interested in either activity, there were a host of drugs to purchase to help alleviate boredom. It started to look like Powder Ridge all over again. The drug dealing was done covertly at first, as people feared being busted by undercover agents posing as hippies. But after it became evident that many of the police were reluctant to make any real show of force other than in traffic control and entry to the festival site, the dealing became more widespread and open.

The police had no desire to buck the intense heat and chase after dealers without a firm statement from upper levels that the festival was definitely off. They wanted direct orders stating a plan of action before beginning any strict enforcing of the law. They seemed content to leave the policing of the campsites and river area to the various motorcycle gangs hired by the promoters to act as security personnel.

In the meantime the Celebration of Life promoters were busy appealing the local ordinance to the Fifth U.S. Circuit Court of Appeals in New Orleans. On Tuesday, June 22, one day after the festival was to have begun, the federal court ruled that a lower court judge had acted wrongfully when he refused to listen to the pleas of the promoters in fighting the ordinance and health permits. According to the decision, the festival would be allowed to take place if basic health facilities were guaranteed. Kapelow and the other promoters agreed immediately to provide water, shower, medical, and sanitary facilities for eighteen thousand festivalgoers and to increase the facilities as the crowds grew throughout the week.

The festival construction crew worked feverishly to finish building the stage and mount the sound system on its supporting towers so that the music could begin on Thursday evening. Truckloads of lumber were piled up near where the thirty-foot stage was being erected. Due to the hastily devised construction plans and the quickened work pace, no one had bothered to thoroughly check the ground on which the stage was being built. Instead of solid earth as expected, the ground under the top soil layer was wet and muddy from underground tributaries of the Atchafalaya River. Sound-system towers were constructed without safety clamping. All the edifices were shaky at best; but still the construction continued.

The rain of the past few days further hindered proper design and construction. Then, during a particularly bad midday thunderstorm, the stage scaffolding gave way and the structure collapsed. Wooden planks and metal tubing came tumbling down, trapping several workers. One young carpenter was severely injured when he was struck with a long metal pipe through his midsection. He was rushed to the nearby hospital, where hours of surgery saved his life.

The sound of the ambulance's siren whining through the crowd became a familiar one as the week passed by. Things began getting ugly as the commencement of the music was routinely postponed due to stage-construction difficulties and problems getting the performers to the site. Many festivalgoers had been at the Cypress Point Plantation for over five days, and food, water, and money were dwindling to critical levels. The limited number of concession stands had run out of most items by Thursday evening, and the town of McCrea, with its one grocery store, had been practically wiped clean. A forty-mile round trip to neighboring communities was the only way for most to get food if their own supplies had run out or had been stolen. The mood at Celebration of Life was by no means congenial. Maybe it was the heat or the delay of the music, but Woodstock harmony was hard to find.

Without any real form of entertainment until Thursday night, most people spent their time getting high, walking around the camping areas, and, after the steamy heat became too much, risking a dip in the river. The murky water offered respite from the heat, but not without a price. During the course of the festival, four young people drowned and countless others had to be rescued from the deceivingly swift current. On Thursday afternoon mass panic broke out when gunshots were heard in

Powder Puddle.

David Gahr

the trees and bullets ricocheted off the water's edge. Members of the Galloping Gooses, Louisiana's answer to the Hell's Angels, strafed the river bank throughout the day. A motorcycle gang member told a reporter that "it was a bitch, man, watchin' the chicks scatter when they heard the shots. It was cool seein' their boobies bounce as they ran for cover, ya' know what I mean?"

As the week went by, the Gooses and the other motorcycle gangs present at Cypress Point became a serious problem. They grew tired of acting like policemen, wanting instead to return to their more fractious ways. It started with the shooting at the river and led to the beating of festivalgoers and almost a dozen cases of reported rapes. As the drug trafficking became more intense and large sums of money changed hands, the bikers took a special interest in holding up dealers and robbing them of their stash and their profits. With the police still busy clearing the roads and attending to emergency situations, the motorcycle gang members acted pretty much the same way the Angels had at Altamont. Senseless beatings were frequent. No one offered much resistance, since most bikers were heavily armed. Many of them brazenly showed off shotguns and holstered Colt 45s in addition to machetes and large chains.

Things got so out of control at the festival site that both promoters and campers asked police to come in and rid the area of the bikers. On Friday afternoon local and state police moved onto the grounds in storm-trooper fashion and began rounding up members of the Galloping Gooses, the Vikings, and the Wheelers. By three o'clock a large group of assorted gang members were stripped of their weapons and escorted out of the festival by police officers armed with shotguns of their own. They were taken to the county line and told that if they returned they would be arrested and confronted not only by police officers but by members of the National Guard as well. One hundred fifty guardsmen stood on alert in nearby New Roads waiting to assist in any evacuation plans that might be necessary at Cypress Point.

The police remained on the festival grounds to implement law and order, and one of the first things they began was a crackdown on the drug dealing. Only Powder Ridge could claim more rampant dealing and more drug-related casualties than this festival. On Saturday a young person died of an overdose of a combination of drugs on the way to the hospital, expanding the number of festival fatalities to five. Another youth that day

Louisiana state troopers ride through the makeshift camping area as festivalgoers await word on Celebration of Life.

was shot either by a narcotics officer or someone in the crowd. The scene was like something out of a bad Hollywood movie.

An undercover police officer had been staking out a young couple who were trying to peddle their remaining drug cache to passersby. A young bearded man stopped and inspected the goods. The couple discussed prices with him and an exchange was made. Seconds after the deal was concluded and the bearded man had walked away with the stash of pills, the officer quickly approached the two, told them they were under arrest for selling and possessing drugs, and handcuffed them together. The couple resisted and began screaming to the crowd.

"Get this pig off us, man! Kill this mother! We didn't do shit and he's busting us!" The girl struggled to get herself free and fell to the ground. Her handcuffed partner followed, and in the scuffle the officer also went down.

The onlooking crowd had now swelled to forty or fifty people. They closed in on the officer and the handcuffed dealers.

"Let'em go. Hey, pig, let'em go!"

"Death to all pigs!"

Someone threw a beer can that hit the officer in the leg. A Frisbee caught the woman in the neck. Everyone in the mob began shouting and whistling. A riot was in the making.

The officer, frightened and not knowing how to handle the situation, drew his gun. Someone in the crowd also had a gun and fired a shot in the air. More people rushed to the scene to see what was happening. The police officer retaliated with another warning shot from his own pistol.

Another shot was fired, but due to all the commotion it was impossible to tell whether it came from the policeman's gun or the one in the crowd. A young man dropped to the ground clutching his leg. Blood dripped through his fingers. The bullet had caught him in the thigh.

By this time the shots had alerted other police officers, who came to the scene. The crowd quickly dispersed, and the wounded man was rushed to the hospital. The two dealers were rushed off to a police car still shouting, "Get the pigs! Kill the pigs!"

The Woodstock spirit? Woodstock? Woodstock? Brotherhoodpeacelovehappinessbrotherhoodpeacelovehappiness.

There was some music at Celebration of Life. On Thursday evening, after a fireworks display, John Sebastian, Chuck Berry, War, and Jimmy Witherspoon managed to get in sets. On Friday, Stoneground, Bloodrock, the Amboy Dukes, and a few others played to the gathered crowd. Rumors flew that the Rolling Stones and the Moody Blues were to play at the festival. Nonsense, of course. Only eight of the twenty-seven rock groups that were supposed to perform actually did. Almost none of the circus and specialty acts that had been announced showed up. On Saturday night the rains that had made such a muddy mess of things earlier in the week returned in full force. By Sunday the festival was over.

The rain was actually a blessing. Celebration of Life had been nothing more than a drawn-out failure and a colossal ripoff. More rain convinced adamant festivalgoers that it was time to go home. They were dirty, wet, tired, hungry, broke, and disappointed. It was time to return to a saner environment.

Three days after the festival ended, tax liens totaling $700,000 were filed against the promoters by federal agents. It was estimated by *Variety* that at $28 per head, gate receipts hovered around the $1.5 million figure.

The Celebration of Life and Powder Ridge left a bitter taste with rock fans and festival participants. Many felt cheated and victimized by promoters, who only cared, it seemed, about the possibility of huge profits. A growing number of young people began to assume that it was wiser not to buy advance tickets to future festivals. Why, they reasoned, shell out $20 or $25 and have it ripped off? It was smarter just to show up at a rock festival and capitalize on the inevitable confusion.

CHAPTER EIGHT

Innocence Forgotten (1970-1972)

Music festivals are not political rallies. People want to rise above politics at a music festival.

—John McLaughlin,
   Randall's Island, July 16, 1970

"It's too damn hot!"

The old, rusted thermometer that hung on the side of the grocery store in Byron, Georgia, registered 101 degrees. And all day the radio announcer with the thickest of Southern drawls kept reminding locals and festivalgoers to expect even higher temperatures for the July 4 weekend.

"Ya'll don't for-get what ah told ya now. A real scorcher of a weekend for ah nation's birthday. Stay out of the sun if ya can, ya hear?"

"Sit on it, buddy."

The Middle Georgia Raceway,

located in the town of Byron, sits ninety-five miles south of Atlanta. Promoters Steve Kapelow (the same Kapelow who would stage Celebration of Life in Louisiana one year later) and Alex Cooley leased the track for the July 4 weekend to hold the second annual Atlanta Pop Festival. No one had anticipated that the worst heat wave of the summer of 1970 would strike on festival weekend. And no one could predict that the most sought-after pill at the site would be composed of, of all things, salt.

Kapelow and Cooley hoped to attract 100,000 paying rock fans from all over the country to Byron. They advertised nationally in many of the underground periodicals and on progressive FM radio stations. But festival tickets were priced high—$35 for three days—and as a result, the promoters had only managed to sell 10,000 tickets in advance.

Kapelow and Cooley were well aware of the talk in underground circles that the Atlanta festival, as well as others being produced that summer, should be "liberated" and transformed into free events. "Power to the people" and "liberation" were fashionable political terms in 1970, and they seemed to fit nicely in rock vocabulary.

Johnny Winter blended blues with rock like no other performer on the festival stage. His performance at the 1970 Atlanta Pop Festival highlighted the event.

Fabio Battaglia

People without festival tickets and with no intentions of purchasing them began milling near the main gate on Friday morning, July 3. The scene was similar to that in Denver at that city's pop festival one year ago, but noticeably absent were helmeted police officers armed with billy clubs and tear gas. By mid-afternoon the temperature had climbed to an unbearable 115 Georgia degrees. That son-of-a-bitch radio announcer had been right. The leaves in the trees hardly moved, and later on in the day, when a breeze did pick up somewhat, it felt as if a giant, slow-moving fan had been set behind a blast furnace.

The atmosphere at the racetrack was ideal for a violent eruption. The intense heat had shortened fuses on tempers, and many in the ticketless crowd outside grew irritable. Those gathered outside the gates weren't baking in the sun for their health. They hadn't traveled hundreds—and for some, even thousands—of miles to perspire, Georgia-style. They had come to hear music and they had come to hear it free. The Atlanta Pop Festival looked as if it would be the best festival of the summer. They wanted to be part of it.

The shouts of "Free festival! Free festival!" began around dusk, as those with tickets passed through the gates in growing numbers. The music was set to start in a few hours. The promoters had taken steps to ward off gate-crashing: A free stage had been built in the main camping area, and local bands and talented or brave campers had access to it at will. The promoters had also printed up flyers that were passed out and tacked up outside the festival site, which read:

> Woodstock was beautiful, but there are fewer large festivals this summer due to fears of other huge financial losses. If you do not help, this may be one of the last big festivals ever. Think about how hard the establishment everywhere is trying to stop festivals. They are afraid of us when we are together. If we kill the festival, we play right into establishment hands. We destroy our own scene.
>
> Peace

"Bullshit, man!"

"Free festival, free festival, free festival, free festival!"

"Open the fuckin' gates. Music is for the people! Power to the people!"

The chanting and shouting grew louder. "Free, free free, free . . ." The promoters let it be known that a "free" day of music would be held on Monday, July 6, for those who could not afford the three-day price of admission. The announcement fell on deaf ears. Besides, that meant those outside the gates would have to wait three days to hear music. What were they to do in the meantime?

The promoters had a quick and serious decision to make. The bikers who had been hired to man the gates were becoming exacerbated and pugnacious. Visions of Altamont. The clubs and chains they carried might become saturated with youthful blood at any minute. A member of the festival staff reported to Kapelow and Cooley that the people outside seemed to be preparing an assault.

"Some guys out by the main gate are tellin' everyone to clasp hands and march toward the entrance."

"How many of them are involved?" asked Kapelow nervously.

"Shoot, I don't know, a few hundred maybe. Man, they don't wanna shut up with the free festival bit and the bikers are really getting pissed off."

A confrontation seemed imminent. Things were getting bad.

"What do you think?" Kapelow wanted a show of solidarity in the decision he knew had to be made. It might cost him and his partner their shirts.

"What do *you* think?"

"Let 'em in."

Cooley looked at the ground. "Let 'em in."

The festival was declared free at 9:30 P.M. on Friday night, as the gates opened. No tickets were collected.

Friday night's concert featured Georgia's own bunch of rockers, the Allman Brothers. The group at the time was almost solely responsible for putting the South on the rock map. Their fiery blend of blues and boogie had made their debut album, *The Allman Brothers Band*, released in the last month of 1969, one of the most critically acclaimed efforts of the year. The album featured the immaculate, spellbinding slide guitar of Duane Allman, matched and backed up by the calculating and equally effective sound of fellow guitarist Dicky Betts. Because of the exciting interplay between them, the Allman Brothers Band possessed one of the most exciting guitar combinations in all of rock. This, combined with the charismatic double drumming of Butch Trucks and Jai Johanny Johanson, the pulsating bass of Berry Oakley, and the ever-resourceful keyboard work and vocal style of Gregg Allman, gave the band all the necessary ingredients to eventually assume superstar status.

The Allman Brothers opened their set amid the kind of applause usually reserved for such rock heroes as Jimi Hendrix and the Rolling Stones. The band was deeply touched by the enthusiasm. They mentioned that it felt good to play for so many friends in their own backyard (the band members lived in Macon).

Duane Allman turned his back to the large crowd, which was quickly closing in on the 200,000 mark. With three nods of his head, the Allmans slammed into "Statesboro Blues" and then "Whipping Post" from their first album. A crack of thunder came out of nowhere. Then another. Rain soon followed, and lightning provided a natural light show in the distance. The rain didn't surprise anyone. It was *supposed* to rain at rock festivals! Ever since Woodstock, rain and mud had become vital necessities for the development of the overall scene. The rain felt cool and refreshing at first; a pleasant change from the torrid temperatures of the day. But after it stopped almost as unexpectedly as it had begun, that sticky, uncomfortable feeling returned. And through it all the Allman Brothers Band played on.

Their set lasted a little over two hours. They played until the rain came again. When the possibility of electrocution became evident, they left the stage, promising to return sometime during the remainder of the festival. They kept their word by reappearing on Sunday morning with a four-hour sunrise set that was one of the longest and most satisfying performances by any group in festival history up to that time.

On Saturday the heat returned, and before long there were only scattered traces of the previous night's thunderstorm. The sun blazed down hard and began to lay out victims. By mid-afternoon the major medical problem was heat prostration as young people succumbed to the near-insufferable conditions. Weakened festivalgoers fainted from the heat with increasing regularity as the thermometer once again topped the 100-degree mark. Thousands of salt tablets were given away to those who felt dizzy weak, and light-headed. Lines at the water spigots were outrageously long; many could not get enough to drink.

Other victims of the sun and heat included those who were severely sunburned. Overheated girls shed tops in vain attempts to get cool and comfortable. Not thinking, many young women suffered aching sunburn on their breasts and sensitive nipples. The pain for many that Saturday night was excruciating when their cherry-red bosoms rubbed against blouses and shirts.

As with just about any other rock festival of considerable size, the drug problem intensified as the event neared the midway mark. But due to the heat at the Atlanta Pop Festival, those suffering from bad trips and overdoses experienced magnified woes. There were verified reports that much of the "orange sunshine" (a combination of LSD and STP) was impure. Other pills known as pinkies blew more than one mind. They contained 90 percent STP and 10 percent strychnine.

By Saturday night a drug- and heat-related medical emergency existed. Doctors at the racetrack requested army helicopters to evacuate the sick and badly sunburned. The roads were still jammed with automobiles, and ambulance service to the nearby hospital had all but ceased. Chaos and confusion reigned; but somehow it seemed fitting. The humming sounds of choppers taking off and landing, the overcrowded medical tents, the warnings of bad acid—it had also become very much a part of the festival scene. It made things exciting. It reminded many of what they had read about or experienced at Woodstock. Groovy. Really far out.

Before receiving the final okay to stage the Atlanta Pop Festival, the promoters had pledged to uptight locals and state authorities that they would actively pursue an antidrug campaign throughout the weekend. Much resentment toward the festival was generated by Georgia state and local officials who voiced concern over the inevitable drug abuse at the event. Governor Lester Maddox held a news conference two days prior to the festival and aired his feelings about the Atlanta Pop Festival and drugs.

"I'm personally not opposed to any musical program that's orderly. I love pop. I love music. I love festivals. I've been accused of popping off too much, in fact.

"But I'm against the breaking of our laws at such events, especially the widespread use of illegal drugs. By having state law enforcement officials on hand, it will serve as a warning to those coming who think it will be a haven for drug addicts."[1]

Kapelow and Cooley kept their word. Sort of. They hired Dr. Sidney Cohen and Dr. Joel Cantor from the National Institute of Mental Health to speak (lecture?) on drug abuse. The promoters also persuaded the Indian yogi, Bhajan, to discuss the virtues of a "drug-free experience of music and love" and an American Indian medicine man to relate the dangers of abusing hallucinogenics. Few listened to what they had to say. For many a rock festival was not a rock festival without drugs.

Drugs gave the scene life and color. It was as important as the music itself. The antidrug speakers satisfied the authorities, but drug use at the festival was as prolific as ever.

For Richie Havens the scene was especially colorful; he recalls:

"Bhajan, the Indian yogi, was onstage preaching whatever it was that he was preaching just as I arrived backstage. I was standing around, you know, talking with old friends and people I hadn't seen since, like Woodstock. I forget what time it was. All I know is that it was dark, nighttime. We're talking, having a good time, when all of a sudden, these brightly lit flying saucers came out of nowhere and began buzzing the back end of the festival area. A lot of people were tripping and whatnot backstage and so everybody's going, 'Ah' and 'Wow, man' and 'Far out!' But it was incredible. I think there were five or six of them, just buzzin' around, checkin' out all those weird people listening to that weird music. It just blew me away, man. The overall symbolism of the situation was incredible. I wonder how many people in the crowd that were tripping on acid and listening to the yogi speak on mystical powers and saw the UFO's and then flipped out because of the heavy scene."

Saturday night was the Fourth of July. Red, white, and blue was everywhere. Cherry bombs and firecrackers exploded throughout the day. American flags topped many tents and campsites. Most were flown upside down in symbolic protest that things were still not right in America. The war was still on. That was the main thing. Nixon promised to end it, but who trusted him? In the spring of 1970 more than 430,000 troops still remained in Southeast Asia, and Nixon had startled the world in April when he announced the invasion of Cambodia. One month later four students were killed on the campus of Ohio's Kent State University by trigger-happy national guardsmen. The war had been brought home, and the violence and brutality of it were there to feel and touch.

Jimi Hendrix played his famous version of the "Star Spangled Banner" that evening after an elaborate fireworks display. He bent and elongated the notes of the national anthem, ripping apart the basic melodic structure until it hardly resembled the original version. Hendrix could still do it. When it came to dramatic intensity, few were better. The Atlanta festival, however, would be one of the last for Hendrix. In September of that year Jimi Hendrix was dead. Drugs. And another festival great, Janis Joplin, soon followed. Rock festivals wouldn't be the same without them.

B.B. King, Mountain, Procol Harum, Rare Earth, the Chambers Brothers, Lee Michaels, Cactus, Cat Mother and the All Night Newsboys, Poco, and Johnny Winter also played the festival. Conspicuously absent were a number of San Francisco bands. A second generation of rock festival artists were advancing to the forefront; subsequently Country Joe, Paul Butterfield, Quicksilver Messenger Service, and some of the others were forced to take a backseat. Rock had matured, and festival lineups such as that at the Atlanta Pop Festival reflected its growth.

The music ended early Monday morning. It was the last time rock fans would gather in such force in the great state of Georgia. Reports of rampant drug use and unchecked nudity circulated in the newspapers weeks after the event. People called for protection against the vices of the younger generation. The legislature and Governor Maddox felt that they had been swindled by the promoters, and they feared a backlash from the embarrassment. Locals looked for a scapegoat and found one in Lamar Brown, the owner of the Middle Georgia Raceway. Brown was pressured into selling the racetrack because of a boycott initiated by racing fans, who were angry because he had permitted the festival to occur on his property.

Eight months later members of the Georgia State Legislature introduced a mass gathering bill which required events lasting fifteen or more hours to comply with strict regulations. The promoters of such events had to post a $1 million surety bond and be assessed $5 for each person exceeding the attendance estimate. The bill also gave the state board of health the power to deny health permits if the facilities at the site were not satisfactory. But most important, the bill passed with a Senate amendment that gave the governor of the state the power to invoke martial law if lawlessness overwhelmed the event in question.[2]

Don Friedman and Robert Gardiner of Brave New World Productions deliberately avoided any widescale reference to the word "festival" when they announced plans in the spring of 1970 for their three-day "pop concert" on New York's Randall's Island. Originally the event was to be billed as the New York Pop Festival, but community backlash against rock festivals, radical political reaction, and bad press concerning gate-crashing and drugs at the Atlanta Pop Festival curtailed advertising the event as such. The promoters emphasized that the concerts would be held in Downing Stadium, that there would be no camping, and at the conclusion of each day's show, the stadium would be cleared.

Their ace in the hole was the fact that the stadium format was a finite and controlled environment. Instead of staging the event out in the country on acres and acres of land, without guaranteed drinking water and sanitary facilities, the stadium's structure possessed these plus an already built fence and wall to discourage gate-crashers and large crowds of kids without tickets. The Randall's Island event did not proclaim to be the heir to the Woodstock throne. Thirty to forty thousand people a day were all the promoters hoped would attend. Friedman had produced other musical events at the stadium in the past. He felt confident that he could pull one more off, even if it was rock 'n' roll.

Randall's Island sits on the outskirts of Spanish Harlem— El Barrio, as the locals call it: the rundown apartment houses, the trash in the streets, the streetcorner hangouts, the neon signs in Spanish. And the smell. The humid and hot temperatures of July accented the potent aroma of spicy Spanish food, the sweat on the streets, and the garbage in the alleys. You smell it once and you never forget it.

Spanish Harlem was the turf of the Young Lords, and Randall's Island was an integral part of their domain. The Young Lords were to the Spanish-speaking community in the late sixties and early seventies what the Black Panthers were to the black community—symbols of ethnic and community pride, youthful romantic revolutionaries, power to *their* people, and *Viva Ché!* Peace and love, yes, but when violence and armed force were necessary, it would be carried out. One was proud to be a Young Lord. People in Spanish Harlem—at least the young ones, anyway—respected the organization. They, after all, were the self-appointed guardians of the community.

Three and one half weeks before the Randall's Island festival (it was a festival framework, regardless of what the promoters said, and young people related to it as such), a group of young revolutionaries representing such groups as the Black Panthers, the Free Rangers, and yippies from local New York chapters presented the Brave New World promoters with a list of demands and ultimatums. Not included in this group, however, were the Young Lords. The bunch billed themselves as the RYP/OFF Collective and, later, the Randall's Island Collective.

Their list of demands was extensive. According to the group, it was absolutely necessary that at least ten handpicked (by them) community bands play at the festival for a price of $5,000 per group plus any expenses. Ten thousand tickets were to be handed out free to young people who could not afford a $21 three-day ticket. If the promoters were going to capitalize on the music and money of the masses to line their own wallets, they should be required to give something back to the community. But that was not all.

In addition, bail funds were to be set up to aid the Panther 21 Defense Committee and to cover all those who might be arrested at the festival. They had also heard that plans were being formulated to film the concerts. Fine. They wanted a copy of the film. And finally, Brave New World was to turn over a portion of their profits to the collective to be shared equally by all participating radical organizations. Gardiner and Friedman felt like they had been hit with baseball bats. The festival was less than a month away. It was bad enough that advance ticket sales had only been trickling in. Now they had problems with young idealistic revolutionaries.

In return for the total compliance of the demands, the RYP/OFF Collective would actively promote the festival in their respective communities. The underground press would support the event, and ticket sales should be brisk in the near future, they promised. They also volunteered the services of their radical troops to act as security personnel and public relations men.

What if Brave New World refused to accept the demands? The collective would pass the word that the Randall's Island festival was a "free people's event" and that no one should buy tickets because the radicals intended to liberate the gates. There would be violence. The festival would suffer an agonizing death. This was a promise.

"We'll negotiate," the promoters responded feebly, still in shock. The radicals got up and left the offices of Brave New World.

When the Young Lords heard about the RYP/OFF Collective and their list of demands, they too insisted on a part of the action. Randall's Island was their turf, if anyone had forgotten, and no one was going to overstep their authority. Let them in on it or the festival is off.

The radicals agreed, and an alliance between the Puerto Rican street-gang-turned-revolutionaries and the RYP/OFF Collective was sealed. The Young Lords would get a financial cut, a bail fund, and a chance to see a few of their community's bands on the stage at Downing Stadium.

Gardiner and Friedman faced a delicate situation. Surprisingly, the radicals consented to negotiate their demands. That, at least, was a plus. They could very easily have remained adamant and referred to any failure in meeting their demands as action worthy of retaliation.

After a second meeting between the collective and the promoters, it was agreed that a bail fund for the Panthers would remain; instead of handing out ten thousand free tickets, people from the community would be allowed in to fill up any empty seats that had not been paid for; the community bands would play, but not at the price originally demanded; stage time and microphones would be set aside for political raps with the audience; the radicals would act as security personnel and ticket-takers; and a portion of the profits would be handed over, but the amount would be determined after the festival was over.

People began entering the stadium facilities late Friday afternoon, even though the music was not scheduled to start until nine. From five o'clock to seven, the RYP/OFF Collective commandeered the stage. In the background carpenters worked quickly to put the final touches on the stage structure. Hammering and the cutting of wood occasionally blended with the revolutionary rhetoric. Not everyone listened. Very few listened with serious intent. Scheduled to perform that evening were Grand Funk Railroad, John Sebastian, Steppenwolf, Jethro Tull, and Jimi Hendrix. It was a first-rate lineup composed entirely of headline acts. Most cared more about the upcoming music than the political fervor on the stage.

Of the 25,000 that saw the show that night, 8,000 had not paid the admission price. As the people entered the stadium, they were handed leaflets by members of the Randall's Island Collective.

"Welcome brothers and sisters. This concert belongs to the people. For the first time, the community, whose culture is being packaged, will also share in the profits of the concert . . ."

The radicals collected the tickets and mingled with the crowd outside the gates of Downing Stadium. It seemed as if only the Young Lords were actively playing the role of security men. They discouraged gate-crashing and made an admirable attempt to keep things under control. The other revolutionaries looked the other way when crashers scaled the fence or ran through the gates. Inside, a tape recording was played through the sound system. An unidentified young woman who claimed to be a member of the militant Weathermen explained how the underground group was going to attack "a symbol of American justice" in the next few weeks.

Backstage was chaotic. Unauthorized people roamed about, and radicals-turned-groupies and rock fans sought to rap with the stars. Pissed-off managers argued with promoters about stage conditions and money.

The festival managed to get through the first night, but things looked as if they would get progressively worse on Saturday. When the artists heard of the gate-crashing on Friday night, they grew skeptical about ever seeing a paycheck. If the people didn't pay to get in, then obviously there would be no money to pay performers. It didn't take a genius to figure that out. So managers insisted that their acts be paid in full in advance, before they stepped out on the stage. The promoters said that it was impossible. Ravi Shankar, scheduled to play on Saturday's billing, refused to go on. Others followed suit. Delaney and Bonnie, Miles Davis, Richie Havens, the Tony Williams Lifetime, and Sly Stone did not even bother to show up.

Outside, the members of the Randall's Island Collective actively campaigned to persuade potential ticket buyers to give their money to the collective in the form of a donation and then gate-crash the festival. There were no cops inside the stadium. The only time they entered the site was to haul down Vietcong and Vietnamese flags. As soon as they took them down, defiant radicals quickly hoisted up another set on the stadium's flagpole.

The gate-crashing was much more intense on Saturday than the previous night. On Sunday things were so out of hand that the promoters gave up and declared it a free festival. All that did was make it official. It had been a free festival for most since its inception. In all, nearly thirty thousand had crashed the event.

Ten Years After and Cactus decided to perform and worry

Jimi Hendrix at Randall's Island.
Courtesy of Warner Brothers

about getting paid later. The New York Rock 'n' Roll Ensemble played for free. Sid Bernstein sent over two of his bands, Elephant's Memory and Rhinoceros, to play for the crowd. Good publicity. But where were the stars, the big acts that were supposed to perform? New York disc jockey Dave Herman told the audience that they had refused to play because there was no guarantee that they would be paid for their efforts. The crowd booed and threw things onstage. He told them too many people had gotten in without paying; there simply was no money to pay performers. More boos. This time a few bottles exploded on and around the stage.

The people filming the concerts put up money to keep the festival going. If the event could be completed and filmed, there was a chance that money could be made from the resulting movie. Dr. John the Night Tripper and Mountain played. Little Richard performed, and when he finished his set, he threw his jacket and boots into the audience. The jacket, however, was trimmed with glass beads, and in the scuffle for the item, many people wound up with bloody hands.

A reporter asked promoter Don Friedman what he thought of the situation.

"The festival spirit is dead, and it happened quickly. I don't know the reasons why. Greed on everyone's part, I guess. The 'love-peace' thing of Woodstock is out. Anarchy. Complete and total anarchy. That's what replaced it."

The festival, of course, was a box-office disaster. The promoters were surprised that they had grossed $315,000. Still, they were more than $275,000 short of their financial expectations. No money was ever given to the collective, and the bail fund for the Panthers collapsed. Some performers were paid; most weren't. It was a flop on all accounts. No one prospered from the New York Pop Festival.

The year 1970 wasn't a banner year for rock festivals. Yet people in the music business realized that large music events still had much life in them. In August Stanley Gortikov, president of Capitol Industries, proposed that a fact-finding commission be set up within the music industry to "assure the preservation and future of rock festivals." Gortikov told *Billboard* magazine that rock festivals were essential for the growth of the music form; it provided an interaction between performer and audience that was unique and highly beneficial.

A few weeks later, in an article written by Jeff Samuels of *Variety*, Jack Holzman, president of Elektra Records, outlined the steps that he thought would make a successful rock festival.

1. There should be a finite number of tickets and everyone should be made aware of that fact.
2. There should be a maximum admission price of $5 per concert.
3. There should be a geographical apportionment of festivals so that kids in different parts of the country would have an opportunity to view the events.
4. A security system similar to that employed at Monterey should be set up at festivals. It would be effective without being oppressive.
5. The performance of big artists should be limited to one day, with seven or eight artists performing over a twelve-hour time span.[3]

Stu Ginsberg of RCA Records added in January of 1971 that the shaky future of rock festivals was the fault of the major artists who "yelled 'revolution' or 'free music' but were the first to demand their checks and royalties." Ginsberg proposed that big rock acts volunteer their services so that the price of tickets could be drastically reduced and festivals made more accessible to the average rock fan.

Two rock promoters, deeply concerned over the festival hysteria and the need for control in their production, wired the White House and asked President Nixon to set up a commission on rock culture. The commission, they explained, could clear up responsibilities of those involved and provide leadership and guidance in the management of the events. The promoters received a form letter from government officials thanking them for their interest and ideas on the problem.

The business end of the rock world was worried. The rock festival was too valuable an institution to allow it to smother under the weight of greed. Record sales were up, stocks were soaring, more new artists had been signed than ever before. The industry was making big money, and the quality of the music was generally respectable in terms of artistic merit. But the rock festival resembled a wild stallion. It needed to be broken and bridled in order to extract its fullest potential. The instability and restlessness of the event had to be eradicated if it was to survive.

In 1972, nearly two years after he had helped produce the second Atlanta Pop Festival, promoter Alex Cooley thought he had found the solution to at least the legal problems surrounding rock festivals. Why bother to fight the mass-gathering ordinances and the other legal stickers designed to prevent the staging of festivals? Instead, he and his business partners came up with an idea that seemed to be a promoter's dream: simply hold the event where there weren't such legal hassles and stipulations. Someplace like Puerto Rico...

Vega Baja is located on the north coast of the island of Puerto Rico. The oceanfront property was once a huge dairy farm of more than 420 acres of beautiful countryside. A stretch of sun-soaked, sandy white beach, the kind that locals and travel agencies love to boast about, separates the farm from the sea. Cooley and his associates rented the land for Easter Weekend. It was on that Friday, Saturday, and Sunday that the Mar y Sol (Sea and Sun) Festival was to take place.

The promoters made arrangements with the airlines so that package deals were offered to festivalgoers flying out of major East Coast cities. From New York City, for example, round-trip airfare plus a festival ticket cost approximately $152. Not cheap by any rock fan's standards, especially those who were accustomed to gate-crashing festivals. Mar y Sol promised to be a small, almost private event. The island and beach atmosphere made the trip to Puerto Rico vacationlike, with the music being an extra added attraction. College kids looking for someplace to go besides Fort Lauderdale, Florida, found Mar y Sol the perfect substitute.

Cooley next contacted various bus lines in San Juan to transport the young people from the airport to the festival site, some thirty-five miles away. The deal was that a flat sum was to be paid to the transit companies to have their drivers waiting with their vehicles as the first load of kids stepped from the first plane. Cooley expected a crowd of twenty-five to fifty thousand. It was not an easy task to transport so many people arriving at virtually the same time. But the deal was concluded anyway. Things looked bright as the first weekend in April drew near.

Out on the festival site a commune called The Family had been hired by the promoters to construct the stage, erect sound and lighting towers, and generally ready the land for the influx of thousands of people. Living the good life, the deeply tanned commune members had been on the site since the beginning of the year. When they weren't working, they spent their time sunbathing, swimming, fishing, surfing, and playing the role of Robinson Crusoe in a 1972-ish sort of way. Somehow they managed to discipline themselves so that nearly all the work had been completed by the time the first festivalgoers began arriving in Vega Baja.

On the surface it appeared that Cooley and his Atlanta-based backers had held up their part of the bargain. It was the other parties involved who botched up the festival plans. Things turned sour a week before the festival, when a San Juan Superior Court judge issued a court injunction that barred any festival activities at Vega Baja because of the possible sale and use of illicit drugs by American hippies. When East Coast newspapers reported the decision of the court, stateside festivalgoers did not know whether to risk a trip to the Carribean island or get their money back by canceling their plane reservations. Some chose the latter course, fearing a report of Powder Ridge or Celebration of Life. Most, however, decided to make the trip regardless of the injunction.

Festival lawyers worked frantically to get the injunction reversed, and miraculously accomplished their goal late Thursday afternoon. Due to backroom compromising the same judge abrogated his earlier decision and permitted the festival to proceed as scheduled. Planes filled with young people began arriving at the airport in San Juan early Friday morning. Once their baggage was secured they searched for the free buses that were to take them to the festival area. There were none. During the court-injunction confusion the transit company hired by the festival promoters had assumed that the festival was canceled and had not assignad any drivers or buses to the airport. When word reached the company that Mar y Sol would take place after all, officials sent all available taxi drivers to the airport to cover for the lack of buses.

The ride from the airport to Vega Baja took almost three hours due to the traffic. It was hot, sticky, and crowded in the taxis as people jammed into them, eager to be part of the first wave arriving at the site. The music was scheduled to begin that evening, but it was obvious, from the chaos, that no live sounds would be heard from the stage until the following day. That gave people time to set up camp, do a little swimming in the warm, refreshing ocean, and get sunburned. Real sunburned. It was only April, and many were sunbathing for the first time that season. As a result, the strong tropical ultra-violet rays turned palish white backs, legs, and chests into sizzling red flesh in a matter of hours.

By late Friday afternoon local Puerto Ricans had set up simple booths and concession stands and begun selling, at outrageous prices, food and other items. One of those "other items" later turned out to be fresh water. Some of the wells that had been drilled exclusively for use during the festival ran dry sooner than expected. Many gallons of precious water were also being used to keep showers going. Locals kindly uttered *"gracias"* in a sinister tone as thirsty festivalgoers at first paid 25¢ and then, at some stands, 75¢ and even a dollar for a glass of water.

When young male Puerto Ricans found out that American girls were using the open shower area, hundreds crowded about to catch glimpses, whistle, and shout signs of approval. They liked what they saw and wanted the girls to know it. The relationship between locals and festivalgoers deteriorated rapidly. No policemen were on the site, security was spotty, and those carrying machetes knew they could do whatever they pleased. When a drunken bunch of locals tore down two American flags and raised the Puerto Rican colors in their place, numerous fights broke out. It was only a matter of time before disaster struck.

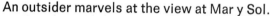

An outsider marvels at the view at Mar y Sol.

David Gahr

Late Friday evening a sixteen-year-old boy from the island of St. Croix, who had been dealing coke during the day and run into some problems with local dealers, slept peacefully in his sleeping bag. Despite the hassles he had had a good day. Saturday would be even better because of the commencement of the music. The moon's light was constantly interrupted by passing cloud formations, and so no one saw a group of locals silently approach the boy. No one heard the sound of the machetes hitting bone or slicing through flesh. In a matter of seconds the body in the sleeping bag became a bloody, mangled mess. The moon and the stars and maybe one or two frightened young people who were deathly afraid to talk were the only witnesses.

Three other people lost their lives at Mar y Sol. A couple swam out past the breakers and were swept away by a fast-moving current. They both drowned. Another young person, this one from New Jersey, attempted to surf where the ocean's floor was lined with jagged rocks. On his last wave he wiped out as the force of the water shot him downward. He cracked his head on a sharp rock and died on the way to the hospital.

There was a marijuana shortage at the festival, which prompted many to resort to powerful tranquilizers, barbiturates, and various hallucinogens. Pot that normally sold for $15 to $20 an ounce on the East Coast was going for a minimum of $50. Surprisingly, however, the medical tent was filled more with sunburn and fight victims than people suffering from overdoses or bad trips.

The music got under way Saturday afternoon and helped ease tension somewhat between locals and festival participants. Nitzinger, Brownsville Station, and folksinger Jonathan Edwards performed enthusiastic sets, but the real energy did not begin flowing until late that evening, when B.B. King and the Allman Brothers played until dawn. The Allman Brothers proved beyond a doubt that they indeed possessed the genuine musicianship and professional edge to overcome the tragic loss of Brother Duane Allman. In October of the previous year, the highly respected guitarist had been killed in a freak motorcycle accident just outside Macon, Georgia. (Bassist Berry Oakley was to die the same way at almost the identical location in 1972.)

Sunday's billing was highlighted by the jazzy sounds of Herbie Mann and Dave Brubeck, to whom the crowd perfunctorily responded; Savoy Brown; and then, as Sunday night turned into Monday morning, Emerson, Lake and Palmer and

Backstage with Black Sabbath.

Alice Cooper. But with the heat and the incessant worry over whether one's tent and personal supplies would be ripped off, the atmosphere at the stage area was not celebratory. Of the thirty thousand who showed up for the festival, only half were interested enough to sit and listen to the music in the afternoon. The remainder of the crowd were either hanging out at the camping area nervously protecting their belongings against theft or on the beach enjoying the warm weather rather than fighting it.

Mar y Sol stretched over into Monday, since there had been no music on Friday evening as originally scheduled. The J. Geils Band, Cactus, Dr. John the Night Tripper, Bloodrock, and

Rod Stewart played late into the night. The inactivity onstage between performers grew longer as the day wore on, and many in the crowd became restless and eager to return home. A number of bands scheduled to perform never showed, and a rumor circulated that there would be no transportation back to the airport.

That rumor turned into fact when one of the promoters nervously announced that there were no buses available to take people back to San Juan. The Transit company that had been hired now claimed that their contract was invalid. The boos and frustrated calls of "ripoff" echoed loud and clear, but after a few minutes a feeling of resignation permeated the festival grounds. The festival was a bummer. Period. The idea was to get off the island where the bad vibrations were so thick one could choke on them and get back to the mainland, where at least one could get a drink of water without having to beg for it.

But how to get to the airport? Panic spread through the crowd as the possibility of missing one's plane became very real and suddenly very frightening. Young people hastily broke camp and started out toward Route 2, the road that led to the airport. Most figured to walk the seven to ten miles to the main highway, and then thumb a ride. Thirty thousand people all had the same idea.

Picture the scene: long lines of young people, ragged, tired, sunburned, and vastly disappointed with what had transpired during the past three days. It was a refugee line if ever there was one. An occasional car or truck that inched its way through the horde of people going in the direction of Route 2 had to fight off attempts of piracy. The situation was pathetic. Was this what a rock festival was all about?

Once again the locals stood to make a profit from the "heepies." When the young people finally reached Route 2 and began hitchhiking, cars recklessly swerved to the side of the road and motioned to the Americans to get in. Maybe the locals were okay after all. It was nice of them to stop and pick up hitchhikers and take them down the road a piece.

"Hi, how's it going?"

"Muy bién, amigo."

The Mar y Sol festival area was so close to the beach that many festivalgoers camped there.

"Are you going in the direction of the airport?"

"*Sí.*"

"Can me and my friends get a lift with you?"

"Sure, *amigo;* twenty dollars each."

"Are you kidding?"

"Twenty dollars or else you walk, my friend."

"Look, man, all I have is twelve bucks and some change. That's all I got, I swear."

"Sorry, *amigo. Adiós.*"

"Hey, wait, okay, okay. I'll give you fifteen dollars. That's all I got, man. Really. That's no shit."

"*Bueno, amigo.* Get in."

(Heard from the backseat in a mumbled tone) "You son-of-a-bitch spic. You're a goddamned ripoff artist!"

Once at the airport, the problems continued for Mar y Sol participants. The terminal was jammed with other vacationers returning to the United States besides the festivalgoers waiting to catch their planes. And what a mess! It didn't matter that you had a ticket that was paid for in advance or a reservation on a specific flight. There were very few available seats on any planes going anywhere in the United States. The place was chaos.

National guardsmen and Red Cross volunteers were sent to the airport. Two huge tents were set up to accommodate those who had no way of returning home in the immediate future. It took hours of standing in line to reach a phone booth. Information centers were inundated with angry customers. Those without any money began to panhandle. Was this a scene from World War III? Had the Martians landed? What the hell was going on?

No one knew for sure. Many young people spent two or more days at the airport waiting to secure a seat on a flight. The energy and spirit of those who had hoped that Mar y Sol would be some kind of superfestival had long been sapped from their systems. Cooley and the promoters left the island claiming they had lost $200,000 on the festival. No doubt they were telling the truth. Puerto Rican government officials wanted them for tax evasion, but nothing was ever done to extradite the promoters. When *Rolling Stone* magazine interviewed Cooley, he stated that, despite the hassles, the festival was a success. A success? The only success that came from Mar y Sol was that it effectively proved that rock festivals were not welcome "cultural activities" in Puerto Rico. It was the first and last to be held on the island.

CHAPTER NINE

Back on the Road Again

I think this was the way it was at Woodstock.

—Festivalgoer at Watkins Glen,
 July 28, 1973.

The traditional concept of the three-day rock festival was being tortured to death. Rock-festival consciousness had strayed so far from its origins at Monterey and the other early fests that it was barely recognizable by 1972. In five short years the rock festival had been conceived, raised to maturity, and begun a rapid deterioration process.

The three-day rock festival was gasping for air, but strangely enough, festival fever remained. Young people still harbored relentless enthusiasm to practice the virtues and habits of the Woodstock Nation. Those who had been too young in 1969 to attend the Woodstock festival anxiously hoped another rock festival of equal importance would be staged somewhere, anywhere. Woodstock, Woodstock. That festival was still the reigning heavyweight champion. Significant events and gatherings were still compared to Woodstock. Gradually its importance had swelled to exaggerated proportions. It became a yardstick; a measuring device of the young and the media to exact intensity and meaning from cultural events. Woodstock, Woodstock. Would there ever be another Woodstock?

No, yes, maybe. If the right promoters picked the right location, hired the right performers, secured the right endorsements, followed the legislators' laws in the right manner, and induced the right vibrations, then maybe a duplication or, more precisely, a reenactment was vaguely possible. Two of the most important components that had made Woodstock what it was were the season during which it was held and the spontaneity of the event. The feeling and the excitement of 1969 could never be brought back. Not in 1972 or 1973, and certainly not in '74, '75, '76, et cetera. Spontaneity could not be achieved if any form of massive planning was instigated. But without such precise formulations, any mammoth rock event staged in the mid-seventies was doomed to failure.

Still, an unbridled interest in such an event was present. As long as the profit motive was tempting, there was always a slight hope that someone would try for the ultimate music festival of the seventies. The smarter promoters seriously began devising ways to bypass the problems and hostilities that had destroyed such festivals as Powder Ridge, Celebration of Life, and, more recently, Mar y Sol. It became increasingly clear that the idealistic pastoral setting was a thing of the past. The staging of successful festivals in the country was a 1960s phenomenon that was no longer viable from a production standpoint. It also was not that important anymore to the youthful masses. Crowds and situations could not be adequately controlled. Such events were cakewalks for gate-crashers. Water and sanitary facilities were insurmountable problems.

Promoters looked toward stadiums and racetrack facilities as the answer. Under normal conditions these enclosed arenas offered the most promising possibilities. Crowds could be kept under control, and most gate-crashers would be frustrated in their attempts. The only problem was the lodging of festival-goers. Where would a couple of hundred thousand young people sleep for two or three days? There was only one answer: They didn't. Overnight camping would not be necessary if the festival lasted only one day. One action-packed, dawn-to-dawn, full day of music presented in a quasi-festive atmosphere. Even though promoters were well aware that thousands would show up days ahead of time, the concept sounded good to the police, town officials, and most others who might resent a rock festival in their town or county. The idea had possibilities.

The first large-scale, successful, single-day rock festival was held in Long Pond, Pennsylvania, on Saturday, July 8, 1972. The Mount Pocono Festival, as it came to be called, occurred at the Pocono International Raceway and featured many of the factors that would later transform the Watkins Glen Summer Jam and Cal Jam I and II into such notable ventures.

The Pocono festival was organized and produced by a three-month-old organization called Concert 10. Realizing that a one-day rock festival was both new in design and potentially quite profitable, the promoters thoroughly researched the scheme and pulled it off with a box-office gross of some $1.4 million. So effective were their advertising and planning that they managed to sell 90,000 tickets in advance at $11 per person and an additional 35,000 at the gate on the day of the show.

Concert 10 proved to the Long Pond community (population 247), Pennsylvania, state authorities and performers alike that their intent was indeed serious. Two hundred and fifty thousand dollars were put into escrow accounts, guaranteeing that musicians would be paid in full and damages, clean-up fees, and other bills would not be disregarded. It was something that was not often done in the rock festival production business, and it went over well with all concerned.

The festival site was just over ninety miles west of the heart of New York City, from where most of the ticket holders would ultimately depart. New Jersey's Route 80 linked the site with the Big Apple.

The festival lineup was made up of fourteen acts, three of which were headliners—Emerson, Lake and Palmer; Three Dog Night; and Rod Stewart and the Faces. The remainder of the billing comprised a far less impressive lot, which only pointed to the fact that the "scene" was now indisputably foremost in the minds of young festivalgoers. The music and the bands that performed placed a distant second. Sign a few big acts, and one could get away with lesser name and lesser quality performers. The financial savings for promoters were substantial.

Of the fourteen acts, two did not show: Black Sabbath and Badfinger. Mother Night, a soul band with a shorter-than-short life span considering the success of the group at the festival; Claire Hamil, an English folksinger; the Groundhogs; Ramatam; Bull Angus; Cactus, which was fast becoming a regular and favorite with festival crowds; Edgar Winter; the J. Geils Band; and Humble Pie rounded out the day.

The promoters expected anywhere between 100,000 and 125,000 people to attend the festival, judging from advance ticket sales. But after the Pennsylvania state police estimated that close to 30,000 people were already in the vicinity of the racetrack by Friday evening, the official attendance predictions were enlarged. In all, close to 200,000 people made it to the festival. More than 50,000 gate-crashed. Regardless of what promoters told the press and law officials, it was virtually impossible to effectively control the gates and fences.

By early Saturday morning state policemen had begun setting up roadblocks that forced festivalgoers to abandon their cars and vans as far as five miles away. The only way to reach the racetrack was to walk. The music began a little after one P.M., as advertised. Mother Night opened the festival with an energetic blend of soul and boogie, and was followed by the softened sounds of Claire Hamil. Next came the Groundhogs, followed by the rain. For those hoping for a real festival atmosphere at Long Pond, the rain and ensuing mud gave the event a degree of authenticity. A large proportion of the crowd was of high-school age; they had heard about mud and rain being integral elements of rock festivals and thus reacted to it accordingly. More seasoned festivalgoers looked upon the weather conditions with chagrin.

The rainstorm lasted throughout the afternoon and destroyed the scheduling of performers. At three-day festivals timing was not that crucial. Sometime during the weekend minutes could be shaved or time made up. But at a single-day festival, this was not the case. The music at the Pocono festival was to have stopped at 11 P.M. It didn't come to an end until 8:45 A.M. the following morning. After the rain came a dense blanket of fog, which blurred the vision of many in the wet crowd. A steady stream of people walked back to their cars after it became apparent that the fog would last throughout the evening. By the time Three Dog Night, the final act, took the stage, perhaps fifteen thousand people remained at the raceway.

Musically speaking, the Pocono festival was without any really lasting climactic moments or highlights. And things weren't much better offstage. One day simply wasn't enough time to nurture the festival spirit. There was no time for an aura to grow into a personable, collective bond between members of the crowd and those who performed on the stage. It was hurry, hurry, get one group on, the other one off. Do some drugs fast; got to get high 'cause I'm at a festival. Got to come down, 'cause I'm on my way home. That was all fine, however, with the newer generation of festivalgoers. They had never seen it done better. For them the single-day festival was a chance to live the stories heard from older friends and brothers and sisters. It was "right on" as far as they were concerned.

The largest crowd that ever gathered for a rock festival did so at Watkins Glen, New York, in July of 1973. Outdrawing the previous high at Woodstock almost two to one, more than 600,000 young people sardined themselves into the Watkins Glen Grand Prix Raceway for a single-day festival known as the Summer Jam. Featured groups were the Grateful Dead, the Allman Brothers, and the Band.

Many historians claimed that the Watkins Glen event was the largest gathering of people in the history of the United States. In essence, that meant that on July 28, one out of every 350 people living in America at the time was listening to the sounds of rock at the New York state racetrack. Considering that most of those who attended the event hailed from the Northeast, and that the average age of those present was approximately seventeen to twenty-four, close to one out of every three young people from Boston to New York was at the festival.

And yet, aside from the stupendous attendance figures, the musical and social significance of the event was minimal compared to, say, Woodstock or even Altamont. Watkins Glen is more important for what it *wasn't*.

It was not a history-making event, in a strict musical sense. Unlike Woodstock, where the lineup consisted of close to thirty acts, Watkins Glen's billing was comprised of only three supergroups. The Allman Brothers, the Band, and the Grateful Dead were established acts (the latter two were Woodstock veterans); all had been on the touring circuit and in the

600,000 at Watkins Glen listen to the Grateful Dead. The turnout was

the largest ever for a rock festival.

recording studios for at least three years. The groups' fans, perhaps the most dedicated around in 1973, had most likely seen them perform live at least once or twice prior to Watkins Glen. They had come to expect certain things from the musicians. In short, there was no overly excited rush to the stage generated by their mere presence at Watkins Glen.

Each of the three groups at Watkins Glen played unusually long sets. The Grateful Dead performed for five hours, the Allman Brothers for four, and the Band for three, including a thirty-minute break due to a thunderstorm. Woodstock had had a continuous change of musical formats and styles. Each time a new act stepped out in front of the massie crowd, a revitalization occurred, creating a renewal of faith in the event and in the power of the music. Energy was forced to flow.

At Watkins Glen a feeling of monotony and tedium constantly challenged the viewers' interest in the music and the proceedings onstage. Long, winding solos were frequent. The heat, the lack of comfort, and the crowded conditions dulled otherwise stirring moments. Many of the 600,000 could barely see the stage, let alone the musicians. And most important, festivalgoers had only one day to soak up the rock-festival aura. Many in attendance were often too busy doing and seeing other things to bother to listen seriously to the music for extended periods of time.

Woodstock also had had two sets of lps and a movie to carry on its significance. No such enduring properties came out of Watkins Glen. Although the Grateful Dead and the Allman Brothers Band had their own sound people record their sets, the Dead would not give their consent to a Watkins Glen album. Their participation was crucial, since they represented over one third of the music and time performed onstage. CBS shot some footage of the event, but the Dead refused to allow it or any other film to be released commercially. Their unyielding position on the matter stemmed all the way back to Monterey, when the band had refused to participate in D. A. Pennebaker's film of the event, *Monterey Pop*. The Dead had always demanded full editorial control of their music and live performances. Whenever they were denied such power, they simply declined to be part of the project.

Watkins Glen did not register with the political portion of the youth culture as had some festivals in the past. To have 600,000 young people at one time in one place would have been the ultimate dream for any sixties radical. But that was just it—the sixties were over. The Vietnam War was over; the peace agreement had been signed in January of that year. Not that there was a lack of issues. Watkins Glen could easily have been an immensely powerful response to Nixon and the Watergate scandal. But the youth of the nation had grown tired of being politically active. Many had tasted the partial delight of seeing some peace in Southeast Asia and felt it was enough. The word most commonly associated with the Watkins Glen festival, according to those reporters who covered the event, was "party." For some young people there Watkins Glen merely represented a summertime retreat from the city that just happened to include the sounds of rock music. For the neophytes, however, Watkins Glen was an opportunity to experience a rock festival in abbreviated fashion, and they relished every minute of it.

All this added up to the fact that the protests, the placards, the defiance, and the true revolutionary zeal of the young had actually subsided. Enter the "me" decade. The 1970s had finally arrived.

But Watkins Glen did point out that rock music was alive and well, and that there still remained within the youth culture a seemingly unquenchable desire to attend rock festivals. Young people still marveled at the power of such gatherings. Young people *wanted* to be there, had to be there.

Shelly Finkel and Jim Koplik, the two promoters of Summer Jam, had been producing rock concerts in Connecticut and had established a regular audience. In 1972 they staged a series of shows in Hartford, one of which was a Grateful Dead concert. During their performance members of the Allman Brothers Band who were backstage were invited to come out for an informal jam. The reception they received from the Deadhead-dominated crowd was lavish and striking.

Finkel and Koplik loved what they saw and heard. The promoters talked with members of the Dead and the Allman Brothers to see if they were interested in a large outdoor concert that would feature the two bands performing separately and then, at the conclusion, merging for one spectacular, memorable jam. The promoters added that the profits could be astronomical for all involved if a large enough concert site was chosen. Both bands were very interested.

Finkel and Koplik searched high and low for an appropriate site. The Pocono International Raceway was considered, but when the promoters heard of the availability of the Watkins

Glen Grand Prix Raceway, they immediately made plans to talk with raceway officials there. Both the town of Watkins Glen and the racetrack management were accustomed to handling large crowds, and since the event was to be a one-day affair, few obstacles prevented a contract from being signed. Finkel and Koplik promised to limit ticket sales to 150,000. Privately, raceway officials doubted whether the rock promoters could sell even 100,000 tickets. But more power to them. They had certainly paid a considerable sum to rent the facilities for the day.

In order to fill out the remainder of the billing, Koplik and Finkel suggested that another band or performer, perhaps Leon Russell, be added to the show. The Dead and the Allmans both agreed to the concept but felt that the Band would be more appropriate than Russell. Besides, they were local New York State boys from the Woodstock area and had a more concentrated Northeastern following than Leon Russell. The Band was approached with the idea and quickly signed a contract.

Two weeks prior to the festival more than 100,000 tickets at $10 each had been sold. The promoters secured permission to put on sale an additional 25,000 tickets the day of the show, since it was obvious that many more people than were originally anticipated would show up. Watkins Glen was to be the first huge rock music event in New York to be produced since the state passed the Mass Gathering Code following Woodstock. Koplik and Finkel adhered to the stringent rules in a precise,

A row of latrines at Watkins Glen one week before 600,000 people stood in line to use them.

Courtesy of Shelly Finkel

almost religious manner. More than one thousand portable toilets were rented and twelve wells were dug to increase the racetrack's water supplies, in addition to strategically locating more than a thousand gallon jugs of mountain spring water throughout the grounds. The promoters even ordered 300,000 premoistened paper towelettes, although no one could figure out what real value they would have at a rock festival. A makeshift heliport was also built.

Henry Valent, president of the Watkins Glen Grand Prix Corporation, was impressed. Jim Koplik and Shelly Finkel seemed to be real professionals. Watkins Glen would not be like those other rock festivals he had read about. It would be different, he thought. It would be a first-class operation.

People began arriving a full week before the festival. Many thumbed their way in or drove campers or vans up early to select an ideal camping location. On the Tuesday before the show, the first of thirty ticket gates had opened. Rather than have the young people mill about the town, the promoters and Valent agreed to open up a bit early. But there was cause for consternation. Summer Jam, as it was called, was supposed to be a one-day affair. Sure, promoters and track officials had realized that many would show up early. That's why they had prepared sizeable campgrounds. But not *this* early. And not this many.

The crowd grew. On Wednesday the New York State police

Promoters Shelly Finkel and Jim Koplik made sure no one went thirsty at Watkins Glen.

Courtesy of Shelly Finkel

estimated that fifty thousand people were at Watkins Glen. On Thursday the approximation more than doubled. By Friday afternoon they were certain that a full quarter of a million kids had made camp in or near the festival grounds. The troopers recalled Woodstock and the nightmarish traffic problems. This was worse. Cars sitting in traffic stretched back almost fifty miles, while the impact of it all could be felt one hundred miles away. They began turning back young people with or without tickets. There was no doubt about it. Summer Jam was going to be bigger than Woodstock. Much bigger.

A sound check was scheduled for Friday. Bill Graham's FM Productions had been contracted to employ the Digital Audio Delay Line system, a computerized sound system designed so that people sitting up front and near the towers of speakers would not be blasted into the universe. It also enabled people sitting way in the back to hear the music just as clearly as those closer to the stage. With such a system, sets of speakers are set up a hundred yards apart. The first set of speakers receives the sound from the stage and relays it back to the second set. This set rebounds the sound to the third set. All this occurs with split-second precision. It is not discernible to the human ear that there is a microlapse in the sound. For both the sound check and the actual concert, the system worked like a charm.

When the Grateful Dead went to do their sound check, more than 100,000 of the 250,000 people present at Watkins Glen were already assembled in front of the stage. Graham suggested what the hell, might as well start the concert early. The Dead consented, and the sound check turned into a two-hour set with a few interruptions to balance out the wall of sound. The Band and the Allman Brothers felt compelled to do likewise. They delivered one-hour and two-hour sets, respectively. In all, a five-hour prefestival performance disguised as a sound check.

After it was over Jim Koplik sat himself in a chair in the backstage trailer and remarked to Finkel, "I'm beat. I feel like everything is over and we actually pulled this off."

Finkel nodded and broke a tired smile.

"I can't believe, though, that wasn't the real thing. Tomorrow is the real thing. Tomorrow is the concert. We have to do it all over again, for at least twice as long and probably for twice as many people."

Koplik glanced over at his partner. Shelly Finkel had fallen into a deep sleep.

The Grateful Dead returned shortly before noon on Saturday to officially open Summer Jam in front of 600,000 people stretched out over every available inch of raceway property. There was the usual threat of rain, but no dark clouds were in sight. Instead the sun shone brightly as the heat grew to noticeable but still tolerable proportions. Stretched out across the ninety-acre grassy knoll that faced the stage was a youthful, exuberant sea of humanity. It was an awesome, emotional sight. And it was scary. What if . . . But negative thoughts were set aside.

The Grateful Dead played and played and played. For five hours Jerry Garcia smoothly rolled out solos like only Jerry Garcia could do. Bob Weir backed him up on rhythm guitar, filling in and closing up weak areas and balancing out a generally tender sound. Phil Lesh on bass and Bill Kreutzman on drums provided Garcia with takeoff and landing strips. Donna Godchaux sang, and her husband, Keith, added bits and pieces on the keyboards. "Uncle John's Band," "Casey Jones," "Friend of the Devil," "Ripple," "Sugar Magnolia," "Truckin'," "Not Fade Away," "Me and Bobby McGee." They kept comin'.

It took little over an hour for the stage crew to disassemble the Dead's equipment and ready the area for the Band's set. Out in the crowd things were good considering the multitude of people. There was a marked decrease in the use of hard drugs and hallucinogens at Watkins Glen, although there were plenty of dealers on hand and pot was everywhere. The ground was littered with empty bottles of Jack Daniel's and Southern Comfort, signs of the large increase in the consumption of hard liquor.

There was an abundance of food and water available, and most of the portable toilets seemed to be functioning, but the lines to use the facilities and the trek getting there were the real problems. A round trip to and from a Port-O-San, including a very brief stay inside it, could take more than three hours. For the sluggish or the stoned, it was like five.

The sun had been overtaken by a series of ominous, dark stormclouds by the time the Band began to crank it up. Not quite an hour into their set, the rain, thunder, and lightning all struck with alarming might. The Band was forced from the stage to wait it out. Thirty minutes later the storm passed, leaving behind 600,000 wet bodies and—what else—mud. Prior to the storm, however, four skydivers had jumped from a circling Cessna, intending to land somewhere on the festival grounds. All of them carried colorful flares to mark both the success of the event and their downward path. The crowd cheered them on as they gradually assumed a shape in the sky. But something had gone wrong up there for one of the chutists. Seconds into his freefall, one of the skydivers' flares prematurely exploded and ignited his garments. Helplessly falling downward, the diver managed to open his chute as the flames engulfed his suit and his body. It was a terrible way to die.

The Band's set lost much of its impact after the storm's interruption. Many people returned to the campsites to cook up some supper and put on dry clothes. Others began the journey back home. But the Band played on—free-flowing, countrified rock with traditional foundations. The instrumentation was defined and exact; the delivery, sharp and authoritative. The Band represented the antithesis of slickness in the summer of '73. None of their music was souped up or hammered out via

One festivalgoer at Watkins Glen climbed a utility pole to get a better view.

Tom Whalley

record-company formulas. Robbie Robertson, Garth Hudson, Levon Helm, Rick Danko, and Richard Manuel offered to rock what the poppish, syrupy bands could not: unadulterated, un-patterned, unmistakable music.

Finally it was the Allman Brothers' turn. The Brothers had the reputation of rarely putting on a less-than-dazzling per-formance. The high-quality compositions and the arousing artistic competency of the band resisted mediocre displays. Dickie Betts had fully assumed the role left vacant by Duane Allman's death. It was a big order to fill, but Betts was just coming into his own. He was confident and, most important, aggressive. He and Gregg Allman were the stars and the leaders that dictated the group's direction. In terms of comparison, neither the Dead nor the Band measured up to the overall ebullience of the Allmans. With the song "In Memory of Elizabeth Reed," it all came together nicely.

It was two o'clock in the morning. The crowd had shrunk considerably, but, as promised, the event would conclude with an all-out jam. Not all the members of the Dead and the Band came out, and realistically, there were too many tired musicians for anything truly memorable to result. More solos. Some basic blues. The last song was a spirited if not overly effective version of Chuck Berry's "Johnny B. Goode."

Watkins Glen had stolen the headlines much the same way that Woodstock had four years before, but with much less intensity and drama and for a much shorter period of time. In the *New York Times* Grace Lichtenstein described the Watkins Glen event as she had seen it:

> . . . At times the scene in the moist darkness resembled a Bosch painting—half naked bodies coated with brown slime, moving rhythmically to the music amid huddled figures curled sleeping in the mud at their feet in barbitu-rate or alcohol induced stupors.[1]

The overall success and incredible turnout at Watkins Glen prompted other rock promoters to think seriously about staging single-day rock festivals. Rock-concert production was steadily growing more sophisticated and professional, and many of the new concepts employed in them were carried over into festival production. This was ultimately accomplished at the expense of the rich, unconstrained, natural improvisations that had made past festivals exciting for the festivalgoers and the media and precariously unstable for the promoters, the local towns-folk, and the police. By 1974 the evolution of the rock festival had finally caught up with the technological, impersonal mid-1970s.

Out in California a former rock manager, Lenny Stogel, went to ABC television after hearing about Watkins Glen with plans for a similar event on the West Coast. He asked the network if they would be interested in financing and filming a single-day rock festival produced at the Ontario Motor Speedway in southern California. Stogel told ABC officials that he intended to bring in eight or nine topnotch recording acts for a twelve-hour concert. He had figured out, he told them, the ways to make it run smoothly, without the problems encountered at Watkins Glen or any of the other festivals.

ABC listened and liked what they heard. They put Sandy Feldman, vice-president in charge of live events, on the job. Together, he and Stogel were to complete plans for what would later be called Cal Jam.

Even though two previous rock concerts held at the Ontario Motor Speedway had been near financial disasters, Stogel felt certain that it was the ideal place for Cal Jam. Its accessibility was perfect; two highways bordered the speedway—the San Bernadino and the Pomona major roads. It was also located within driving range of Los Angeles, San Diego, and all of Orange County. Southern California ranked with the New York metropolitan area as possessing the most voracious rock appe-tite in all of America. Ontario had parking for fifty thousand cars and was far enough away from any immediate population centers so that traffic would not be catastrophic. Ontario was the place.

At first Stogel and Feldman hoped to lure either Led Zeppelin, the Band, or the Rolling Stones into signing contracts, but this never materialized due to the awesome fees of the supergroups. The promoters next went to proven stars such as Emerson, Lake and Palmer; Black Sabbath; and Deep Purple to headline the show, backed up by Black Oak Arkansas; Seals and Crofts; Rare Earth; the Eagles; and Earth, Wind and Fire. Admittedly the lineup was not spectacular, but the promoters counted more on the "event" rather than the groups to attract a big crowd to Ontario. Many people out on the West Coast had not partici-pated in Watkins Glen. Cal Jam would be their chance.

In order to prevent the problems that had dominated rock festivals in the past, Stogel felt that the audience must be totally captivated for the entire twelve hours of the show. Once the kids grew restless, the event was in trouble. Keep them busy, keep them seated, make them feel they would miss something important and interesting if they didn't pay attention. That, according to Stogel, was the key to success.

The promoters hired Imero Fiorentino to design the stage, which he conceived as a complex structure of hydraulic lifts and movable platforms built on railroad tracks. This way, as one band on one platform finished its set, another act on another platform was ready and waiting to be slid into the spotlight. A maximum lapse of fifteen minutes was all that was to be tolerated. Due to the excessive amount of equipment used by Emerson, Lake and Palmer, a separate platform was constructed for the English trio. Throughout the day skydivers, stunt men, skateboarders, and other entertainers would keep the audience occupied.

Cal Jam occurred on Saturday, April 6, 1974, and drew 200,000 fans paying $10 a ticket. The gross of $2 million was one of the largest in the history of rock. ABC filmed it and televised the concert on their "In Concert" series. It had all gone so smoothly. Rare Earth, the opening act, took the stage fifteen minutes *ahead* of schedule. The crowd was orderly. There were very few drug problems and almost no gate-crashers.

California Jam II, 1978.

Jana Howard

They expected 200,000 to attend and that's exactly the number of people that showed up. So structured, so systemized, so calculated.

There were mixed reactions to Cal Jam. Most marveled at the precision and organization. The event was the epitome of efficiency. The media dubbed it a computerized rock festival. Others, however, looked upon it with disappointment. There was no room for creativity or a do-your-own-thing attitude. The musicians were forced to perform in a machinelike fashion. No excitement; too predictable. Boring.

During an interview in June of 1979, just a few weeks before his death in Chicago in a DC-10 plane crash, Lenny Stogel recalled Cal Jam.

"When I knew I was putting on a show for 200,000 young people, I didn't want anything popping off unexpected. I wanted to be in total control and know exactly what was happening that moment and what would be happening in the next few hours. Two hundred thousand kids was a big responsibility. I used to get a funny feeling in my stomach whenever I thought about it. I had to be in control—for the preservation of my sanity."

The financial achievements of Cal Jam necessitated a sequel to the event; thus another Cal Jam was held in March of 1978. It was basically a repeat of the original formula: efficiency plus organization equals success and big bucks. Instead of 200,000, Cal Jam II attracted 250,000. It was held at the same location and produced by the same promoters. It was filmed for television, and this time an album also resulted from the concert.

The lineup was once again less than outstanding. Actually the billing reflected the stagnation that had gripped rock, especially mainstream rock, at the time. It also revealed that the younger portion of the vast rock audience was not really bothered by the situation. Only Santana, Dave Mason, and, to a lesser extent, Heart, played music reminiscent in style to the old festival sets. Most of the other bands uncorked a numbing, combustible orgy of manic power that bullied its way through the speakers. Hard rock was being abused; it was being exploited for its colorful audacity more than anything else. Aerosmith and Ted Nugent blitzed the crowd with frenzied and furious energy. Mahogany Rush and Rubicon tried to follow suit but failed. Bob Welch had members from Fleetwood Mac come to his aid.

The festival spirit was only superficially present at Cal Jam

Jana Howard

The van used by Heart to transport the group to and from the Cal Jam festival area.

II. Some members of the crowd clutched to remaining threads of the past, while a few of the performers tried to simulate an emotion vaguely remembered by the older members of the crowd. Rock had become big business, and like Cal Jam were, to many, just big-business ventures.

The performers had their choice of either being helicoptered from the Beverly Hills Hotel to the festival grounds or chauffeured there in lavish, customized vans with paintings of the band's latest album cover on the exterior panels. Backstage requests were ludicrous in many cases. Some performers wanted pinball machines for their amusement. Others required specially prepared dishes. One band wanted plates of M&Ms placed in their dressing rooms, but no yellow ones were to be included. As a result, a Cal Jam employee had to sift through the mounds of candy, separating the yellows from the rest.[2]

Cal Jam I and II were hybrid forms of the old rock festival phenomenon. Cal Jam's promoters sought to present a festival atmosphere in a highly regulated and supervised environment. Eight or nine years back a rock festival would have smothered under such conditions, but for the late seventies it was the right way to handle such events. It was easy to determine the differences that existed between an outdoor rock concert and an outdoor rock festival. It was also easy to comprehend that in terms of rock music and rock events, 1968 and 1978 were really and truly a full decade apart.

CHAPTER TEN

A Long Way From Monterey

Rock festivals are dead—aren't they?

—the question most often
   asked of the author

The term "rock festival" has been battered and abused, its definition stretched and exaggerated, and its media connotation certainly exploited. Some promoters, eager to capitalize on the term's tight relationship with the youthful masses, have labeled as festivals ordinary rock concerts staged in ordinary outdoor rock arenas. Others have insisted that their five-hour, four-group indoor concert was also a festival of sorts. At a concert featuring Richie Havens and the now-defunct Ten Wheel Drive at an ice-skating rink in southern New Jersey, a local disc jockey who

Ten years after. Site of the Woodstock festival,
August 15, 1979.
Robert Santelli

assumed, for the evening, the role of emcee, kept calling the show a mini-Woodstock even though fewer than two hundred people were in the audience. The only thing that resembled Woodstock that night was the driving rain that hammered and finally leaked through the building's roof.

Today rock festivals exist only in the form of memories. Some people enjoy nostalgic recollections of the festivals they attended. Others possess sour ones. Bad drugs account for a number of the latter. Let's face it, rock festivals perished along with other by-products of the sixties in the maturing process of the Woodstock generation. The festival idea is permanently tucked away somewhere in a rock 'n' roll graveyard. Perhaps it's located in New York State or down the highway a bit from San Francisco.

Is a resurrection possible? Not really. Any rock festival scheme of substantial size would undoubtedly lose the battle with the various political, social, and economic forces of the day. Promoters would need a surplus of funds to enter the inevitable legal fray. They would need to be adamant in their conviction so as to endure the seemingly endless array of reactionary roadblocks set up by the general public. Promoters John Morris and Michael Wadleigh can attest to that in regard to their plans for a second Woodstock, or, as they later called it, The Second Gathering.

The two, both veterans of the original Woodstock (Morris was one of the stage managers and Wadleigh filmed the event), announced in April 1979 their plans to celebrate the tenth anniversary of the event with another festival. Morris and Wadleigh sought to rent land in New York State as near to the original site as possible and stage the fest on August 15 to 17, the exact dates of the anniversary. They told the press that thirty groups would play the festival: ten acts from the original Woodstock, ten supergroups of the late seventies, and ten bands not yet internationally famous but with bright futures predicted for the 1980s.

They never pulled it off. The reason: no festival site. Morris combed the state for a town or village interested in having perhaps a million kids as weekend guests. There were no takers and, consequently, no festival. Morris had to settle for a grossly disappointing reunion concert on Long Island in early September that attracted eighteen thousand people, many of whom went home before the music ended.

The next question is whether a resurrection of the rock festival idea is truly desirable. A few big-time promoters, some members of the media, maybe Warner Communications executives, and a smattering of performers might nod their heads in enthusiasm. But the interest stops there. These days few rock people seem interested in sardining themselves on a hill with a half million other souls. Times have changed.

Then there's the ecological repercussions of rock festivals. The vision of a green, pastoral setting with rock as background music is deceptive. As David Wolman wrote in an article that appeared in *The Village Voice* during the Woodstock II proclamation, "Despite the good will and the ecological conservatism embodied in the lyrics of Woodstock, the event did cause hardship to a small town and damage to its land. Farm ponds were left with glass and debris on their bottoms. Cows got hardware disease from eating cans. . . ."

A viable alternative to the traditional rock festival is the urban fest—a series of concerts that run through the day and/or evening on successive days in large stadiums, arenas, or parks. At such events camping is prohibited, gate-crashing is minimized, a fair view of the stage area is usually possible due to the limited number in attendance, and yet some semblance of a festive feeling is preserved. The jazz and folk idioms have, in many cases, been successful with this sort of thing for quite some time.

Aside from the legislative barriers that precluded a continued proliferation of rock fests, the "me" decade (the post-Watergate seventies) spawned a collection of rock groups and performers who simply advanced a counterfestival mood with their music and stage antics. A metamorphosis had indeed taken place; rock began to symbolize the decadence and technological domination of society in more frightening ways than ever before. A musical style was created that was highly dissimilar to the format and philosophy of rock when festivals were in their heyday. The second half of the 1970s witnessed the increased popularity of groups that featured acts of violence onstage (the Sex Pistols and other punk-rock bands) and a generally self-oriented, self-centered lyrical expression. A necessity for some groups to incorporate visual and often elaborate theatrics into their performance quickly evolved. There existed a subtle need for the rock genre to reconfirm its importance as a creative musical force. Many felt that rock had strayed too far from its roots and original intentions.

New wave and punk rock began showering a strong influence on mainstream rock. Such artists as Elvis Costello, Graham Parker, the Sex Pistols, Patti Smith, and others demanded intimacy with their audiences in order to be truly effective. The indoor auditorium or club setting was the environment most apt to stir up an emotional reaction to their music. Even such superstars of the late seventies as Bruce Springsteen have repeatedly eschewed outdoor settings for concerts. Springsteen and others like him have pointed to the poor sound, strained visibility, and plethora of minidisturbances that frequently go hand in hand with outdoor performances. Precise lighting and direct communication with the audience are mandatory for many of the genre's top acts today. These are difficult to achieve outdoors.

It is difficult to deny the mark that rock festivals made on contemporary music and cultural history. But along with this, the rock fest also mirrored the darkened innocence and shattered spirit of a generation. The Woodstock generation.

Appendix: Festival Factsheet

Human Be-In

Date: January 14, 1967.
Site: Golden Gate Park, San Francisco, California
Attendance: 20,000
Performers: Grateful Dead, Jefferson Airplane, Quicksilver Messenger Service, Dizzy Gillespie, Allen Ginsburg, other lesser known local bands, and spur-of-the-moment performers.

Although this was not a festival in the true sense of the term, the origin of rock festivals is directly linked to this event.

Fantasy Faire and Magic Mountain Music Festival

Date: June 10, 11; 1967.
Place: Mount Tamalpais, California

Attendance: 15,000

Performers: Jefferson Airplane, Country Joe and the Fish, Doors, Byrds, Dionne Warwick, Smokey Robinson and the Miracles, other local acts.

The first actual rock festival. Nonprofit in nature (admission $2), the proceeds went to charity groups.

Monterey International Pop Festival

Date: June 16, 17, 18; 1967.
Place: Monterey, California
Attendance: 50,000
Performers: The Association, Paupers, Johnny Rivers, Animals, Simon and Garfunkel, Big Brother and the Holding Company, Electric Flag, Paul Butterfield Blues Band, Blues Project, Canned Heat, Country Joe and the Fish, Hugh Masekela, Steve Miller Band, Al Kooper, Quicksilver Messenger Service, Buffalo Springfield, Jimi Hendrix Experience, The Who, Grateful Dead, Mamas and Papas, Otis Redding, Moby Grape, Laura Nyro, Jefferson Airplane, Byrds, Booker T. and the MGs, and Ravi Shankar.

Aside from Woodstock, this was the greatest rock festival in history. Monterey's success set off festival fever in the late sixties.

Newport (California) Pop Festival

Date: August 4, 5; 1968.
Place: Costa Mesa, California
Attendance: 100,000
Performers: Sonny and Cher, Steppenwolf, Chambers Brothers, Tiny Tim, James Cotton Blues Band, Canned Heat, Country Joe and the Fish, Electric Flag, Paul Butterfield Blues Band, Jefferson Airplane, Grateful Dead, Iron Butterfly, Blue Cheer, Eric Burdon and the Animals, Byrds, Quicksilver Messenger Service, Illinois Speed Press, other local acts.

Newport unveiled the problems that rock festival promoters would ultimately face in the future.

The Sky River Rock Festival and Lighter Than Air Fair

Date: August 31–September 2, 1968.
Place: Sultan, Washington
Attendance: 15,000
Performers: Country Joe and the Fish, Grateful Dead, It's A Beautiful Day, Santana, Muddy Waters, James Cotton Blues Band, Big Mama Willie Mae Thornton, Ramblin' Jack Elliott, New Lost City Ramblers, Dino Valenti, Youngbloods, Mark Spoelstra, plus many local acts.

Sky River is considered an important festival due to its non-profit nature. It was also one of the few festivals to occur two years in a row.

The Miami Pop Festival

Date: December 28, 29, 30; 1968.
Place: Hallandale, Florida
Attendance: 100,000
Performers: José Feliciano, Terry Reid, Procol Harum, Buffy Saint-Marie, Country Joe and the Fish, Three Dog Night, Chuck Berry, McCoys, Booker T. and the MGs, Fleetwood Mac, Pacific Gas and Electric Company, Steppenwolf, Marvin Gaye, Grateful Dead, Hugh Masekela, Lester Flatt and Earl Scruggs, Paul Butterfield Blues Band, Joni Mitchell, James Cotton Blues Band, Richie Havens, Box Tops, Iron Butterfly, Turtles, Canned Heat, Grass Roots, Junior Walker and the All-Stars, Sweetwater, Joe Tex, Ian and Sylvia, and the Charles Lloyd Quartet.

The first successful large scale rock festival to be held on the East Coast.

Newport '69

Date: June 20, 21, 22; 1969.
Place: Devonshire Downs; Northridge, California
Attendance: 150,000
Performers: Jimi Hendrix, Joe Cocker, Spirit, Taj Mahal, Ike and Tina Turner, Creedence Clearwater Revival, Steppenwolf, Buffy Sainte-Marie, Eric Burdon, Jethro Tull,

Young Rascals, Chambers Brothers, Booker T. and the MGs, Johnny Winter, Byrds, and other local bands.

Newport '69 marked the first incidence of large-scale violence at a rock festival. It was also the first large festival of the summer of 1969—the golden year of rock festivals.

Denver Pop Festival

Date: June 27, 28; 1969.
Place: Mile High Stadium; Denver, Colorado
Attendance: 50,000
Performers: Big Mama Willie Mae Thornton, Flock, Frank Zappa and the Mothers of Invention, Joe Cocker, Zephyr, Rev. Cleophus Robinson, Aorta, Aum, Jimi Hendrix, Poco, Tim Buckley, Johnny Winter, Creedence Clearwater Revival, Three Dog Night, Sweetwater, Taj Mahal, and Iron Butterfly.

Mace, billy clubs and tear gas. Need I say more?

Newport Jazz Festival

Date: July 3–6, 1969.
Place: Newport, Rhode Island
Attendance: 78,000
Rock Performers: Jeff Beck, Blood, Sweat and Tears, Jethro Tull, Ten Years After, Sly and the Family Stone, Led Zeppelin, and James Brown.

For the first time rock groups appeared at the traditional jazz festival. It was also the last time.

Atlanta Pop Festival

Date: July 4, 5; 1969
Place: Atlanta International Speedway; Atlanta, Georgia
Attendance: 140,000
Performers: Pacific Gas and Electric Company, Delaney and Bonnie and Friends, Sweetwater, Ten Wheel Drive, Creedence Clearwater Revival, Canned Heat, Johnny

Rivers, Ian and Sylvia, Johnny Winter, Booker T. and the MGs, Paul Butterfield Blues Band, Dave Brubeck, Al Kooper, Blood, Sweat and Tears, Janis Joplin, Led Zeppelin, Spirit, Joe Cocker, Chicago Transit Authority, Tommy James and the Shondells, and the Staple Singers.

The deep South stepped into the festival age with good music and, surprisingly, good vibes.

Seattle Pop Festival

Date: July 25–27, 1969.
Place: Woodenville, Washington
Attendance: 70,000
Performers: Chuck Berry, Doors, Bo Diddley, Vanilla Fudge, Youngbloods, Spirit, Led Zeppelin, Byrds, Ike and Tina Turner, Ten Years After, Chicago Transit Authority, and lesser known and local bands.

Unlike the Sky River festivals, the Seattle Pop was a commercial venture, and a successful one at that.

Atlantic City Pop Festival

Date: August 1–3, 1969.
Place: Atlantic City, New Jersey
Attendance: 110,000
Performers: Tim Buckley, Jefferson Airplane, Creedence Clearwater Revival, Paul Butterfield Blues Band, B.B. King, Hugh Masekela, Booker T. and the MGs, Lighthouse, Byrds, American Dream, Biff Rose, Joni Mitchell, Chambers Brothers, Procol Harum, Iron Butterfly, Johnny Winter, Mother Earth, Dr. John the Night Tripper, Chicago Transit Authority, Crazy World of Arthur Brown, Buddy Rich, Janis Joplin, Little Richard, Sir Douglas Quintet, Santana, Joe Cocker, Three Dog Night, Buddy Miles Express, and Canned Heat.

The first rock festival to occur in the New York-Philadelphia metropolitan area. Many who attended the Atlantic City festivals made the journey to Woodstock two weeks later.

Woodstock

Date: August 15–17, 1969.
Place: Bethel, New York
Attendance: 400,000
Performers: Jimi Hendrix, Blood, Sweat and Tears, Joan Baez, Creedence Clearwater Revival, The Band, Janis Joplin, Jefferson Airplane, Sly and the Family Stone, Canned Heat, The Who, Richie Havens, Arlo Guthrie, Crosby, Stills, Nash and Young, Ravi Shankar, Johnny Winter, Ten Years After, Country Joe and the Fish, Grateful Dead, Incredible String Band, Mountain, Tim Hardin, Joe Cocker, Sweetwater, John Sebastian, Melanie, Santana, Sha Na Na, Keef Hartley, Quill, Paul Butterfield Blues Band, and Bert Sommer.

When people think of rock festivals, they think of Woodstock— the legendary event, the apex of the rock festival era.

New Orleans Pop Festival

Date: August 31–September 1, 1969.
Place: Prairieville, Louisiana
Attendance: 25,000
Performers: Janis Joplin, Jefferson Airplane, Grateful Dead, Byrds, Country Joe and the Fish, Santana, Cat Mother and the All-Night Newsboys, T-Rex, It's A Beautiful Day, Chicago Transit Authority, Canned Heat, Youngbloods, Dr. John the Night Tripper, and The Who.

One of the smaller festivals to occur over the Labor Day Weekend. A bad festival for drug users.

Texas International Pop Festival

Date: August 30–September 1, 1969.
Place: Dallas International Motor Speedway; Lewisville, Texas
Attendance: 120,000
Performers: Canned Heat, Chicago Transit Authority, James Cotton Blues Band, Janis Joplin, Johnny Winter, B.B. King, Herbie Mann, Rotary Connection, Sam and Dave, Grand Funk Railroad, Led Zeppelin, Delaney and Bon-

nie and Friends, Incredible String Band, Santana, Nazz, Sly and the Family Stone, Spirit, Sweetwater, Ten Years After, Freddie King, Tony Joe White.

Johnny Winter and Janis Joplin's homecoming.

Second Annual Sky River Rock Festival

Date: August 30–September 1, 1969.
Place: Tenino, Washington
Attendance: 25,000
Performers: Steve Miller Band, Terry Reid, James Cotton Blues Band, Big Mama Willie Mae Thornton, Country Joe and the Fish, Quicksilver Messenger Service, and many local acts.

The New Orleans Pop, the Texas International Pop, and the second Sky River fest all contributed to perhaps the greatest rock festival weekend.

Altamont

Date: December 6, 1969
Place: Altamont Speedway; Livermore, California
Attendance: 300,000
Performers: Rolling Stones, Crosby, Stills, Nash and Young, Jefferson Airplane, Flying Burrito Brothers, and Santana.

What Woodstock was, Altamont wasn't. After Meredith Hunter had been stabbed and murdered a few feet from the stage, rock festivals began a downward slide.

Wild West

Date: Canceled
Place: Kezar Stadium; San Francisco, California
Scheduled performers: Grateful Dead, Janis Joplin, Quicksilver Messenger Service, Jefferson Airplane, Country Joe and the Fish, Santana, Sly and the Family Stone, Steve Miller Band, and many other lesser known San Francisco bands.

Political bickering killed plans for this ambitious event.

Powder Ridge Rock Festival

Date: July 30–August 1, 1970.
Place: Powder Ridge Ski Resort; Middlefield, Connecticut
Attendance: 30,000
Scheduled performers: Sly and the Family Stone, Led Zeppelin, Janis Joplin, Chuck Berry, and many others. Only folksinger Melanie performed, however.

There wasn't much music, but experienced festivalgoers rated this aborted fest number one in terms of drugs.

Celebration of Life

Date: June 21–28, 1971.
Place: McCrea, Louisiana
Attendance: 50,000
Scheduled performers: At least 27 rock acts were to perform. Only John Sebastian, Chuck Berry, War, Jimmy Witherspoon, Stoneground, Bloodrock, the Amboy Dukes, and a few other local groups actually played.

Celebration of Life—a black mark in rock-festival history.

Atlanta Pop Festival

Date: July 3–5, 1970
Place: Middle Georgia Raceway, Byron, Georgia
Attendance: 200,000
Performers: Jimi Hendrix, B.B. King, John Sebastian, Mountain, Procol Harum, Jethro Tull, Rare Earth, Chambers Brothers, Poco, Johnny Winter, Cat Mother and the All-Night Newsboys, Lee Michaels, Cactus, Allman Brothers, Savage Grace, Gypsy, and other lesser known bands.

Jimi Hendrix plays the "Star Spangled Banner" on July 4th for 200,000 people.

Randall's Island Rock Festival (New York Pop Concert)

Date: July 17–19, 1970.
Place: Downing Stadium; Randall's Island, New York
Attendance: 30,000
Performers: Little Richard, Elephant's Memory, Rhinoceros, Dr. John the Night Tripper, Mountain, Jimi Hendrix, Grand Funk Railroad, John Sebastian, Steppenwolf, Jethro Tull, Ten Years After, and Cactus.

Politics and greed turned this festival upside down.

Mar y Sol

Date: April 1–3, 1972.
Place: Vega Baja, Puerto Rico
Attendance: 30,000
Performers: Allman Brothers Band, John Baldry, Cactus, Dr. John the Night Tripper, Jonathan Edwards, Emerson, Lake and Palmer, J. Geils Band, B.B. King, John Mc-Laughlin and Mahavishnu Orchestra, Herbie Mann, Nitzinger, Osibisa, Dave Brubeck, Alice Cooper, Black Sabbath, Brownsville Station, Savoy Brown, Bloodrock, Elephant's Memory, and Rod Stewart.

The Allman Brothers' set made all the hassles getting to the festival site worth it.

Mount Pocono Festival

Date: July 8, 1972.
Place: Pocono International Speedway; Long Pond, Pennsylvania
Attendance: 200,000
Performers: Emerson, Lake and Palmer, Three Dog Night, Rod Stewart with the Faces, Mother Night, Claire Hamil, Groundhogs, Ramatam, Bull Angus, Cactus, Edgar Win-

ter, J. Geils Band, Humble Pie. (Badfinger and Black Sabbath were originally on the slate, but did not show.)

The first successful single-day festival.

Watkins Glen Summer Jam

Date: July 28, 1973.
Place: Watkins Glen Grand Prix Raceway; Watkins Glen, New York
Attendance: 600,000
Performers: Grateful Dead, Allman Brothers Band, The Band.

The largest gathering of rock fans ever—and for only three bands!

California Jam I

Date: April 6, 1974
Place: Ontario Motor Speedway; Ontario, California
Attendance: 200,000
Performers: Emerson, Lake and Palmer, Black Sabbath, Deep Purple, Black Oak Arkansas, Seals and Crofts, Rare Earth, Eagles, and Earth, Wind and Fire.

A hybrid form of the original rock festival concept, Volume One.

California Jam II

Date: March 18, 1978.
Place: Ontario Motor Speedway; Ontario, California
Attendance: 250,000
Performers: Santana, Dave Mason, Heart, Aerosmith, Ted Nugent, Mahogany Rush, Rubicon, and Bob Welch.

A hybrid form of the original festival concept, Volume Two.

Notes

Chapter 1

1. William J. Schaffer, *Rock Music* (Minneapolis, Minn.: Augsburg, 1972), pp. 54–56.
2. Ralph Gleason, "The Tribes Gather for a Yea Saying," *San Francisco Chronicle*, January 14, 1967, p. 53.

Chapter 2

1. Pete Johnson, "Something New—A Festival for Musicians," Los Angeles *Times*, June 4, 1967.
2. Robert Christgau, "Anatomy of a Love Festival," *Esquire*, January, 1968, p. 154.

Chapter 4

1. Pettyjohn, Marge, "Texas Fest Corrals Sales," *Billboard*, September 27, 1969.
2. Editorial, Atlanta *Journal*, July 3, 1969, p. 22.
3. Philadelphia *Enquirer*, "Mass Drug Orgy Charged at 3 Day Rock Festival," August 5, 1969, p. 21.

Chapter 5

1. Editorial, *New York Times*, August 19, 1969, p. 46.
2. *Variety*, "Woodstock Talent Payroll," September 17, 1969, p. 45.

Chapter 6

1. From the song "The New Speedway Boogie," lyrics by Robert Hunter.

Chapter 7

1. "NY State Law Fences in Pop Fests With Long List of Stiff Regulations," *Variety*, June 24, 1970, p. 63.
2. Bill Graham's letter ran in *Variety* and *Billboard* magazines in August 1970.
3. "Any Day Now! (Festival News from the Wild West)," July 18, 1969, p. 1.

Chapter 8

1. Gene Stephens, "Patrol, GBI to Combat Drugs at Pop Festival," Atlanta *Constitution*, July 1, 1970, p. 74.
2. "Georgia Passes Strict Pop Festival Bill," *Variety*, March 24, 1971, p. 61.
3. Jeff Samuels, "Greed Kills Love Rock Fests," *Variety*, August 19, 1970, p. 67.

Chapter 9

1. Grace Lichtenstein, "Festival at Watkins Glen Ends in Mud and Elation," *New York Times*, July 30, 1973, p. 1.
2. Robert Hilburn, "Jam II: 300,000 Bit Players in Ontario," Los Angeles *Times*, March 20, 1978, p. 42.

Selected Bibliography

Books

Belz, Carl. *The Story of Rock*. New York: Oxford University Press, 1972.

Boeckman, Charles. *And the Beat Goes on: A Survey of Pop Music in America*. New York: Robert B. Luce, 1972.

Christgau, Robert. *Any Old Way You Choose It*. Baltimore, Md.: Penguin Books, 1973.

Eisen, Jonathan. *Altamont: Death of Innocence in the Woodstock Nation*. New York: Avon, 1970.

Gleason, Ralph. *The Jefferson Airplane and the San Francisco Sound*. New York: Ballantine Books, 1969.

Grossman, Lloyd. *A Social History of Rock Music*. New York: David McKay, 1976.

Hopkins, Jerry. *Festival!* New York: Macmillan, 1970.

Lydon, Michael. *Rock Folk: Portraits from the Rock 'n' Roll Pantheon*. New York: Delta Books, 1968.

Marcus, Greil. *Rock and Roll Will Stand*. Boston: Beacon Press, 1969.

Roberts, John, and Rosenman, Joel, with Pilpel, Robert. *Young Men with Unlimited Capital*. New York: Harcourt Brace Jovanovich, 1974.

Rolling Stone, ed. *The Rolling Stone Reader*. New York: Straight Arrow Publishers, 1974.

Schaffer, William. *Rock Music*. Minneapolis, Minn.: Augsburg, 1972.

Magazine Articles

Bailey, Andrew. "Rock Fests Nearing Finale?" *Variety*, August 19, 1970.

Brady, John. "An Afternoon with Max Yasgur." *Popular Music and Society*, 3, 1974.

Carroll, Kent. "Woodstock Talent Payroll." *Variety*, September 17, 1969.

Chenoweth, Lawrence. "The Rhetoric of Hope and Despair: A Study of the Jimi Hendrix Experience and the Jefferson Airplane." *American Quarterly*, Spring, 1971.

Christgau, Robert. "Anatomy of a Love Festival." *Esquire*, January, 1968.

Farrell, B. "Second Reading: Bad Vibrations from Woodstock." *Life*, September 5, 1969.

Ferris, Timothy. "Puerto Rico: Some Music at Last." *Rolling Stone*, April 27, 1972.

Fouratt, Jim. "Denver Festival: Mace with Music." *Rolling Stone*, July 26, 1969.

Freeland, Nat. "Calif. Jam Best Run in Rock and Tops in $$." *Billboard*, April 20, 1974.

Gleason, Ralph. "Aquarius Wept." *Esquire*, August, 1970.

Hansen, Barry. "First Annual Monterey Pop Festival." *Downbeat*, August 10, 1967.

Holden, Joan. "Shooting Up a Rock Bonanza," *Ramparts*, December 1969.

Hopkins, Jerry. "Lou Adler." *Rolling Stone*, December 21, 1968.

Lentz, Paul. "Festival of Life: A Deadly Rip-Off." *Downbeat*, September 16, 1971.

Logan, Dan. "Monterey Pop Revisited." *Downbeat*, March 5, 1970.

Lombardi, John. "Atlantic City: Pop Goes the Boardwalk." *Rolling Stone*, September 6, 1969.

Marcus, Greil. "The Woodstock Festival." *Rolling Stone*, September 20, 1969.

Miller, Tom. "A Melting Pot at Sky River Festival." *Rolling Stone*, October 4, 1969.

Peterson, Richard. "The Unnatural History of Rock Festivals: An Instance of Media Facilitation." *Popular Music and Society*, Winter 1973.

Reeves, Richard. "Mike Lang + John Roberts = Woodstock." *New York Times Magazine*, September 7, 1969.

Rubin, T. "Watkins Glen: An Almost Ordinary Event." *Christian Science Monitor*, July 31, 1973.

Samuels, Jeff. "Another Woodstock Unlikely as Coin, Civic Problems Squeeze Promoters." *Variety*, May 6, 1970.

———. "Greed Kills Love Rock Fests." *Variety*, August 19, 1970.

Sander, Ellen. "A Decade of Pop Completed." *Saturday Review*, December 27, 1969.

———. "The Most Festive Festival of 1968." *Rolling Stone*, February 1, 1968.

Siegel, Joel. "Watkins Glen Jam Tops Woodstock: 600,000 Fans." *Rolling Stone*, August 30, 1973.

Tracey, Pat. "Birth of a Culture." *Commonweal*, September 5, 1969.

Williams, Richard. "Woodstock." *Melody Maker*, May 23, 1970.

Williams, Tom. "Atlanta Pop Fest a Gate Crasher." *Billboard*, July 18, 1970.

Willis, Ellen. "Rock Etc.: Woodstock." *New Yorker*, September 6, 1969.

Index

Winter, Edgar, 242

Winter, Johnny, 84; at Atlanta (1969), 108–9; at Atlanta (1970), 216, 222; at Denver, 94, 97; at Newport Jazz Festival (1969), 105; at Newport '69, 91; at Texas International Pop, 115–18

Winwood, Steve, 92

"With a Little Help from My Friends," 145

Witherspoon, Jimmy, 212

Woodstock, N.Y.: fame of, 2, 122; as rock festival site, 124; rock star retreat proposed for, 122–23

"Woodstock" (song), 110–11

Woodstock (Wadleigh film), 142, 149–50, 184–85, 190

Woodstock and *Woodstock Two* (lps), 149, 150

Woodstock Music and Art Fair (Woodstock Festival), 121–53; 3, 72–73, *130*, *134–35*, *136*, *137*, *144*, *148*; Altamont contrasted with, 184–85; antiwar protest at, 133, 142; arrangements for, 122–29, 131, 170; attendance figures, 7, 88, 127; as business venture, 123, 131, 149–51; disaster-area theme of, 128, 136, 143; drug problems, 128–29, 138; electrocution danger, 139–40; exploitation of, 189, 259–60; fees paid to performers, 153; film, 142, 149–50; finances, 122–29, 131, 149–51; food and water supplies, 136, 138, 143; influence, 18, 110–11, 119; legend, 1, 147–49, 162, 182–83, 239–40; lps, 149, 150; medical situation at, 133, 137–38, 143; music, 131–33, 140–42; *New York Times* stories on, 136; political efforts at, 142–43; prob-lems due to overcrowding, 128, 133, 136–38, 143; publicity, 123–24, 136, 147–49, 177–78; sanitation problems, 143; security staff, 128–29; site (Bethel, N.Y.), 125, 137, 138, 151, 258; Sly Stone at, 140–41; stage construction, 72–73; tenth anniversary of, 260–61; traffic jams, 127–28, 129–30, 143; vibes, 131, 133, 136–37, 138–39, 145; weather, 2, 131, 133–36, 138–39, 145–46, *148*; The Who at, 142

Woodstock Nation, 3, 187; aging of, 6, Altamont's effect on, 18, 182–83; birth of, 141–42; Hoffman on, 1, 143; naming of, 143; rock music and, 182–83

Woodstock Nation: A Talk-Rock Album (Hoffman), 143

Woodstock Ventures, 123–26, 128, 129, 141, 150–51; Hoffman and, 142–43

Workingman's Dead (Grateful Dead album), 183

Wyman, Bill, 156–59, *164–65*

Yasgur, Max, 1, 125–27, 151

Yippies, 65, 142–43, 190, 223

Young, Neil, 146

Youngbloods, 74

Young Lords, 223–26

Young Men with Unlimited Capital (Roberts and Rosenthal), 142

Young Rascals, 91

Young Socialists, 93

youth culture, *see* counterculture

Zappa, Frank, 29, 95, 96, 104

Zemel, Louis, 198–200

Zemel brothers, 203

Zephyr, 96, 98

Index

291

About the Author

Robert Santelli is a free-lance writer in South Jersey who specializes in rock subjects. He is a regular contributor to numerous rock publications. This is his first book.